Through a Divi

"In *Through a Divine Lens,* Sue Frederick shares the secret of the universe: We are each aspects of the Divine, and we're all connected as part of the One. Everything that happens in our lives is designed to help us see that truth and recognize our life's purpose. The empowering practices Sue presents here are not about deflecting painful emotions but rather learning to see events from a higher perspective—a divine lens—and to tap into what our souls already know. Reading this book is like coming home to yourself. It's life-altering."

KATY KOONTZ, EDITOR IN CHIEF OF *UNITY MAGAZINE*

"*Through a Divine Lens* is an empowering book that uplifts, inspires, and teaches how to view life and one's spiritual journey through a dynamic new perspective. All too often people become victims by surrendering to circumstances they feel are beyond control. While it is difficult to be optimistic through misty optics, Frederick guides the reader how to leave behind the victim mindset and to take control of one's own journey through life by changing perspective. The author's perspective is not one of an aloof clinician but an intelligent, sensitive, and spiritual person who has walked the journey of pain and through the steps she shares emerged into the light of understanding that we truly are the masters of our own happiness."

MARK ANTHONY, JD PSYCHIC EXPLORER AND AUTHOR OF *THE AFTERLIFE FREQUENCY*

"I didn't just like *Through a Divine Lens,* I loved it! There are very few books on the metaphysical like this one. I felt like I was on a journey with a very loving guide—one who had taken a journey all by herself and then returned to guide me. Having the ability to make the journey that personal is a gift. A God-given gift. I loved the stories and the lessons, so much so that I actually took notes to reflect on later. Sue tells us to wait for the shift. She speaks of reinvention points—those points in our lives where the winds shift and our direction has changed—usually forever. Sue talks of exit points and how she is grateful for the heartbreak. Then she tells us why. The pain lets us know that our soul is still alive—despite our greatest losses. Sue talks of past lives and soulmates. She takes us on adventures into past lives and sacred councils. The lessons go right to the heart, and the stories are like echoes from a canyon. A deep personal canyon. This book is a must-read. Again and again."

Joe McQuillen, author of My Search for Christopher
on the Other Side and We're Not Done Yet, Pop

"*Though a Divine Lens* is a guidebook to surmounting grief after tragedy. Sue describes many beneficial tools to allow the reader to experience spiritual growth, including past-life regression, numerology, helping others, and expressing gratitude. At the same time, she intersperses practical methodologies with autobiographical stories to illustrate her important, thoughtful messages. I highly recommend this healing work, written by a cherished provider of Helping Parents Heal, which serves as a practical handbook to healing and living one's best life."

Elizabeth Boisson, president and
cofounder of Helping Parents Heal, Inc.

"There are times in your life when you meet someone and know intuitively that they are a bright light, what some of us refer to as an Earth angel. Sue Frederick is definitely one. When a child transitions many of us refer to the before and after, acknowledging that our lives are forever changed. We find ourselves on a spiritual journey seeking information and looking for authors who will help us through their words to find purpose and meaning. Sue has helped many understand the concepts of soul planning, numerology, and the impact and role they play in our lives and in the relationships we have with our loved ones in spirit and those on Earth. In her book *Through a Divine Lens,* she details the roles and impacts of soul planning and provides tools we can use to help us navigate this earthly journey. I highly recommend reading this powerful book."

Irene Vouvalides, vice president and board member of
Helping Parents Heal (HPH)

"Sue Frederick has simply shared a beautiful and in-depth knowledge of spiritual growth and understanding. The tools she's given us to turn life struggles into strength are simply perfect. Sue, thank you for sharing the light within your soul in the pages of this book."

Fara Gibson, psychic medium and author of
Heaven's Voice Is Within Your Soul

Through a Divine Lens

Practices to Quiet Your Ego and Align with Your Soul

A Sacred Planet Book

Sue Frederick

Park Street Press
Rochester, Vermont

Park Street Press
One Park Street
Rochester, Vermont 05767
www.ParkStPress.com

Text stock is SFI certified

Park Street Press is a division of Inner Traditions International

Sacred Planet Books are curated by Richard Grossinger, Inner Traditions editorial board member and cofounder and former publisher of North Atlantic Books. The Sacred Planet collection, published under the umbrella of the Inner Traditions family of imprints, includes works on the themes of consciousness, cosmology, alternative medicine, dreams, climate, permaculture, alchemy, shamanic studies, oracles, astrology, crystals, hyperobjects, locutions, and subtle bodies.

Cataloging-in-Publication Data for this title is available from the Library of Congress

ISBN 978-1-64411-732-3 (print)
ISBN 978-1-64411-733-0 (ebook)

Printed and bound in the United States by Lake Book Manufacturing, LLC
The text stock is SFI certified. The Sustainable Forestry Initiative® program promotes sustainable forest management.

10 9 8 7 6 5 4 3 2 1

Text design and layout by Debbie Glogover
This book was typeset in Garamond Premier Pro with Minion Pro and Gotham used as display typefaces

To send correspondence to the author of this book, mail a first-class letter to the author c/o Inner Traditions • Bear & Company, One Park Street, Rochester, VT 05767, and we will forward the communication, or contact the author directly at **www.SueFrederick.com**.

To Elizabeth Boisson and her children in spirit,
Chelsea and Morgan, who inspired her to bring healing to
the world through the non-profit Helping Parents Heal.
And to all the departed spirits who push us to recognize that
there is no death. We're so grateful that you've awakened us!

When I'm on path and aligned with divine order,
I feel of use to the greater message, the larger truth, the highest
good. Love moves through me like a ray of light piercing
everything, a laser beam opening my heart.
I am finally out of my own way.

When I forget about divine order, nothing makes sense.
My sadness is legendary. My hunger is hopeless. Heartbreak
brings me to my knees in despair. Everyone betrays me:
my mother, brother, sister, lover, friend. I'm a boat without a
mooring. Fear blocks my inner voice.
My mind tricks me. I let it.

When I remember to throw out the ego lens and reach
for my divine lens, I see the loving God-ness of our universe.
Sacred wisdom once again pours through me, showering the
world in diamonds, each one forged from the
fire of tremendous loss. Forgiveness abounds.
I'm held by the angels.

Contents

Foreword

By Dr. Linda Backman

Webster defines a lens as something that influences or facilitates perception, comprehension, or evaluation. Kobe Bryant, the humanitarian and master athlete, told us, "Everything negative—pressure, challenges—is all an opportunity for me to rise." Life must be lived as the glass half-full, rather than half-empty.

Sue Frederick's book of wisdom is an autobiographical weaving and demonstration that walks us squarely in front of our own mirror and asks: Are you a victim of your ego lens as a result of what you deem as tragedy in your life? Or are you open to a new and crucial vantage point? Your soul, known as your Higher Self, along with your spiritual guides, implores you to embrace a divine perspective of how opportune life events enhance the evolution of your soul and your human self.

Often, we speak of the forces of light versus the forces of dark. Sue's pithy compendium tells us that our self-serving, judgmental, dark side originates in the dualistic perspective that we are not worthy or good enough and that we must have done something bad and are being punished as we view our personal life, with all its losses, health challenges, relationship issues, and the like. The divine light, which is our light, shines brightly when we examine our daily life from our soul's perspective, which is our inner wisdom. Our divine lens reveals the heavenly purity and evolutionary nature of life to advance us both individually and collectively.

What are your life events that your dark ego might label as trauma? Have you faced loss like Sue did when her first husband passed? Has your child been diagnosed with a complicated illness? Did you have a baby born prematurely and die, as I have? What mountain have you climbed as you were thrust headlong into seeking to understand certain life events? For me, the beauty of deciding to risk a third pregnancy, which produced our baby daughter, who came after the passing of our premature second child, might not have happened. All was designed on the higher planes with purpose, intention, and love.

Seek to understand your soul's journey is Sue's key principle, flashing like a neon sign. When, and only when, we grasp that our soul's evolution and our current incarnation are inextricably bound together do we realize the great design of life. Every lifetime includes purpose and confrontation with the ego self. Will you fall prey to grief, depression, anger, jealousy, and more? Or will you realize that our free will allows us to choose our soul's divine lens in which we can examine the events of our life to find meaning and advancement?

In 1993, an unexpected opportunity to choose the light side of divine consciousness came to me, seemingly out of nowhere. As a psychologist in private practice, my original colleague in the practice, quite sadly, passed away at age thirty-two from lung cancer. Within forty-eight hours I knew beyond a shadow of a doubt that I was receiving intuitive communications from him and being shown scenes of past lives we had shared. Over time, my life, which is my lens, was permanently altered. Many years later I met Sue Frederick, an experienced soul who had been brilliantly supporting grieving clients and others with her wisdom and intuition.

As I worked to conquer my fear of transitioning from conventional psychology to soul regression therapy, worrying about losing my credibility as a psychologist, I simply couldn't help myself. I was compelled to learn about soul evolution so that I could guide my clients to seek revelations about their soul's journey from lifetime to lifetime. Years later, I was blessed to meet Sue, who chose to study her own soul regression and then learned how to guide others in their soul regressions.

In chapter 8, Sue shares the immensely powerful regression details of her client Patricia. For twenty-eight years now I have been guiding clients to realize their soul-level, divine lens specifics of past lives and the relationship to life today. Patricia's story provides all of us who are reading this book a plethora of disclosure about her soul's learning, from her past lives up to the present lifetime. What can we learn from Patricia's regression, masterfully facilitated by Sue Frederick? Yes, each of us experiences past lives of trauma related to karma and free will choices. Free will is a unique quality of life on Earth. Also, in this regression case study we taste something of past lives of soul accomplishment, or dharma. Patricia demonstrates how she was abused simply because she was different due to her indigenous past-life heritage. In addition, she speaks of the calm and peace that she experienced upon physical death, and the release of her soul energy, which caused her to live and breathe. Soul regression is a powerful revelatory tool for understanding our deep past as it influences our life today. Sue shares her client's key regression element: to not give up her power in life today as she did in a past life. This kind of past-life "bleed through" occurs for so many of us, as our past-life experiences, both evolutionary and karmic, are triggered in our life today. Patricia is told by her team of spiritual guides, "Just be yourself. Don't try to be someone else. Just be completely yourself. Don't be afraid to let yourself show completely. You can't heal someone if you've never been broken."

In 1993, my passion to help others cast aside their ego lens in order to know who they are as souls came squarely to me, such that I was compelled to alter my conventional approach to the practice of psychotherapy. I believe that when you adopt new glasses by which to view your life, you will see your soul's intention.

Sue Frederick is an exemplar for following your soul's guidance. In this inspiring, extraordinary book, she teaches by example. I invite you to drink in every drop of her wisdom. When you are willing to be open to your opportune wounding, then you are truly on the journey to evolve your soul and the soul of humanity.

DR. LINDA BACKMAN is a psychologist and regression therapist with forty-four years of experience in private practice, including over twenty-five years guiding thousands of soul regressions in person and remotely. Linda has been conducting Past Lives and Between Lives Soul Regression training since 2002. She is the author of *Souls on Earth: Exploring Interplanetary Past Lives; The Evolving Soul: Spiritual Healing through Past Life Exploration;* and *Bringing Your Soul to Light: Healing through Past Lives and the Time Between,* all published by Llewellyn. Featured on many broadcasts and webcasts, including *Dr. Oz, Coast to Coast AM,* and *Gaia TV,* Linda regularly interviews spiritual way-showers on her widely syndicated *Souls on Earth* podcast. Linda founded the RavenHeart Center and Training Institute in Boulder, Colorado, in 1997.

Preface

I've been knocked flat, in bed with a 103-degree fever and a scary cough that leaves me nauseous and unable to eat. This potent combination of high fever and days without food has cleansed my body, shaken my brain, and broken me wide open. Between bouts of fever, I feel like a newborn baby, joyful and grateful to be alive. Yet it will take weeks in bed for my ego mind to fully understand that I've been knocked flat so I can surrender, let go of old patterns, and embrace new realizations downloaded from the Divine, and that these transmissions will take my soul and my work to the next level.

During one memorable night when my fever rose above 103, the thin veil lifted, and I had a vision of our planet on its evolutionary journey of consciousness-awakening. There was a moving river of light spreading around the globe, one light sparking another and another, until bands of illumination circled the entire planet, enlightening all the dark crevices. Suddenly I realized that this is the story of human evolution, sparking from one light of divine consciousness into billions of such sparks of light, which gradually overcome the darkness. It was clear how much more light there is in our world than darkness, and I felt assured that the light is winning, no matter how tragic the news may seem or what new events may unfold in the future. This fever-fueled vision inspired me with new ideas and concepts to write about. Much of what I dreamt and understood that night I couldn't remember when I first woke up. I did remember my sense of knowing that all is well with the world, which is moving in the right direction. I felt transformed by this out-of-body experience, and for days I struggled to articulate these ideas to family and friends.

The experience of feeling reborn led me to a new level of work, which began to solidify into specific ideas over the next few weeks, until I was consumed with the concept of the divine lens versus the ego lens as the two primary ways we perceive events in our lives. This new concept and how to reap the benefits of divine lens viewing is what this book is all about.

So how does this work?

As you can see from the vision described above, many things can precipitate an out-of-body experience that can reveal the divine realms, including illness and fever. From the time I was little I've had precognitive dreams and clairaudient and clairvoyant experiences. More often than not, my nighttime dreams were out-of-body experiences, journeys into mysterious realms or states of consciousness where I saw sacred beings, extraordinary landscapes, and met with departed loved ones. I always awakened from these dreams feeling exalted, uplifted, and eager to return there.

When I began claiming these gifts and using them to create my life's work and inspire my books, I longed for a way to help clients experience these states of higher consciousness themselves. I knew their healing and insights would have more sticking power if they had the experience themselves. A few years ago I gratefully received training in soul regression from Dr. Linda Backman, founder of the RavenHeart Center, so that I could do exactly that: guide others into the realms that I knew and loved so well from my own journeys.

As a certified Past Life and Between Lives Soul Regression therapist, I have had the great blessing of guiding clients through meditative journeys into the divine realms for therapeutic soul healing. In these intensive sessions, the client experiences a significant past lifetime and a return to the divine realms to meet their spirit guides and Council of

Elders for advice and guidance. These sessions are a complete immersion into the soul's story, a way of seeing life through the divine lens. The experience brings a new and empowering perspective to whatever challenges the client is facing, such as the pain of grief or physical illness.

For two decades, I've also done intuitive numerology coaching sessions with thousands of clients. This work has helped many of my clients understand their soul mission and soul agreements for their current lifetime. When they follow these numerology sessions with an intensive soul regression (like the ones you'll read in this book), they get a completely immersive experience of merging with their divine essence. That perspective is a transformative divine lens shift.

From my personal experiences and those of my clients, as well as from conversations and visions with my beloved departeds, here's what I have learned: We leave our bodies easily during certain brain-wave states of deep relaxation, such as meditation or deep sleep. During those times when the mind quiets, the soul travels. And we can learn to be conscious of the experience and remember it when we return to the body.

Slipping into that exalted state has always been easy for me, almost too easy, in this lifetime. It's a painless, exalted state of awareness where our everyday concerns disappear. We know everything we need to know in those moments. In that state, we meet souls we've loved for many lifetimes, who wrap us in unconditional love and compassion; they've returned to their greatest divine potential after crossing over at the end of life. These souls are marinating in the loving consciousness of divinity, where forgiveness is effortless and eternal.

During these journeys, our primary spirit guides usually step forward. These are the evolved beings who have guided us between each lifetime and have helped us manifest our life plans for evolutionary purposes, for the highest good. We have intuitive knowingness conversations with these beings and can ask them how we've been doing in our many Earth journeys, and what we need to know in order to do better. For example, a guide may tell you to request their help more often because they're always available to lift you into a higher state of consciousness, even during your moments of deepest pain. Yet they can't step in unless we request their help, so our participation is required. And our requests are always answered.

If we desire, our guides will take us to meet the group of highest evolved beings, known as the Council of Elders. It's their job to oversee the growth and learning of all souls reincarnating on Earth. And yes, they also help individual souls whenever help is requested. We experience a higher vibration, a sacred presence, as soon as we step into their meeting space. We often feel a bit humbled and grateful to be in their presence while asking for insight and guidance about whatever challenges we're facing; they will answer every question in a way that serves our inner growth.

If we so desire, we can visit the Library of Souls to study and learn more. This is a place in the divine realms that I've visited so many times in this lifetime, yet did not have a name for it. I love the calm energy, wisdom, and knowledge that permeates this library. It's like stepping into the most beautiful space of learning you've ever experienced. Dr. Linda Backman taught me that this is called the Library of Souls because every piece of knowledge about incarnations on Earth and elsewhere is contained there, as well as higher knowledge about why we chose Earth as a place of learning. We have access to all knowledge when we visit this place of higher learning, even if we sometimes can't consciously bring all of that knowledge back to Earth with us. One of my beloved departeds, my best childhood girlfriend, Crissie, who was brilliant in her human lifetime on Earth, is one of the workers and teachers in this library; I often get to see her when I visit there.

There is another place that I've visited occasionally, where we can learn why we chose our particular body for this lifetime and how it is perfectly designed to help us learn what we came here to learn. This place is similar to a pavilion where we can study and absorb the lessons and gifts inherent in each body type we may pick for a lifetime. Much healing is gained here about why we've struggled with certain health issues or poor body image, and the purpose of it all. As we return to the earthly realms, we carry the love, wisdom, and insight we've gained in those realms.

When I guide a client's soul regression, they're the ones receiving the guidance, and I ask them to speak it out loud as they receive it; this way they can hear their own voice sharing this wisdom whenever they listen to the audio recording I make. Clients find those recordings extremely helpful because as time goes by, the conscious mind begins to forget parts of that profound experience.

In this book, I've shared the edited transcripts of several of these soul regression sessions, which I believe you'll find helpful as you absorb the ideas outlined in this book and the process of soul regression. It's my goal that you, the reader, will have your own journeys to the divine realms for insight and healing, and that this book will precipitate that sacred experience for you.

Introduction

You either believe in divine order or you don't. It's an all or nothing thing. Either you're aware that all events occur for your soul's growth, your highest good, and the highest good of all, or life feels chaotic, painful, and meaningless. Each day provides numerous opportunities to shift back and forth between those two views until you fully align with the view that empowers you the most and moves you forward in a positive direction. Only then can you fulfill your soul's mission and live up to your greatest potential.

Wearing your divine lens is like putting on a new pair of prescription glasses and suddenly seeing a world you never saw before: the small miracles in everyday life, the divine order behind each challenge, the love hidden in every painful interaction. For example, when you get a new job, your business becomes successful, you fall in love, or you have a baby, you may find yourself saying, "Things happen for a reason." You slip on your divine lens in those moments and offer gratitude to a loving God or a benevolent universe that operates for our highest good.

When things aren't going so well, however—when you lose that great job, when you're facing bankruptcy, when your spouse divorces you, or if your child dies in a tragic accident—you may feel angry at a cruel God who would cause such suffering. Or you may rage at an unjust universe, where tragic events unfold for no apparent reason. Yet each crisis offers a potential awakening, a fresh opportunity to discover if you're living from your soul's perspective, which is your divine view, or from your ego self. Once you're aware of these warring perspectives and their consequences, you can choose to view life through your divine lens. That choice changes everything for the better.

We can think of the divine lens as being like the lens of a camera. We can view the world through a macro lens or close-up, where we aren't aware of the bigger picture and don't understand where the leaf or a rose petal fits into the larger scope of a rose bush, a rose garden, a region, a country, or a world. This is what we do when we view our greatest pain (for example, the tragic loss of a loved one or the ego-crushing experience of being fired from a great job) as the largest and most significant event in our life, with nothing from the past or the future to serve as a reference point that allows us to place it in a larger perspective. Through this macro view lens, we aren't able to understand that our pain is but a bump in the road in the long journey of our soul—a challenge perfectly designed to move us into greater spiritual wisdom and higher consciousness for the highest good of all, including the highest good of our departed loved one. We don't see how linked we are to all other souls who also feel great loss and find their way through their pain. This detail-focused view is the ego lens view.

Or we can use the panoramic lens on the camera and suddenly see a larger world with endless possibilities and meanings, which we can realize when focused on one moment of great pain. We can understand our soul's story within this larger panoramic view of all of our shared soul stories. This is our divine lens. It shows connections and threads where our ego lens sees only pain.

We can also imagine using different filters on the camera lens that either highlight the shadows within the frame or highlight the light within the frame. When we're using the ego lens, we see mostly shadows wherever we look. When we're using the divine lens, we see light even in the darkest corners. This is where our wisdom lives—within the light of the darkest corners of our lives.

Whenever you're afraid, grief stricken, shut down, or angry, it's time for realignment with your Higher Self. The ego self has lied to you and taken you far from who you came here to be. Your ego lens only reveals a small piece of your story—a moment of utter loss that separates you from your Higher Self and from the Higher Selves of others. This separation from your soul shows up in your life as fear, confusion, depression, addiction, and anger.

Fear, addiction, pain, and despair occur when we lose our connection to our Higher Self, our divinity. Of course, we *all* experience moments of great pain and despair. It's part of our human journey here on Earth. Yet the moment we cry for help from our Higher Self, everything changes. It's as simple as saying, *Please, divine guides, God, or Higher Self, help me shift into my soul's wisdom to see the lesson in front of me. Quiet my ego mind and open my heart.* Take a deep breath and wait for the shift. Listen to the inner voice that speaks with love and not fear. At that moment, you're lifted into the divine view of life and reminded that you're a powerful soul who came here to evolve and help others. Unexpectedly, you see divinity in everything, the golden glow of love in each painful and joyful moment. You feel expanded, unafraid, open, and clear on how to move forward. Your divine lens is activated.

The ego mind tells you you're here to win, manipulate, accumulate, conquer, protect, and defend. The divine lens shows you the grand view of your soul's perspective. It reveals that you agreed to be born in this lifetime to face these exact moments of crisis and view them with love, gratitude, and wisdom; to understand the pain of others who may be hurting you; to realize that everyone is doing exactly the best they can given their level of consciousness; and that all is forgiven in the end.

Your divine lens reveals that you are a highly evolved soul who intended to shine your wisdom on the painful, dark moments of your life, and to help others do the same. You came here to shine love on your fear, to pour light on your greatest pain.

Every single day of your lifetime has been perfectly designed to help you remember your divinity and shift out of the frightened ego view that's rooted in our physical experience of being human. In one moment of recognizing this, one heart-opening shift of perspective, your life changes, your soul speaks up, and your next step is revealed.

PART ONE

Ego Lens or Divine Lens?

Please divine guides, align me with my highest self and lift me above the limited perspective of the ego; help me see the lesson in this challenge and gift of this moment.

At this very moment, your Higher Self is battling your ego self to determine how you'll experience this day. Your Higher Self whispers, *This is your greatest moment. Choose love over fear. Step into the light and become the source of love for everyone.* Your ego self counters with, *I'm not good enough or strong enough. Life is unfair. I'm in too much pain.*

Today, despite whatever challenges you are facing, you can gain a new and enlightening perspective by putting on your divine lens. When you embrace this new perspective, it empowers you to live every day in alignment with your soul's wisdom. When you perceive life this way for a few minutes each day, awareness will begin to grow within you until your life is moving forward gracefully, your relationships and career are thriving, and your pain is diminished. This is the gift of your divine lens.

I believe that once you experience the rich benefits and the mind-altering shift into your divine lens, you'll never leave home without it.

You'll react differently to every challenging situation as you learn to remove your ego lens and slip on your divine lens. It truly changes everything.

The most wonderful thing about being human is our ability to choose. In this earthly realm we're allowed to experience the perfect combination of destined soul mission and free will, every moment of our lives. We come here with the soul intention to live up to our greatest potential, align with our Higher Self, and do great work that helps others. Yet we also hit bumps in the road: loss, illness, financial challenges, childhood pain, and relationship turmoil.

Free will allows us to decide exactly how we'll view each challenge and how we'll use every gift we've brought with us. No one else chooses our viewpoint for us. We are the ones who determine how we view our life story. We can choose to view this world as purely physical and material, with random tragedies and meaningless coincidences, or we can choose to view life through the eyes of our soul. When we align with the wisdom of our soul, we see things differently. Light pours through us and reveals the hidden beauty in each moment. We see that each challenge was perfectly designed for our highest good before this lifetime began. We understand that the purpose of each bump in the road has been to help us grow and awaken, which is the primary reason we incarnated into this physical realm.

Life on Earth is a human consciousness experiment that we've all agreed to participate in. We're expanding consciousness to penetrate this dense realm, and this evolutionary process has been going on for billions of years.

1

Spiritual Crisis

Are You Religious, Spiritual, Both, or Neither?

Since my earliest memory, I loved going to Catholic Church. I felt God's presence among the towering statues, flickering candlelight, pungent incense, and stained-glass windows that depicted a compassionate Jesus placing healing hands on a child, or the barefoot St. Francis of Assisi kneeling in prayer while birds rested peacefully on his shoulders. These loving beings filled my dreams and spoke to me when I prayed. But it was Mother Mary, with her long hair and flowing blue gown, who was my constant companion. I prayed the rosary to her nearly every day and knew without a doubt that she was my loving mother. I turned to her in every childhood moment of pain, and her graceful presence comforted my heart.

As I grew older, I began to understand the implications of the Catholic Church's dogma: the burden of "original sin" that they said I was born with; the poison of "mortal sin" that could send me to burn in hell forever; and the persistent need for daily "penance" to atone for my sins while embracing the suffering of the cross.

My blossoming adolescent sensuality, according to the nuns, was a perilous slide toward mortal sin. In daily religion class we were instructed to avoid looking at our own bodies when we bathed for fear of slipping into mortal sin and everlasting damnation. As much as we prayed, went to Mass, and devoted our lives to Jesus and Mary, one tiny mistake could ruin everything, according to the priests and nuns.

Catholic dogma grew increasingly impossible for me to align with. There was a growing rift between the religion I was born into and my inner knowingness. Eventually my discomfort with the teachings of the Catholic Church caused me to search for new answers that better aligned with a forgiving God whom I intuitively knew did not punish. I loved Jesus and Mary with all my heart. Their daily presence in my life did not line up with the cruel God described in Catholic doctrine.

My soul refused to believe the Church's claim that all souls that are not Catholic—Hindus, Buddhists, Jews, Muslims, Presbyterians, Episcopalians, Baptists, Methodists, and so on—are condemned to hell for eternity. This never resonated as true for me. I would have been willing to forego sex forever if God demanded that of me, but I simply knew in my gut that every being on Earth has a beautiful soul and is doing their very best. This I knew for sure whenever I trusted my inner wisdom.

When I left home for college in 1969, a new world opened up. I saw fliers advertising Theosophy, yoga, and meditation classes on campus bulletin boards and was instantly drawn to learn what those things were about. This part of my life launched what became a lifelong journey of spiritual exploration, with, at various times, residencies in New Age and Native American studies, Buddhism, Hinduism, the Unity Church, and other metaphysical studies. During my twenties I learned from the school of nature, living outdoors for months at a time, absorbing the spiritual truths found in nature while teaching mountaineering for the Colorado Outward Bound program. I was drawn to places and people who exhibited the kind of spiritual wisdom I wanted to absorb.

From my journey, I've come to believe that religion is a starting place, not a destination. A church may launch our spiritual exploration, but religion's main purpose is to hook us up to the Divine, to help us experience something beyond the physical world, to get us asking the big questions: Who am I? Why am I here? Where do I go when I die? Once religion has gotten us to this point, however, we need to find our own personal connection to the Divine and follow the path that resonates for us as true, that does not dictate our behavior through fear-based dogma, but instead wraps us in love and wisdom.

We can do both. We can maintain our connection with the religion whose community and sacred traditions comfort us, while also nurturing our own personal spiritual connection to the Divine in the manner that feels true to us.

Once you've embraced a spiritual (not religious) point of view, you've found your soul's reference point. The essential next step is to create a disciplined daily practice of personal connection to the Divine. This daily personal practice is something you can do while also following the traditions of Judaism, Christianity, or whatever religious community you're comfortable with. It doesn't have to be all or nothing, religion or spirituality. But spirituality does require a daily discipline of connection. Whether you choose twenty minutes of mantra-based meditation, contemplative prayer, or chanting, your daily spiritual practice is as necessary for a healthy life as brushing your teeth. It's your moment to slip on your divine lens, quiet the ego mind, and connect to your soul's wisdom. A consistent daily practice allows you to experience the enormous benefits of divine-lens viewing every day.

Your soul knows the difference between fear-based doctrine and enlightened wisdom, and will nudge you to run away from dogma. Your disillusionment with a church is only the beginning of your spiritual journey. A daily personal practice of sacred connection is required for life in the physical world, where we so quickly forget our divinity. This juncture is where many people get lost. They feel deceived by religion and so mistakenly think that God has betrayed them, so they turn away from all things sacred. Yet God is embracing them all the while. If they choose to listen to their soul's wisdom and pick up their divine lens, they'll remember this.

Sometimes it takes a painful loss, a reinvention point, to reopen our search for spiritual truth. We begin seeking answers again in moments of pain, which eventually leads us away from our comfort zone and into true spiritual awakening. This is the gift of our pain.

YOUR SPIRITUAL AWAKENING

Be wary of any spiritual teaching or teacher who makes you feel afraid or bad about yourself, or who doesn't resonate as true. Quiet your mind, listen to your inner wisdom, and you'll know the truth.

You're a divine spiritual explorer who came here to evolve and help others. It's your job to cross boundaries, question everything, and search for meaning. If you're living your life in fear and aren't sure of what you believe, it's time to break the rules. You have nothing to lose and everything to gain.

If you were taught that God punishes us, condemning us to hell for transgressions, you'll probably hunker down to fit into this fear-based system for much of your life. If you leave your church, you may feel guilt-ridden and believe that now you'll go to hell for breaking the rules. This is your ego mind speaking, not your Higher Self.

If your parents were punishing and controlling, you may believe that it's your job to unquestionably obey everyone, including the Church, because that's what you were raised to do. This is a sign that you've turned away from the voice of your soul's wisdom in order to survive a painful childhood. Your inner wisdom still awaits you. It's the voice of love found deep within your heart. Fitting into others' expectations and beliefs is the fastest road to disconnecting from your inner wisdom.

God is love. That's all you need to know. This simple
truth contains everything necessary to live your best life
and fulfill your soul's mission.

You are made of loving God consciousness; it flows through each one of us unobstructed—when we allow it. When we quiet the mind.

Divine order is always acting in your favor. No matter how shut-down or off-path you've been, your soul will create a wake-up call for your highest good. This will arrive as a divorce, bankruptcy, job loss, or the loss of a loved one. Suddenly you'll be asking the important questions again and refusing to settle for answers that don't resonate as true. This is your soul taking charge instead of your ego, getting your life back on the path. Your divine lens has been reactivated. If you step out of bounds for the first time in your life you'll be amazed to discover that you're not condemned to hell. That instead you feel alive, fearless, loving, and joyful. You have rediscovered your inner truth. You're following your inner compass, which is your intuition. Eventually you will travel to the edges of the world to know what can be known, to discover the wisdom that can't be learned within the boundaries of convention.

You've found your way home to the Divine.

◉ Explore the Spirituality Question

There's a difference between spirituality and religion. Religion is a set of beliefs and rules governed by a church. If you've been comforted by your church and don't question those beliefs, that's terrific. But if your church's beliefs don't fully resonate with you, are you willing to step out of your comfort zone to explore new ideas and develop your own personal connection to the Divine? Consider the following:

- Do you follow a religion or do you have a daily spiritual practice of some kind? Is spirituality a focus of your daily life or not? Do you pray or meditate every day? If so, describe what you do.
- Reflect on the details of your spiritual journey. How were you raised? What do you believe in now? Have you explored other religions beyond the one you were raised in? What do you believe about the nature of God that's different from your childhood beliefs?

- Where do you believe your departed loved ones are now? Where do you believe you'll go when you die?

- Do you believe you're a soul on an intentional journey for your highest good? Why or why not?

- When you're in pain—especially the grief of loss—ask yourself, *Why did this happen? Where is my loved one now? What is the point of my life now?* By exploring these questions from a broader spiritual (not religious) perspective, you may find answers that are truly healing. This loss can be your spiritual awakening, calling you to experience firsthand your own divine nature. Your pain will diminish the instant you have an experience of communicating directly with your departed loved one or with your divine guides and feeling their presence. Not only that, you will also have confirmation that the unseen realms are real.

- To explore a bigger view of spirituality, would you be willing to go on a spiritual exploration? Would you consider spending time at a monastery, ashram, or spiritual center, or taking a meditation class? Would you be willing to visit a Hindu ashram or a Buddhist center, a Unity Church, a Science of Mind Church, or a Kabbalah center? Would you at least be willing to read some metaphysical books? Such a spiritual exploration might help you understand what others believe about the afterlife so you can see if those ideas resonate with you.

2
Self-Doubt

How the Ego Lens Destroys Confidence

When we think of being in an ego state, we imagine this means that we're overly confidant, arrogant, and boastful. But it's actually the opposite of this. When we're using the ego lens to view our world, to view any situation, we're looking at ourself and others as limited beings with limited potential, all of us competing to survive. The ego lens tells us we need to struggle to get what we need because there's never enough to go around, and we're never good enough to get it done, so we must be better than everyone else to succeed. The ego lens thrives on seeing differences.

When you allow this view to dominate your life, you pull the plug on your inner wisdom, the source of your personal power. This drains your energy and leaves you feeling defeated and exhausted. The stress of having to be the best—which your soul knows is impossible—will push you far from the unique path you came here to experience. The ego lens hides the truth. It blocks your ability to clearly see your unique gifts or the gifts of others.

The ego lens sees only the surface of life. The divine lens, on the other hand, makes no assumptions. It reveals the deeper truth behind every story, the pain hidden in each misbehavior, the soul journey behind every wounded personality. It reveals similarities rather than differences. The divine lens is your prescription for compassion. It aligns you with your soul's wisdom and empowers you to be your greatest self. It reveals that you're perfectly who you're supposed to be at this very moment—which is exactly as powerful, beautiful, and brilliant as you're meant to be today. This perspective allows you to shine, even when your mind tells you that you're inferior, powerless, or not good enough.

The divine lens illuminates each moment of your life with wisdom. It pours light into your wounds. It fills every dark space with love. Wearing your divine lens, you understand that the gifts of others are perfectly unique to them and what their soul came to accomplish. You see that you're absolutely radiant when you speak your soul's truth, share your wisdom, and speak from your heart instead of from your mind.

Never doubt that your soul will always put you exactly where you're meant to be for your highest good and the good of others. Your task is to embrace each painful moment and flip it into gratitude for the gift of what you're learning and the gift of knowing that divine order is already helping you move through this perfectly designed lesson.

Whenever you call out to your Higher Self for guidance, you open to source energy and flawless wisdom. You open your channel of inspiration. Divinity pours through you. Then you become the goddess, the prince, the golden child. All meaningless ego comparisons seem ridiculous and fall away. You carry the light within. You get the job you're not qualified for, the standing ovation, the partner you thought would never notice you. Your work, which is your holy sacrament, shines with resonance. This is divine lens living at its finest. And it's available to you 24/7, just for the asking.

IF I'M A DIVINE BEING, WHY DO I DOUBT MYSELF?

If today your ego mind is tormenting you, saying you've messed up, made wrong choices, ruined relationships, and aren't good enough, reach for your divine lens. It's the antidote to self-doubt. It reveals the perfection of your soul's journey of evolution despite how your ego views it or labels it.

Yet since the day you were born, you've been hypnotized into trusting your ego. As a child you were taught that you don't know the truth, and only outside "authorities" do. This is the voice of self-doubt, born of the ego and its limited perceptions. This idea is forced on everyone who takes a human lifetime. As children, we're taught that our elders know better than we do, and that we must listen to them and trust them.

Yet children have an inner voice of wisdom. They've only recently arrived from the divine realms, and their intuition is unrestricted. They may not be able to navigate their physical bodies yet or understand the rules of the society they've incarnated into, but they're filled with inner wisdom, truth, and knowingness.

You too were this conscious and aware when you arrived here. If your childhood was difficult, it means that your soul posse, your parents and siblings, were struggling to do what they were capable of understanding as right action, even though you may have suffered because of their unenlightened behavior. Your soul agreed to these experiences as part of your higher education. You still had choices within each painful moment.

As a child, your inner voice advised you to stay away from some adults and stick close to others. You sensed energy and navigated through the sixth sense of intuition rather than the five physical senses. You were a sixth-sense being until you stumbled, hit your head, or put your hand on a hot stove and learned that the physical world has different laws from those in the divine realms, and that you needed to focus on learning the physical laws of survival. This narrowed focus diminished your awareness by necessity. Input from your intuitive sixth sense took a backseat. This was all required in order to learn how to live on planet Earth, how to navigate a clumsy body through the dense energy of gravity. Yet the downside of learning these things was that you began to shut down your inner knowingness, your sixth sense. Advice from well-meaning parents, siblings, teachers, friends, and clergy became too overpowering to ignore.

As expected by your elders, you surrendered to the complete human experience of the ego self, which was very different from your previous existence in the divine realms. You diminished everything about yourself in order to survive here. Thus your inner struggle between the ego self and the Higher Self began, with the ego winning as you became more successful at navigating the physical world. This was the natural process of adjusting to life in this realm.

At first you mourned the loss of those divine realms and the seeming loss of your Higher Self. You felt homesick for something you couldn't quite remember or describe. Your toddler tantrums expressed the frustration of life in a physical body, which was so different from what you remembered. Gradually, your divinity slipped away from your grasp as you learned the laws of appropriate behavior. The adults around you approved of this transformation. They complimented you for turning into such a "good" boy or girl. In this way you became defined by your environment, shutting out the extra information available from your sixth sense because it was too confusing and unacceptable.

If you were sensitive and had not fully closed off from your intuition, you may have felt confused by the contrast between what your elders advised and what your inner voice longed for. Your longing to reconnect with something you could not quite remember and your urge to follow your own path was powerful. Because of this longing, you may have chosen the path less traveled as soon as you stepped out to live life on your own terms. This choice would eventually lead you to a life in alignment with your unique soul mission.

If you followed the path laid out for you by others, you would hit reinvention points later on, possibilities for changing direction. If you listened to your inner wisdom at those turning points, you would also find your way to fulfilling your highest potential. Divine order always provides openings, small miracles, and sacred opportunities that show up exactly when we need them.

WHY DO I SECOND-GUESS MYSELF?

Viewing your life through your ego lens inevitably makes you doubt yourself. If your intention is to speak your soul's truth and share your wisdom, you'll often be misunderstood by others. Your ego will tell you this is because you're a loser and you're too different to fit into or succeed in this world. But once you remember that you carry a light inside you that cannot be extinguished, you'll no longer doubt yourself. Your uniqueness is your gift.

Your physical self is part of the reason why you struggle so much. Your body is a great weight that you carry in this heavy dimension. Sometimes this heaviness is too much and pulls you away from your divinity. But your body is also a great gift that can be used to connect to the Divine.

There are several practical steps that can help lift you into the higher frequencies. These include physical movement, getting outside in nature, feeling gratitude and laughing with others; there is also meditation to quiet the mind, crying to release the pain in your heart, and sending compassion and forgiveness to those who misunderstand you. Once you remember that you're here to enlighten others and be a teacher, you'll stop being disappointed by those less evolved than you. By aligning with your Higher Self, you'll see the pain that others carry and you will become the healer. No one can wound you when you stand in alignment with your soul. Those less evolved than you will be drawn to you because you carry the light inside you. It's because of your open heart, your powerful soul's wisdom, that others who need healing will show up in your life. But if you allow yourself to be wounded by the judgments of others, when they don't react as you'd hoped, by step-ping into *their* divine light as you have, you might feel discouraged or defeated. This only pulls you out of your divinity.

Feeling worthless and discouraged is an enormous waste of time. There is no soul that is worthless. There is no soul that has any reason to feel discouraged. All is evolving as it should. You are evolving as you should.

The judgments of others reveal infinitely more about them and their seeming unwillingness to grow than they reveal about you. How many lifetimes will it take for you to learn this, to see their criticisms and contempt as misunderstandings due to their low level of consciousness, rather than as a statement of your worth or value?

Once you absorb this lesson, you will never be hindered by criticism from yourself or others again. You'll become the source of loving wisdom for others, and everywhere you walk you'll fill the room with light.

◎ Shift into the Confidence of the Divine Lens View

- Take one deep, slow breath; follow it in and out. Repeat.
- Chant a mantra like *Om Namah Shivaya* or say a prayer such as the Lord's Prayer for several moments.
- Make your request: *Please help me see my soul's perspective on this challenge. I pray to be hooked up to the wisdom of my Higher Self and of the divine realms and the guidance of all the divine beings. I pray to align with this wisdom now in order to see from my soul's perspective, and choose my words and actions from that perspective.*
- See yourself and others as one expanded soul on a shared journey. Invoke the Divine with the request, *Help me to see the path my sister/brother walks, understand their pain, and realize how to love them best in their journey, knowing that their limitations and mistakes have nothing to do with me.*
- Ask, *How do I move forward through my doubts and fears?* Write this question over and over until you begin to sense the answers channeled from your Higher Self. You'll know that the words are coming from your Higher Self because you'll be writing quickly, without thinking or editing what you write. This is how divine guidance comes to us.
- Complete these sentences:
    I am grateful for . . .
    I open my heart and send love to . . .
    One positive step I can take today is . . .

3
Fear

The Favored Lens of the Ego

Love is an ocean. Fear is what we imagine is lurking beneath the surface—the shark circling our legs, the crab biting our toes. Yet we've come here to swim in this ocean of love. Love is the essence of our DNA.

Fear is a creation of the ego mind. We need the ego to survive in this physical world, but it pulls us away from love. The ego doesn't understand love except as something to acquire from others. The ego mind is linear and logical and nothing more.

We connect to love, divinity, intuition, and creativity through the right brain. We rely on the rational left brain to process the mundane aspects of everyday life. We arrive in this dense realm fully accessing both sides of the brain, left and right. But as we mature, we're slowly talked out of love. Western cultural beliefs and values support left-brain logic over right-brain intuition.

Our souls inherently love everything and everyone. Love is the fabric of the higher realms and the energy we're composed of. We're designed to be channels for infinite, divine love. Our minds are simply filters to help us navigate this physical world. But once we arrive here, we're taught to worship the mind over the heart and soul.

Our left-brain, ego-driven world tells us that receiving love is the priority and the key to happiness. This is completely backward. True happiness exists only when we allow ourselves to channel divine love to others, to become a source of infinite love and forgiveness. Once we realize that quieting the left-brain ego mind allows us to love fearlessly, we've found the key to a meaningful, joyful life. We've realigned with our soul.

The soul is not designed to take from others. The soul is designed to be the channel for divinity, grace, and light for everyone, and to forgive fearlessly. Love is the only antidote to fear. When you're afraid of anything or anyone, it means your ego voice has the upper hand and has drowned out the voice of your soul. You're out of alignment with your divinity.

When love is not given freely, your energy becomes stagnant, which creates neurosis, dependency, psychosis, and fear. These are symptoms of misalignment with your Higher Self—basically, spiritual constipation. The remedy is to choose one person in your life to begin practicing unconditional love toward. Send pure love and gratitude to them for several minutes a day. Don't ask for or expect anything in return. Requiring love in return destroys love. Your mission is to understand your ability to love freely and reawaken your fierce and powerful heart.

This reawakening will transform your life. It'll cure whatever ails you, heal all wounds, and create loving relationships. It will change the way you think and behave toward others. It will shift you directly into your divine lens view and shatter the ego lens.

If you find yourself thinking that someone doesn't deserve your love or has hurt you too much to forgive them, it means you've shifted back into your ego mind and are no longer wearing your divine lens. These are fear-based beliefs coming from the ego mind. They're out of alignment with your Higher Self and who you came here to be.

Your Higher Self sees that we're all here on a shared journey of awakening, and that the unawakened need more love, not less. Pouring love and compassion on those who have hurt you eventually sparks them into higher consciousness. Only when we're all awakened will consciousness shift and the highest realms finally merge within this physical realm to create true perpetual love that shines light into the darkest crevices, where lost souls have lingered.

Angelic beings have been working toward this goal for eons. At first they worked alone. Now humans have evolved enough to perform angelic duties here on Earth, helping to transform the dense matter into light.

Jesus, Buddha, and many other enlightened teachers brought this message to Earth. But our human ego interpretations of their ideas twisted and distorted their original words and turned them into fear-based doctrines and stringent rules that hid their original message of divine love. We're awakening now, however, beginning to remember who we are as we distance from the poison of the ego mind, which destroys the fire of love burning inside all of us. The ego's fear-based reign is not permanent. It never wins in the long run. The soul is infinitely more powerful than the ego. And love trumps all.

> *It takes just baby steps to break a lifetime pattern of ego-*
> *and fear-based living. Seeing just one painful moment*
> *through your divine lens changes everything.*

Little steps can change everything. A lifetime immersed in ego-based living can shift in a moment of love and compassion—a moment of seeing a loved one's tragic death as being in divine order, or a parent's betrayal as a symptom of their need for love.

From my soul to yours

Fear is the great crippler, the dark force, the energy void. It's the Achilles' heel that all humans share. It's what we push against so that we can choose courage and love instead, and thereby light our way through the darkness.

Thank your fear for being such a powerful teacher, for waking you up at night with heart tremors; for unplugging you from Source; for taking on the illusion of bills to pay, a business to grow, a book to write, children to provide for, a husband dying of cancer, a boyfriend leaving, and terrifying self-doubts. Such magnificent lessons!

God bless you, fear, for getting my attention more than anything else, more than anyone, more than love, more than joy. You found me when no one else could. You sought me out, pushed me into corners, made me weep, made me angry, and broke me in half. Finally, fear, you broke me wide open. For that moment of total surrender to the Divine, I am deeply grateful. Only then did I embrace my soul and step fully into the light, refusing to ever go back into your dungeon, refusing to be your prisoner again.

Fear, my old friend, I recognize you now when you come to me in the night disguised as worries, illness, heartbreak, grief, or disappointment. I recognize you, master of disguises. I recognize you by the stirring in my gut as you approach, the quickening of my heart, the frantic pacing of my thoughts. Ah, it's you!

And you, fear, are not real. You are the boogeyman I planted in my closet. The one I told to awaken me in the middle of the night so I would learn to dance with you instead of cry, so that I would learn to use you as fuel to help me reach my next level. So that I would ultimately see that you are my friend, my fertilizer, my divine companion on this journey to rediscovering my soul.

I embrace you, fear, because without you I would be nowhere. I would never have jumped off a cliff into the unknown. I would never have stepped into my first terrifying adventure that changed everything. I would never have found my voice. Because without you, fear, I would still be sleeping.

You can stay in the closet or you can dance with me. It makes no difference. My light cannot be diminished. It never could. But it took you showing up for me to discover that. Now I love you so much, fear, that I can't find you, no matter how hard I look. My love has destroyed you, flooded your darkness, washed away your disguises, illuminated every crevice where you once hid.

When I turn to face you now, I see only divine order in your place.

I feel only my burning heart pulsing with gratitude, my arms reaching up to grasp the light.

Let me tell you a story . . .

In the spring of 1976, I was a twenty-five-year-old Montessori preschool teacher living in Missouri and looking for reinvention. My first love had moved out and broken my heart. I was drowning in self-doubt. When a friend mentioned that he'd once taken an Outward Bound survival course and it had changed his life, I was in.

After a few phone calls to Outward Bound headquarters in Hurricane Island, Maine, I packed some clothes and drove my little Honda Civic across the country for a three-week June course held on a thirty-foot-long, eight-foot-wide open boat with two sails and twelve oars. I'd heard stories of being dropped off alone on a tiny island for three days with only a tarp and some water. I knew about the required morning jumps from the edge of a seventy-five-foot cliff into the freezing Maine water, where you could die of hypothermia in twenty minutes. I was both terrified and elated.

I'd never done anything like this. I'd grown up in the 1950s, in the conservative South, where girls behaved and men created the rules. I found my posse of true friends when I dropped out of the University of Missouri in 1970 to march against the Vietnam War and ultimately to launch a dream. Mostly disowned by our conservative families because of our alternative beliefs, my newfound college-dropout friends and I worked menial jobs, opened health-food restaurants, bought land, grew our food, and lived organically before that was a thing. We discussed, debated, and practiced new kinds of spiritual awareness such as meditation, metaphysics, and simple living. I completely loved that part of my journey. But the "real world" beckoned as we each awoke to the realities of financial survival on untamed land in the middle of Missouri. Most of us left the farm in pursuit of more meaningful careers and the training they required. I became a teacher.

I did okay as a Montessori preschool teacher, but it soon felt like it wasn't enough, like I was starving for something more, never having taken my true path—whatever that was to be. And when my first love moved out, I became untethered, without boundaries, adrift. My soul was hungry for new direction, for rebirth. I felt I had nothing to lose.

From the first moment arriving at Hurricane Island in Maine, everyone in my Outward Bound group was treated like a military grunt in basic training. We were given duffle bags to stuff our few pieces of clothing into, assigned to bunk beds, run through obstacle courses, and taught basic nautical navigation with compass and sea charts. We were required to run at least three miles around the island every morning at sunrise, culminating in the morning cliff jump. I'd never run before. I'd been a dancer. This was 1976—long before the movie *Rocky* changed our culture, turning us into fist-pumping fitness addicts. I was winded and exhausted from the very first step of every early-morning run.

I'll never forget my initiation into cliff jumping, as dozens of cold and terrified people just like me lined up to take our turns running and jumping off a cliff that clearly led to a hideous death far below, either smashed against the rocky shore if we didn't leap far enough, or drowning in the tumbling waves of the deep blue sea. I was trembling and nauseous with fear as I got closer to the front of the line. But my wise instructor whispered, "Don't think. Just run and jump. Feel the fear and do it anyway."

In that moment, my life truly did begin to change. I took a deep breath, opened my heart, and ran for it. I was suddenly soaring over the water, screaming, laughing, then underwater, fighting for the surface. When I emerged, I heard cheers and felt the most immense joy I'd ever known. Pure elation. I'd done a terrifying and impossible thing, and I loved it.

For the next three weeks, the hardest weeks of my life thus far, I found myself overcoming fear a thousand times a day. I'd been randomly assigned to a "mobile course," meaning that after our initial four days of basic training on Hurricane Island, twelve of us lived together for twenty-two days on an open wooden boat with two sails and twelve heavy oars, enough for everyone to row endlessly on the windless, foggy sea. Hypothermia was a constant threat as we slept in sleeping bags thrown on top of oars laid crosswise across the boat. We sailed or rowed from island to island, sailing through storms that left us puking and rowing through windless days for back-breaking hours. When we arrived on an island, we hauled our gear to the beach and instantly went for long runs together.

Our instructors read to us every day and night, sharing inspiring stories of famous adventurers who'd trekked into the unknown to discover new lands, or who'd climbed previously unclimbed peaks in impossible conditions. The message was simple: Human potential is immeasurable and its imagined limits are always being stretched. Step up to your untapped potential. Break through your limitations. Fear is simply energy. Use it to move forward.

My instructor was badass and wise all at once. When I lagged behind on a morning run, he would jog beside me whispering about finding my inner strength and not being a wimp. When we rowed around an island to discover a towering, hundred-foot rock cliff rising straight up from the open sea, he taught us to rock climb. I felt strong and smart on my first-ever climb. With the sea to my back and the promise of heaven above, I stretched and reached and pushed like a dancer on a vertical stage. When I reached the top, my instructor told me that I was a graceful and talented natural climber, and that I was stronger than I knew. I drank in his words like water.

I believed my first lover had left me because I wasn't good enough, because I was deeply flawed and too insecure. I was wrapped in self-doubts since childhood, raised by a mother who never knew how to love me, and shamed in a family where my kind of sensitivity, intuition, and spiritual awareness was discredited. I was the oldest, and my role was to be perfect and to raise my younger siblings, which I did until I turned eighteen. That was my job, especially as my mother surrendered to the pain of miscarriage and depression. I swore I'd never be like her.

But leaving home at eighteen, I didn't know a single good thing about myself except that I could write.

Alone for three days during my solo experience on that tiny, freezing island off the Maine coast, nestled under a flimsy tarp strung between evergreens as storm after storm blew through, I was terrified at night by the howling wind and pounding waves, the deep black sky, the sense of utter isolation from the world. Left with nothing but my fear and my tears, I began to remember who I was. I found my radiant, indestructible soul. I was reborn into someone strong and good. Fear was now my ally. Fear and doubt became my fuel for reinvention.

After that course was over, I returned to Missouri, became an avid rock climber, and worked my way through college to get a degree in psychology. Two years later, I became a Colorado Outward Bound mountaineering instructor, which led me on the journey to be who I am today.

When we bravely say yes to life, open our hearts, and jump into the deep blue sea of fear, we emerge stronger than we ever believed we could be; we awaken to our true self. We shift from the ego lens to the divine lens, and everything changes for the better.

◎ Dissolving Fear

Love is the most powerful positive force of all, and it always trumps darkness.

- When you're afraid, send love to what you fear. It's like turning on a light in a dark room. Open your heart and pump the love. Darkness will disappear.
- When you're afraid, sit in meditation until you can feel love for just one person in your life. See that person wrapped in your powerful love. Pump your love to this person until you see them smiling and laughing. Now extend that love energy out to the entire space around you, filling it with golden light.
- Now pump your love out to the entire world. See our planet wrapped in golden love and light, and all of its peoples looking peaceful and happy. Spend time with that image. When you open your eyes, the room you're sitting in will shimmer with love and light. Your fear will be gone.

4

Anger and Jealousy

How the Ego
Fires You Up

Anger and jealousy are part of our collective human experience. As consciousness evolves, we begin to understand that when we stand in anger, we see people and events through the ego lens rather than the divine lens.

The ego lens shows us that we're separate from others, disconnected, victims of those more powerful than us. The ego mind tells us there is injustice in the world and so our anger is justified. This approach to life and to painful events is fine—at first. In our youth we may use our anger to move forward, fight for freedom, get out of bad situations or relationships, and accomplish things that seem impossible. Anger can be used as a positive force for personal or collective change, especially at the beginning of the soul journey.

As we evolve, however, we reach a point where we become aware of more enlightened ways to respond to life's pain. When we explore our anger to see what truth it is revealing, we realize there's another way to look at who or what makes us angry. We can slip on the divine lens and see the larger play of light and dark, of awareness and unconsciousness. We begin to understand that every soul here is behaving exactly as nobly as their consciousness allows and as appropriate for their stage of soul growth. They're capable of nothing more until they evolve to a higher level of consciousness.

In other words, the murderer is so unconscious and unevolved spiritually that the inner darkness of their fear-based mind becomes their own personal hell. Only when they ask for wisdom, when they reach out and search for meaning, are they pulled into the light and become capable of living from a state of greater wisdom, awareness, and compassion. Until that moment of awakening, however, the murderer lives in a private hell of their own creation, even though the outside world does not see or understand this. The murderer gets away with nothing, even if he's never caught.

Your job as an awakened being is to help awaken higher consciousness in others—through love and wisdom rather than anger and blame. Your job is to become a beacon of light for those who live in darkness. You must bathe in love and wisdom, surrender the pitiful ego lens, and learn to live mostly within your divine lens. Once this is achieved, you're capable of changing the world, of reforming the murderer, whether he lives inside or outside you.

*Only when we all awaken in consciousness will we be
free to live fully in the light of divinity. As long as one soul
walks in darkness, none of us is free. As long as one soul
is unforgiven, we are all unforgiven.*

Today you may choose to act or think with anger. This is your free-will right as a human on planet Earth. But observe how anger feels in your body. Observe the aftereffects of your angry thoughts, words, and actions. Then ask yourself: Did I change anything or anyone for the better with my anger? Did I help an unevolved soul wake up? Was I in touch with my soul's wisdom when I acted in anger? Or did it feel like I acted from my lower ego self, fighting with the world for the sake of fighting?

What Lies beneath This Anger I Carry toward the World? Is it perhaps my deep longing to be back home in the divine realms, where we're wrapped in love and light? Am I angry that I'm here and not there? Here and not "home"? Have I forgotten that I chose this earthly experience? Have I forgotten that I chose to help others evolve?

Am I angry that there is so much unconsciousness here? How does my anger help bring others into the light? Could sharing my wisdom be more effective in helping others awaken? How different would that feel inside my body? Inside my heart? What would be the effects of sharing my wisdom to help others rather than relying on old patterns of anger and blame? How might my life change then?

There's a brief moment of silence before we react in anger. Within this brief, silent moment lives your choice point. This silence is the gateway to your soul. If you take a deep breath, take a step back, and call out for divine guidance, you'll quickly feel yourself lifted out of the reactionary anger of ego, which is the need to attack, defend, justify, and blame. Grab hold of that spirit hand reaching down to lift you up and pull you toward the wisdom of divine perspective.

The question is: Do you love the feeling of anger more than you love beauty or grace? Do you understand that by choosing anger you're denying grace and blocking its flow from your own life?

Look at your worthy opponent standing in front of you, the one who sparked your anger. Bless that soul for arriving at this exact moment to show you your next level of inner growth, to give you another chance to pass your soul's test and rise to a higher level of consciousness, a level where beauty, love, and grace abounds.

All that's required of you in this moment of anger is to see the other person as a wounded soul doing the best they can from their own level of awareness. Love them for their pain and struggles because you're just like them. By loving them, you're loving yourself. Rise above the unconscious ego behavior they're showing you, because it's ugly, selfish, and desperate, and that's not who you are. That's not who you aspire to be.

Look at this lost and pained soul standing before you who has just hurt you and acted from their ego self, and know that you no longer want to look like them or act like them. They're showing you a part of yourself that you're ready to surrender.

One simple breath and a request for guidance pulls you away from habitual reaction and raises you a notch toward your great soul potential. Thank the messenger, your worthy opponent, for the lesson; thank the soul standing before you who triggered your reaction. Your anger is revealed so that it can be healed.

The next time someone says or does something that triggers your anger, you'll already be removed from the ego experience, more in touch with your soul's wisdom, watching it all unfold from your divine lens. You'll pause, take a breath, adjust your lens, and choose your words gracefully. Compassion will pour through you when you allow it. Quieting the mind and opening the heart is how you allow it.

This is the gift of your anger. This is the gift of your opponent arriving with their sword drawn, eager to slice a piece out of you. In that moment of sacred recognition, everything changes: you realize that nothing and no one can ever hurt you or tarnish your lovely soul when you view life through your divine lens.

JEALOUSY, COURTESY OF THE EGO LENS

When we view the lives of others through our ego lens, we see only the illusion of who they're pretending to be. We see the illusion of perfection that they've created for protection. We all create this same illusion, although some of us are better at illusion-creation than others.

Every single soul comes here to learn and evolve. If you believe that anyone on Earth has it easier or better than you, you're not seeing their soul journey. You're using your ego lens and seeing only the illusion.

We assume we understand who people are when we look at the superficial circumstances of their lives. But we're only looking at their ego story instead of seeing beneath the surface to understand their soul story. When we wear the ego lens, we can't see the desperate pain, the tragic losses, and the crippling self-doubts that live inside everyone. If we did, if we took the time to understand their soul story, to feel the abuse they suffered in childhood, the heart-wrenching losses they experienced in early adulthood, or the crippling self-doubts they wake up to every morning, then we would understand they are the same as us, whether they live in a mansion, a palace, or as a beggar on the street. We're all souls on a journey of evolution, having a shared experience here on Earth. From this divine perspective, everyone is worthy of your love, compassion, and forgiveness.

You may tell yourself that you could be happy if you lived in a mansion or a palace or a beach house on the ocean, that all you're missing is financial abundance. But this simply means that the lesson you're facing right now is around owning your power through money and career. It's about finding your true work despite your self-doubts. What you're learning today as you struggle with a lack of money is exactly what you need to learn in order to evolve to your next level of soul growth.

If you're facing life's lessons with anger, bitterness, or jealousy, then you're not learning what you're meant to learn, and you're delaying your own growth. When you judge a wealthy neighbor or a celebrity for their superficial lives, you're using your ego lens. You're refusing to see the soul journey and the perfection of each person's journey to consciousness. In your jealousy, you're flunking your soul's lesson and sliding backward in your own journey to consciousness.

Study the person you're jealous of. Discover their true story. Seek to understand their soul journey. What lessons did they come here to learn? What is their greatest pain? What is their greatest gift? As you dig deeper and truly see what they've experienced in this lifetime, you'll eventually be very glad that their path is not yours. You'll see that their hidden pain and private challenges are not anything you would choose to take on. You'll realize that you prefer the struggles and blessings of your own journey. Then you'll find it easy to offer anyone love, wisdom, and compassion.

Whenever you feel jealous, meditate and ask to be lifted from your ego view and shown the soul story of the one you envy. Ask to understand their pain so you can feel compassion rather than jealousy. This will elevate you into divine consciousness and pull you out of your own pain. You're now wearing your divine lens to view the lives of others, and you can check jealousy off of your list of soul lessons yet to learn.*

From my soul to yours

I've been having a near-death experience, looking down at this life, bewildered by what I see, confused by how lost we are. I struggle to get my boots back on the ground, assume the position, and just *be* here. I land in the dirt; it hurts my eyes. But I came here on purpose, just like you.

I need to see the golden cords tying all of our random and tragic world events together, revealing the divine order. I see them sometimes. Not today. Today I feel the weight of fear and despair on my shoulders.

Our crushing human flaw is our focus on the material world and not the spiritual purpose behind it. "It is what it is," we say, shrugging our shoulders. This misguided focus repeatedly creates a painful spiritual crisis, one from which we all will eventually evolve.

Do you tell yourself every day that you have to work in an industry you dislike, doing work that isn't your soul mission, just to get a paycheck and benefits? It's what you have to do, you say to yourself, forgetting that this physical world is *your* dream, *your* illusion.

---

*Numerology is a powerful tool to help you understand your birth path and to see yourself as a soul on a journey. See "Calculating Your Birth Path Using Numerology," the appendix of this book. I've also described this technique in my previous books: *I See Your Dream Job: A Career Intuitive Shows You How to Discover What You Were Put on Earth to Do* and *I See Your Soul Mate: An Intuitive's Guide to Finding and Keeping Love.*

Do you tell yourself that your loved one's too-early death was a meaningless tragedy from which you don't intend to recover because what's the point? And why feel happy when your loved one is gone?

Do you look around at others to blame for the trivial and tragic moments of life? Everyday traffic (those idiot drivers!); your chronic illness (those stupid doctors!); your failing business (this terrible economy!).

When your pain gets so great and your life crumbles, do you suddenly cry out for different answers? Do you frantically struggle to clean up your spiritual oil spill, the black mess spreading across the waves of your higher consciousness?

Can't we evolve without crisis? Or does it take a world tragedy to get us to ask different questions, to search for deeper meaning? Can't we live every day remembering who we are and play this earthly game from a higher perspective? Will you have to die before you remember who you are? Will you have to die before you remember that this is a game we came here to play, and that the winners are the ones who live in love and help everyone else?

You came here to remember your death while still walking on the sands of this shore, to stand in both worlds at once. Impossible? No, or we wouldn't have come here. It's only a simple reaching for your divine lens that's required, a deep breath, and a request for inner guidance that changes everything.

Daily Energy Shifters

Here are some daily energy shifters to help you keep your divine lens perspective, especially when the dark emotions of anger and jealousy arise:

- Open your heart and love recklessly.
- Refocus your thoughts.
- Tell a new story.
- Shift from superficial to superspiritual.
- Laugh like there's no tomorrow.
- Forgive with abandon.

- Get wildly grateful.
- Sweeten up.
- Move your chi.
- Feed your chi.
- See your best future.

5
Sadness, Depression, and Anxiety
Ego Cataracts

.

Sadness comes to you wrapped in illusion. It tells you a tall tale—that you're longing for a loved one on the other side, a lover who left you, or a career that betrayed you. But that's never what your sadness truly is. Sadness is a pool, an ocean, a river that sweeps us away when we disconnect from our Higher Self and our soul's wisdom. Sadness and depression are signs that we're living in alignment with the ego instead of the soul.

A physician will tell you that sadness and depression are nothing but chemical imbalances to be righted by a drug. And you may even try to reach enlightenment through pharmaceuticals, for a while . . . But chemical imbalance is not the source of your sadness. Chemical imbalance is the side-effect of the long-term use of the ego lens. Chemical imbalance occurs when the soul disconnects from the Higher Self. This separation from the soul's wisdom causes your ego mind to dwell on negative thoughts. Living submerged in such fearful emotions will throw your body chemistry into chaos. You become a victim of your negative thought loops, which you've chosen to indulge in for too many years (or perhaps lifetimes).

You should never discontinue taking prescribed medications unless you're under medical supervision. And I'm certainly not a medical professional. But in my experience with thousands of clients and students, I'm convinced there are effective ways to correct such a chemical imbalance other than pharmaceuticals. One of them is by quieting the mind through daily meditation and calling for guidance to help you view life through your divine lens. When we ask for divine guidance, we always get answers. This divine intervention helps us break our negative thought cycle.

It's essential to understand the chain of events that creates emotional imbalance. It's not simply one incident in life that throws us into chronic depression, anxiety, paranoia, or schizophrenia. Those diagnoses arrive on the heels of years of making lifestyle and emotional choices not in alignment with our Higher Self. These choices include things like a poor diet that lacks the B vitamins our nervous system requires, alcohol and drug use that throws us off our natural chemical balance, and allowing the ego lens to fill us with fear so that we endlessly make choices based on fear rather than trusting the wisdom of our soul.

A diagnosis of any form of mental illness is a sign of a deep spiritual and emotional crisis that has been slowly brewing after years of negative, fear-based thinking and being disconnected from one's Higher Self. To turn this negative cycle around requires reversing all habitual patterns, from lifestyle choices to spiritual beliefs. And it's crucial to recognize our addiction to the emotion of fear.

Often, by the time a person is diagnosed with a mental disorder such as depression, they *do* need chemical intervention in the form of prescription medication to break the cycle. But medication is only the beginning of realigning with the soul. The person must also take steps on all recovery fronts, including nutrition, exercise, vitamin supplementation, counseling to understand the nature of the mind, and spiritual exploration to find greater purpose in life. This doesn't have to mean religion or church. It can mean going on the spiritual journey of learning to meditate, taking classes in New Thought* ideas, and reading books once considered taboo because they were too unconventional or New Age.

Establishing a personal daily practice of connecting to the Divine, to something beyond the physical world, is essential for a healthy life. We can meditate, pray, quiet the mind, or walk in nature as we reestablish our connection to our Higher Self. As well, it's important to understand the true nature of prayer. True prayer is about asking for guidance, wisdom, and love—not material things. Many religious followers become disillusioned because they've been taught that God is basically their Santa Claus in the sky, someone who answers their prayer requests for a new job or car. If that job or car doesn't appear, they turn away from God and refuse to ever again believe in anything beyond the material world.

Yet when we pray for things instead of spiritual intangibles, we aren't acting in alignment with Source and are not in divine order. Those prayers are seldom answered. When we ask for light, love, and clarity, we're immediately surrounded by divine guides, breaking us wide open with wisdom and filling us with love. True prayer is a request for guidance. The ego prays for things; the soul prays for wisdom and courage. The soul's prayers are always answered.

Our Higher Self will caution us against living a life that's not in alignment with our great potential. This guidance shows up as dreams and strong feelings that are nearly impossible to ignore. Our divine lens reveals that living such a life drains us of soul power, also known as energy. The divine lens always reveals the first step that will move us into a life of light, inspiration, and love. But *we* must take the first step.

Whenever we feel alone, abandoned, and afraid, remember that somewhere, sometime, there was a place that felt different to us, that felt

---

*The New Thought movement, which emerged in the nineteenth century, sought to understand the divine mysteries through the power of thought, maintaining that true human selfhood is divine. It said that one's thoughts could unlock secrets to living a better life, free from the constraints of religious doctrines or dogmas.

loving, that felt like home. Our soul longs mightily for this elusive realm, this vague memory of when we once lived in the light, where our soulmates embraced us and we learned our soul's lessons effortlessly through grace. In this other world that we vaguely recall, we felt completely and absolutely loved in ways that we've only briefly experienced on Earth.

Right now, you're on Earth because this is the school you agreed to attend. It offers the exact challenges and lessons you agreed to master. It allows your true essence, your unique gifts, to take full form and be fully shared. You volunteered for this experience because you knew it was for your highest good and the highest good of others.

What could be better or more fulfilling than the evolution of your soul? Once you step onto this path with total surrender, you'll live in divine grace and joyful fulfillment. There's nothing finer, sweeter, richer than this life that awaits you here when you fearlessly embrace it.

Yes, you're desperately homesick for something "other"—a vague dream, a fading memory of a loving home you once knew. You're hungry for the light, and you pursue it in all the wrong places. But you will be returning to that light soon enough. And when you do, you'll see that this lifetime was a brief opportunity, merely the blink of an eye in your soul's journey. You'll understand that this was the lifetime when you intended to let your gifts pour through you to enlighten the world and banish fear with love.

Your ego cries out, *Why am I here all alone in this empty, meaningless, unconscious world?*

Your soul answers, *Because you chose to come here for your highest good and the highest good of all. You came here to evolve. Embrace this moment, seize the opportunity for growth and wisdom, and know that you're never alone.*

This earthly realm feels heavy, dense, scary, and sometimes dark—especially compared to the lingering impressions of the higher realms we experienced before we incarnated. Depression and sadness are part of our collective human experience in this dense energy. But when we reach for light and call for divine guidance, we're instantly pulled into the light and freed from the murky waters of depression and sadness.

Sadness and depression are gifts of opportunity.
They break us apart until we finally say, "Enough!
I'm disgusted with my ego lens and its pitiful view.
I will try to view this differently. I'll reach for my
divine lens because I truly have nothing left to lose!"
In that moment everything changes. We're lifted
gracefully into love.

Deep sadness has been with me throughout my lifetime. It has washed over me at every challenge, arriving on the heels of each loved one's death, each job loss, each moment of confusion and fear. I've known sadness as an endless longing. It wrings me out. Only when I find myself broken open, sitting in the mud, tears streaming down my cheeks, do I finally open up, call out for the Divine, and ask to be shown the reason for my pain.

In the instant I make that call for inner guidance, send that plea, whisper the words, reach my arms up to the Divine, a blanket of loving comfort is wrapped around my shoulders. I'm shown how to get up and move forward.

But then I must make the effort to get up. I must make that choice. And in finding my strength to get back up again, I learn the meaning of the lesson and feel the reward of leaning into the pain and stepping into my wisdom.

From my soul to yours

The moment you shed your tears, open up, give up, surrender, and admit you know nothing, everything gets better. Way better. Magically better . . .

When you wrap your arms around your departed beloved, the one who won't be coming home again, and you lose your heart, feel it lifting up and taking wing, leaving like the daylight leaves at sunset, you see that nothing here is real. And the person you thought you were is gone, left behind, empty handed.

Later, when you've traveled home, stood in your bedroom staring at nothing, you see that the only thing left behind is you—bare naked, stripped down to your soul. Who is that? How long has it been? How long have you managed the details of your life and forgotten to check on your soul?

That feeling of not knowing who you are now or what matters anymore is your new beginning. It will kick the wind from your stomach, knock you to the floor, and leave you without words, empty, waiting to be filled with Spirit.

One day soon you'll be the newborn baby you once were, bright and shiny, with no story attached. No history. No definitions or titles. Just a radiant soul made of energy and love, excited about a new beginning. This is the blessing of your loss.

Throw out your trash. Rip off your clothes. Forget your name, your story, your tragedies. Feel the joy of knowing nothing and being no one. This fresh energy will soar into your newly opened heart like mother's milk. It's what you've needed for a long time. It's necessary to help you realign with your great work.

Release each belief you've held so dear, every idea of who you should be, every fear of not being perfect. You've carried this carefully crafted identity, your burden of lies, for too many years. Now the universe has made its own plans for stripping it all away to help you remember something essential.

That's always the purpose of your loss.

You didn't come here to be someone else or hide behind anyone. You came here to be you, laden with gifts and blessed with challenges. You intended to grow—to push past your fears and expand. You knew coming in that change would be required. When did you forget that?

Look in the mirror and ask: Who am I now? Is this who I intended to be?

Strip it all away. You never know what lies beneath your tarnished surface until it's all gone. Then you'll see the gold, the beauty of your naked soul. You don't have to figure it all out to know which steps to take for the next five years. You need only take the first step. Divine order arranges the rest.

Get out your pencil and erase the spreadsheets, delete the to-do lists and the five-year plans, walk into your yard, climb the fence, swim in the lake of your unspoken dreams. Heal yourself.

Turn away from those who remind you of who you've been. Walk out of rooms that keep you small. Take a step into the impossible. This is your new life.

Someday when you've forgotten who you used to be and what you used to want, and you believe in things you never would have considered and do things you never would have had the courage to do, you'll catch a glimpse of your beloved—the one who would never come home again, the night your new life began. You'll see him in the corner of the room, watching you, nodding his head with a smile, sending you the greatest love you ever felt. And you'll know that you never lost anything on that wicked day when you thought you'd lost it all.

◉ Shifting into the Soul's Perspective

Practice this technique whenever life feels difficult:

Take one deep, slow breath; follow it in and out. Sit in silence.

Repeat a mantra such as *Om Namah Shivaya* (in Sanskrit, "I bow to the Divine Self within") or a prayer such as the Lord's Prayer for several moments.

Make your request: "Please help me see my soul's perspective on this challenge."

Finish these sentences:

- I am grateful for . . .
- I open my heart and send love to . . .
- One positive step I can take today is . . .

MAKE POSITIVE LIFESTYLE CHOICES

Become aware of the importance of physical, emotional, and spiritual nutrition to your mental and emotional well-being. Everything you eat, drink, read, view, think about, or pray about affects your mental and emotional health.

Embrace the physical habits that heal you, such as eating fresh, unprocessed, unsweetened foods; rising early in the morning and going to bed before midnight; taking nutritional supplements such as herbs and B vitamins (preferably as advised by a doctor of naturopathy); eliminating all alcohol and drugs; reading inspiring and uplifting books; exercising or moving at least twenty minutes daily; and spending time with people who inspire you.

Make a daily checklist of the foods you eat, including the beverages you consume, the amount of sleep you get, the amount of time spent in prayer or meditation, the people you're around, and the amount of exercise you get.

Keep track of how these daily activities influence your mental and emotional well-being. When you're ready to heal, you'll have a roadmap of which activities, people, and foods serve you best.

See a counselor or therapist who helps you feel positive and optimistic about your future.

◉ Use Your Pain as Fuel

Consider the possibility that all of your pain—every wound you've ever experienced, every loss, every disappointment, every frustration—was exactly what you needed and chose in order to arrive at this point in your life, which is exactly where you're supposed to be. Realize that your soul chose to experience this pain to open your heart and strengthen your connection to the Divine in order to push you onto your true path and inspire you to accomplish your soul's mission. Your greatest work offers to the world what you wish had been offered to you in your moment of greatest pain. Consider:

- Pain fuels your greatest spiritual and emotional reinvention; it breaks your heart wide open and sends you searching for the truth of who you truly are.
- Pain brings a clarity and focus to your life's purpose that gives you a powerful advantage in everything you do.
- Pain will drive you to see beyond the surface and embrace a truly spiritual perspective in every area of your life.
- Pain heals us by giving us a chance to refocus on what's important: who and what we truly love, why we are here, and what great work will fulfill our Earth mission.
- Pain can only be healed when we allow ourselves to fully feel it—for a minute, an hour, a day, or every day.
- We have to surrender and feel in order to heal.

6

Perfectionism and Stress

The Ego's Macro Lens

There's no brilliant without crazy, no wisdom without ignorance, no love without hate, and no courage without fear. Yet we hope to be one without the other—a rose without thorns. We forget our agreement— to fully experience the light *and* the dark, which is to be human.

We can't own our gifts or our divinity without also owning our piti- ful self and our stupidity, without realizing that our mistakes are what we came here for. They can offer our greatest moments of awakening.

There's no north without south, no found without lost, no laughter without tears, and no sunrise without sunset. We come here to feel and express it all: to move through the crazy to find the brilliance, to move through hell to find heaven. Only then can we clearly choose light over dark, love over hate, and courage over fear. This is our mission here in this dense realm.

Pretending to be perfect—all good, brilliant, enlightened—is an impossible dream here on planet Earth, for we are imperfect human beings. Yet how we waste time longing for it and seeking it in others. When our beloveds' weaknesses are fully revealed, we stone them, hate them—just as we despise ourself—for being fallible. But this is to miss the point of being human.

How eager we are to see another person's flaws, to forget that we too have flaws, are made from the same fabric, have spoken the same words, and made the same mistakes. To realize our divine nature is to know that we are all made of this same imperfect fabric.

Create your beautiful life. Sew perfection into every moment. But embrace the defects hidden in your cloth. Know that under the surface, your beautiful life is woven with the same anxieties, fears, hatreds, and mistakes as the life of your greatest enemy. Then you'll realize why there's nothing ever to forgive.

Offer a hand to the one who hurt you the most; you'll help them see their gifts and remember their divinity. You'll help them be who they came here to be. Doing this will save you.

The moment you see that your greatest shame, your greatest pain, is also your greatest gift, you'll understand why you're here and who you are.

Love your pain and fear, embrace your darkness. It will lead you to your gifts, your courage, and your divinity. It will open your heart. Love the entire story of your imperfect life, especially the grotesque mistakes and ugly self-doubts. Release your need for perfection in anyone or anything, yourself most of all. Love the thorns along with the rose. Become the person who embraces the thorns and the gifts in everyone, including yourself. Know that one can't exist without the other. Doing this will heal you. And it will save the life of everyone you meet.

THE IMPERFECTION OF PERFECTION

There is no perfection here, but we long for it, like longing for a dream. The impossible perfection lives elsewhere, in another realm from whence we came. It's the perfection of love, wisdom, and spirit. It's higher consciousness.

Our attempts to recreate perfection here on Earth are often focused on the outer self, the ego, and the details of our material world. We seek to perfect the trivial. Or we demand perfection from others. All of this is misguided.

This world, this realm, is not perfect and never will be. That is not its purpose. If you spend your life on Earth expecting perfection from yourself and others, you will live in constant disappointment and bitterness and lose touch with your soul's wisdom. Or you can spend your life seeking true perfection as you once knew it on the other side: the perfection of spirit. This is soul alignment. It allows perfect wisdom to flow within you and through you to others. This type of perfection aligns you with divinity and empowers you to become a source of endless love and wisdom. This is the true perfection that you're ultimately seeking, not the false perfection of an imperfect physical world that your ego lens focuses on.

You already know everything. You already know the
parts of your story you'll regret. You already know which
pieces you'll be proud of. And you already know that
your story ends someday.

Take an inventory of true perfection in your life. Are you focusing on spiritual growth above all else? Are you asking for divine guidance in your moments of greatest pain? Are you reaching for love and forgiveness when you feel angry and blameful? Are you a channel of divine inspiration in your work? Do you use your unique inner gifts to change the world? If so, you've achieved true soul perfection. This is what you came here to achieve. It's the only perfection you're meant to strive for. Once you achieve this, your life aligns with grace and divine order. You see light where others see darkness. You know the answers to all questions. You become fearless in adversity. Your heart urges you forward. You accomplish what you came here to do.

If you've gotten caught in the painful trap of false perfectionism, forgive yourself for being misguided, for forgetting what you came here to do. You didn't go through the enormous effort it took your soul to condense into a physical body and walk through this dense physical world simply to rearrange meaningless details. How do you know they're meaningless? Ask yourself if they will matter to you at the end of your life when you review your lifetime. When you see the ripple effect of each action you took on Earth, each word you spoke, you'll understand then what was essential. You can understand this now, if you so choose.

Where are you seeking perfection today? Do your efforts leave you disappointed, depressed, angry, or afraid? If so, you're not seeking divine perfection. Turn that powerful human drive for perfection toward your inner self, your soul's growth. Seek to have a perfectly loving heart and a sense of inner peace from living in alignment with your Higher Self. Seek to become a fearless channel of divine wisdom and to find work that helps enlighten the world.

Now your perfectionism is being used for your highest good and the good of others. It's serving its true purpose—correctly focused, like a powerful laser, on exactly what you came here to do and who you came here to be.

STRESS, ASTIGMATISM OF EGO

When we lose touch with the voice of the soul, we feel alone in the world, untethered, shaken, fragile, and overwhelmed by impossible details. We believe that making a mistake will ruin everything. Our creativity is blocked with fear. This is the distortion of the ego lens. Viewing life through the ego lens, we aren't able to see the cords of divine light illuminating our path or hear our inner guidance comforting us. When we abandon our higher self we feel beaten down, worried, and afraid.

The ego lens reveals only the most trivial details. It obscures the higher purpose, the greater path, the overarching gift of the moment. Seen through the ego lens, each detail matters equally. Priorities are confused. We cannot move forward.

You are never alone, especially when you feel overwhelmed. Every divine guide who watches over you and each member of your soul family is available to instantly offer wisdom, to reveal a new idea, to fill you with inspiration, to light your way and pull you out of the darkness.

Why can't you feel this? You can—by changing lenses. This inner shift begins with the breath. A simple, deep inhalation and slow exhalation begins to align you with Spirit and with your soul's wisdom.

Notice how shallow and rapid your breathing is when you feel stressed. When you take a deep, slow, delicious breath, inhaling fully, exhaling slowly, you begin to move into the light. You infuse your body with divinity. You realign with your soul. This is the real reason why smokers are addicted to cigarettes—it's the only time they breathe deeply. A long inhalation on a cigarette changes their energy for the better, until the cigarette habit destroys their bodies and thus depletes their energy. Learning to breathe deeply—minus the cigarette—is very helpful to anyone trying to break this addiction.

After taking some deep breaths, call out for guidance. Speak your request out loud. Ask for inner clarity and enlightened wisdom. Ask to be pulled out of fear and instead to feel loved and supported and to clearly see your next step. Ask for strength and courage. These requests are always answered. These prayers are always heard.

In that moment of prayer you will suddenly realize you've been sitting at a feast, a table laden with nourishment and abundance, but you've been unable to see it. The ego lens has blinded you to what's right in front of you. You've been starving when all along everything you've ever needed is right in front of you, within reach. You ache with fear when more love than you could ever imagine is already on your plate.

A simple shift into focusing through your divine lens reveals the feast of opportunities that await you, the abundance of love within easy reach. It helps you reorganize your priorities. Suddenly you feel as fearless as a hero and as loving as an angel.

◉ Tell Your Soul Story

Writing can open you up to the many possibilities of seeing from a higher perspective, especially when that view is obscured by stress and the obsessive drive for perfection. Consider the following questions, and without premeditating, write in your journal the first thing that comes to mind.

- How would you view your life from your soul's view? What moments do you recognize as gifts of opportunity and divine guidance that you did or did not recognize at the time?
- Speaking from your soul and not your ego, what would you tell yourself today to inspire you to move forward without the need to make everything perfect?
- Look for any patterns in how your perfectionism manifests and make choices to act outside of your fear of being "less than." When you've chosen from inspiration and courage, where did those choices get you?
- Highlight the moments in your life when an opening appeared and you took it, even though you were afraid of being judged, and that choice brought you into a better life.
- Spend a few minutes quieting your mind, then take a deep breath and release it, asking for divine guidance: *Please help me see my journey as I intended to fulfill it here—living with wisdom, love, and light.* Now begin writing your story in the third person, as if you're telling a story about someone other than yourself. Start with your childhood and move forward all the way to the present, observing those times when self-judgment and perfectionism blocked you from moving forward, and those times when you overcame those ego tendencies with the gifts of grace and forgiveness.
- Explain how you helped others and fulfilled your soul's mission or could have done so. Write about the relationships you attracted (both those that were painful and those that were wonderful) and the love you ultimately embraced or did not embrace. Write about your graceful exit through your future death as your soul has planned it for you. Write quickly so that it pours through from your right brain, your intuition, your soul.
- Now take another breath and ask for more wisdom. Read through your story, keeping in the painful challenges that you've faced but filling in your steps after those challenges with even more love and wisdom at every turn until you tell the story of your richest, most fulfilled potential lifetime. When it feels right to you, keep it. This is now your story—the only one you'll ever tell again.

7

Addiction

Ego Lens Side-Effects

When we become addicted to anything or anyone, it's because our ego mind has taken over and drowned out our soul's wisdom. Our ego voice tells us that life is too difficult and physical pleasure is our only relief from suffering in a pointless world. The ego also tells us that we need the love of another person to complete us, to feel happy, when we already have a constant divine companion, our Higher Self, as well as many sacred guides and departed loved ones who are available to comfort us at any moment.

The more we indulge the ego mind and its desires, the more separated from our Higher Self we become. Overuse of alcohol, drugs, sex, shopping, and food steadily replaces prayer. These compulsive behaviors cloud our connection to the higher realms. They block our access to the sweet nectar of divine wisdom that flows freely from Source and is infinitely more pleasurable and empowering than physical addictions.

Yet the very act of pursuing drugs, alcohol, or any addiction is the act of a hungry soul seeking meaning in an empty world. It's the soul crying out for connection to something greater than the physical world. Your soul craves the bliss and love of the divine realms, which you remember vaguely and can briefly recreate in that moment of getting high, before the terrible crash occurs, as it always does, leaving you in a lower, less connected, and more fragile and terrified state than before.

Your addiction, whatever it may be, is actually the soul's search for spiritual fulfillment, for release from the mundane. It's a cry for relief from the depressing ego lens perspective you've been drowning in. With addictive behavior you do not realize that you hold within you a divine lens that alleviates the emptiness of the ego mind more profoundly than any compulsive behavior or mind-altering substance ever could.

Your self-destructive behavior is a cry for salvation, even though you may not realize this and those around you may not either. But your soul does understand and waits patiently for you to realign with the Divine so that all pain can be healed. Your soul sees that you're choosing this lesson as a final step into the darkness before you climb into the light. But how far will you fall into that darkness? How long will it take you to crawl out? Will you stay so long that climbing out and into the light becomes nearly impossible? Only you can decide this.

ADDICTION AS
A TEMPORARY REPRIEVE

Within all addictive behaviors exists a brief moment of bliss that is vaguely reminiscent of the higher realms. We feel temporarily comforted. We feel at home, briefly, until the fall from grace that always arrives on the heels of addictive behavior.

Addictive acts are not the pathway home. They only take us deeper into the abyss, which is devoid of love, wisdom, and joy. There's no greater pain than this abandonment of the soul, so we continue with our compulsive addictions to alleviate the pain in a never-ending cycle.

The only solution is to shift into higher consciousness without the aid of a substance or a behavior. We're required to choose our divine lens. This takes discipline and courage after we've spent so much time swimming in the muck of unconsciousness. Yet it's possible for anyone suffering from addictive behavior.

As humans, it gives us great comfort to know there is something more to this physical world. Yet if we've reached for that experience through the self-destructive behavior, although providing a temporary reprieve from our soul-level pain, this comfort is fleeting. Afterward, we feel even more depleted and depressed than before. The crash that follows getting high is a moment of utter terror, as we become completely submerged in ego and separated from our Higher Self. Our body chemistry goes out of whack due to becoming fully immersed in fear rather than love. Continually reenacting addictive behavior disconnects us from Source, such that we can no longer embody the high-frequency energy that we need in order to reach out and reconnect. At this point one becomes a lost soul.

> *Taking a deep breath and calling for guidance*
> *will always pull you back into the light.*
> *But the addict rarely realizes this.*

The addict forgets that they live in a physical body in a physical world, with certain sacred laws that must be followed to keep the body filled with the life force and the personality aligned with the soul. When these rules are violated, we suffer from the lower vibrational energy we've created within the body. This low-vibrational state manifests as a hangover, withdrawal symptoms, depression, and anxiety.

The ego mind tells us there's no other way to restore balance than to repeat the same unhealthy behavior. But the body chemistry is now out of whack, and it becomes nearly impossible to reestablish a base level of contentment. The addict has fallen deeply into a hole that is ruled by the ego, and the ego is now fully in charge, doing its best to block the soul's wisdom. This is what's known as hell.

But the soul is always whispering loving guidance. In brief moments, between bouts of pain, we experience this inner voice of wisdom. Maybe it arrives while we're laid out on the bathroom floor, examining a negative bank balance, or looking in the mirror in the morning after a lost night out. In every moment of surrender, the soul speaks up.

If you choose to take a deep breath and listen, to ask for guidance and seek another way, you'll be lifted into the light, given a new chance, and pulled out of the hole that the ego has dug for you. This is called spiritual awakening. You can call it a twelve-step program, daily meditation, Christianity, Judaism, Hinduism, Buddhism, or metaphysics in general. It doesn't matter what form it takes. You're now beginning to embrace your soul's wisdom once again. You're learning to separate from the hell of the ego mind.

Your awakening can cure any addiction. It can heal your broken body. It can mend your broken heart. But it takes work. Inner strength can be developed only in the same way your muscles are strengthened—through discipline and repetition.

If today you suffer from some form of addiction and you're reading this book, you are being called to awaken. You're being asked to align with your soul's wisdom and experience the true bliss of the Higher Self. This bliss trumps everything. It's the lesson you came here to learn, and it's the next step of your soul's journey.

WHY ARE WE ADDICTED TO THE EGO LENS?

There's only one answer to this question: because we're afraid. Ironically, we fear our own divinity, our soul's wisdom, our great potential. If we owned our divinity, we wouldn't be capable of living small anymore, of dwelling in blame, rage, hate, and fear. Those states are powerful drugs in themselves, which the addict favors over the effort it takes to cultivate love, wisdom, and understanding. These higher frequency states ask us to stretch our beliefs, release old patterns, ignore the crazy chatter of the world around us, and disregard others' opinions of us, and instead follow our untested inner wisdom.

◎ Breaking Through Addictions

Take these baby steps to help you pull away from the ego's desires and shift into your Higher Self.

Meditate for twenty minutes twice daily to quiet your fear mind. Use the Sanskrit mantra *Om Namah Shivaya.* Don't think about the meaning. Just repeat the Sanskrit phrase and keep redirecting your focus away from your thoughts and back to the sacred mantra.

Treat your physical body as if you're recovering from an illness. Eat only live, fresh, and/or raw foods and healthy proteins like baked chicken or fish. Drink fresh water throughout the day. Avoid all sources of sugar and all processed foods. Supplement with B vitamins to boost your nervous system, and vitamin C to boost your immune system. Move at least twenty minutes a day—walking, jogging, biking, or some other form of exercise, especially one that takes you out in nature. Try to break a sweat at least once a day, to release toxins.

Get a spiritual coach or partner to join you on a spiritual exploration journey. Read and discuss books outside of your comfort zone that stretch your mind with new ideas on how our universe works, who you are, and why you're here on Earth.

Immerse yourself in the sacred. Visit a Buddhist or Hindu ashram and spend a weekend in silence and quiet contemplation, or visit a nondenominational church such as the Unity Church, or study *A Course in Miracles.* Create an altar to delineate a sacred space in your home for drawing your focus to the sacred, or mindfully walk in nature, breathing consciously.

Open your heart completely. Forgive with abandon. Imagine your life if you truly believed that God is love, pure and simple, and that there's no such thing as a punishing God or punishing karma. Imagine that you've landed here in Earth School for a temporary journey of spiritual evolution, knowing that your soul chose your particular life circumstances as the perfect fertilizer for your inner growth. Consider that you're exactly where you were meant to be so that you could wake up today and realize you're here to make a difference in the world, to help others as a result of the wisdom you've acquired from your pain. Consider that pursuing this meaningful work and bringing healing to others is the long-lasting bliss and joy you've been seeking all along through drugs, alcohol, love, sex, or food.

Stay away from toxic friends and situations that diminish your sense of self and fuel your addiction to ego gratification.

Find an addiction specialist and follow their recovery program every day.

8

Cynicism

20/20 Vision or Glaucoma?

When you view life with cynicism, you're wearing your ego lens. Its dark filter is revealing shadows while obscuring the light. This is a macro view of the world that focuses only on the shadowy corners while entirely missing the golden light that illuminates everything.

You may believe that your cynicism protects you, shields you from ignorance, and keeps you from being duped into believing what isn't true. However, cynicism is a very low-frequency energy that does not serve you, protect you, or enlighten you. Cynicism at its core is fear. Fear is the opposite of love. And love is the essence of this divine universe and what we came here to swim in.

Cynicism arises from the rational left brain. It only shows you half of the picture while blocking the essence of what you really need to know. The higher truths come from your divine, "illogical," intuitive right brain. The higher truths usually defy logic.

It's the job of your left brain to filter out everything that lies beyond logic, beyond your five senses, so that you can focus primarily on this physical world to survive, find food and shelter, and navigate through Earth's dense energy.

Yet without your inner guidance, your right brain's access to the

Divine, you're completely lost, unable to see the essence of things or remember who you truly are. Without your divine perspective, which is free of logic and unbridled, in the creative flow and immersed in sacred knowledge, you quickly become a lost soul. Cynicism blocks access to your right brain and its inner guidance. Cynicism does not exist in the divine lens perspective.

Wearing your divine lens, you understand that everything is evolving for your highest good and the good of all souls. From this higher perspective, your heart knows that each soul, no matter how they may appear, is just doing the best they can. You clearly realize that you came to this physical world to help shift consciousness, to shine your love and wisdom on all the lost souls and to help them evolve, too.

Cynicism only hurts you. It protects you from nothing and no one. It closes off your heart and disconnects you from divine guidance and flawless intuition. It blocks love. Cynicism in relationships is a deal-breaker, a love-destroyer. It brings you into a low-vibrational frequency where love does not exist. Opening your heart and focusing on the divine essence of another person, seeing them for who they came here to be, for their intrinsic greatness, allows you to help anyone embrace their potential.

Yes, you may learn some painful lessons here, just as you agreed to before you arrived in Earth School. These lessons are for your highest good and your soul's evolution. You may avoid these lessons by stepping over them (using love and wisdom to navigate). But when you live in cynicism, anger, and fear, you will find yourself painfully slogging through each and every hard lesson you lined up for yourself in this lifetime.

The higher realms are cynicism-free zones.
In those realms your heart is wide open, your love is
fierce and unstoppable, and your essence is trusting.
You embrace wisdom above all else.

Call it what it is: cynicism is fear. Nothing more, nothing less. When you live in the murky waters of fear, you suffer. You fall far from grace. You swim among the sharks. You plummet into the hell realm rather than swim in the sweet ethers of divine love.

Cynicism does not protect you. To be protected, you need clear access to your divine intuition. Your soul reveals truth to you 24/7. You may have gotten used to silencing this voice, this divine whisper, but your inner wisdom, which comes from the heart and speaks in the voice of love, is the key to your success and happiness on Earth. This wisdom tells you where to take your next step, who to love, and what career to embrace.

Your cynical mind pushes you into doubt, where you will live in a world of evildoers, tragic events, meaningless work, and futile effort. Nothing you do is ever good enough. Nothing anyone does for you is ever good enough. People are selfish and out to get you, according to the cynical mind. You must be on guard, says the ego, because evil is more powerful than you are.

This is all true when you're not hooked up to your soul's wisdom and divine intuition.

Cynicism attracts lower frequency experiences and less evolved souls. Cynicism attracts empty jobs, meaningless work, and futile efforts. Everywhere you look, you see the harshest lessons, the cruelest acts, the most unkind people. And you have now become one of them. You have become what you feared most. And your fearful energy contributes to the darkness of the world.

WHY DOES THE WORLD SEEM MORE CYNICAL THAN EVER?

Why is this, you ask? Ironically, it's because the energetic vibration on our planet is rising. As the vibration rises, our spiritual growth accelerates. And as with all change, resistance to change mounts an equal force against the gathering momentum of expansion. We're at a tipping point:

fear versus love, cynicism versus consciousness. Which side are you on? What is your prevalent viewpoint? Are you a cynic? Do you immerse yourself solely in conspiracy theories? How does that make you feel? Do you find all kinds of logical reasons to embrace fear-based viewpoints?

Yes, there are many corrupt people in positions of power. This has always been true for as long as humans have existed on Earth. Those who have much to learn ascend quickly to power partly because of their unconsciousness, their inability to see the essence of things and remember their soul's mission. This gives them the kind of ruthlessness required to gain power in a low-consciousness political system. These unconscious and greedy people are frequently in the spotlight. We're fascinated by them for a reason: watching their inevitable downfall enlightens us. Our soul is taking notes.

Yet view it this way: as each unconscious person is brought into media scrutiny, their inner growth is being spurred. This is a byproduct of the enormous attention humans receive in the public eye. This energy accelerates the individual soul's vibration until the person comes face-to-face with their greatest soul lessons, which then unfold before us. Any intense focus on a person's life serves as a soul catalyst, though you may not always see this growth unfolding on your television screen. The seeds of growth are within all of us, and the hot lights of the media burst these seeds into life.

There are infinitely more awakened and conscious beings living on this planet than unawakened beings. If you are reading this book you are one of the awakening ones, working behind the scenes to shift us into the light.

Divine consciousness is ultimately more powerful than the unenlightened acts of unconscious souls. This higher consciousness exists on both sides of the veil. The spiritual teachers, healers, writers, and artists among us are the ones holding the light on this side of the veil, even if these people are not famous or less conventionally successful than the unawakened. All lessons are learned in the end. Light trumps the darkness every time.

SOUL STORIES
PATRICIA: THE EXHAUSTED CAREGIVER

The following is a transcribed and edited session (identity hidden) of a client who was exhausted from caring for her dying mom, grieving the death of her father, struggling to get along with her siblings, and feeling very alone because she was single and in her fifties. Patricia came to me for a past-life soul regression session, and as a result of learning to see through her divine lens, she experienced an enormous amount of healing.

I first instructed her to take some very long, slow, deep breaths with me. I suggested that as she breathed in, she feel a sacred essence in the room with her, an essence of deep peace and relaxation. I then guided her into a deeply relaxed meditative state.

Here's how the session unfolded:

Sue: *You've just arrived at an important, significant past lifetime. I'm going to ask you some very simple questions about what you may be seeing or feeling, and you can respond out loud with the first thing that comes to mind when I ask the question. Are you outdoors or indoors?*

Patricia: *Outdoors.*

Sue: *Can you describe what you see?*

Patricia: *I'm in a forest.*

Sue: *How does it feel in this forest?*

Patricia: *It's not dark. There are boulders. Not big ones, but big rocks, and it's quiet.*

Sue: *Can you tell if it's day or night?*

Patricia: *It's daytime.*

Sue: *Can you feel the temperature on your skin? Is it warm or cold? Is there anything in particular that you smell?*

Patricia: *Pine trees. Yeah. It's not hot, but it's warm. It's not cold.*

Sue: *Get a sense of how you're dressed and how you look. Begin by looking down at your feet or bending down to touch your feet. Then notice what's on your legs. Observe the clothing you're wearing—the colors, textures.*

Patricia: *I see my skin is brown, Native American, and then I see I'm wearing leather . . . cowhide leather, beadwork, and suede.*

Sue: *Are you male or female?*

Patricia: *I'm a young girl.*

Sue: *What do you feel?*

Patricia: *A bit of fear and lost, loneliness . . . There's an animal presence. I see a horse. I keep getting the words* lost direction *and* fear. *I don't know what the fear is from . . .*

Sue: *Is there anything you wish to add about this scene that you're becoming aware of?*

Patricia: *I'm seeing more of the clothing I'm wearing and then a campfire. A horse is there; the horse is my companion. Birds are flying overhead. I'm not sure what to do next, not sure where to go.*

Sue: *Let's move to the next significant scene in this lifetime. One, two, and three. Now you're in a different scene in that same lifetime. Where are you now? What's happening?*

Patricia: *I'm running from a guy on a horse. He's a soldier, and he looks like one of those cavalry men. He's coming after me, and I'm running away from him through the forest.*

Sue: *Can you tell where you might be geographically? What part of the country?*

Patricia: *United States. It could be East Coast. It could be Midwest . . . Oklahoma, Middle America . . .*

Sue: *Ask your guides to tell you what year it is.*

Patricia: *1856. They said North Carolina.*

Sue: *Perfect. I want you to look into the eyes—*

Patricia: *He wants to kill me. He says he wants to kill me.*

Sue: *I want you to look into his eyes for a moment and see if you recognize him as someone from this lifetime.*

Patricia: *He has a mustache. No, I don't know him. Not this lifetime . . .*

Sue: *Okay. At the count of three, we're going to move to the final scene in this lifetime, the death scene. We're taking three deep* *breaths: one, two, and three. Now you're in the final moments of this lifetime. Where are you?*

Patricia: *There's a base camp with a campfire in the middle and tents, I guess. I hear the word* rape, *but I don't think he . . . I don't feel that I was harmed or attacked in that way. I guess he wanted to, but he didn't. I don't know. He wasn't successful.*

Sue: *What else do you know about this moment and how you got here?*

Patricia: *I ran away from my family. I was alone in the forest. When the man saw me, I was that brown girl they wanted to catch, make an example of. He says, "I'm going to kill you. You're not human." Words are just coming into my head. I'm just saying what comes in, right?*

Sue: *Yes.*

Patricia: *"You're nothing. You're nothing. I'm just going to kill you. You're a savage. No one will know. No one will know."*

Sue: *Can you tell how old you are on this last day of your life?*

Patricia: *Maybe fifteen or sixteen.*

Sue: *I want you to trust your soul to show you how to take your last breath, how this lifetime comes to an end. You can describe it when you're ready.*

Patricia: *I try to fight back because of how I was raised, and the horse knows this, the horse is making a lot of noise. It's tied up. The horse is trying to help me, but it can't. I call out to the Great Father to take the pain away. I look at him and I say, "I'm not afraid." Then I just see white. I don't feel any pain.*

Sue: *Those are your last words, correct?*

Patricia: *Yes. I didn't want to look at him and I looked at him. He's really white. He has strawberry blonde hair and a handlebar mustache. I don't know him from this lifetime. He's got rage, and I say, "I'm not afraid." Then it's . . . Yeah, I don't feel any pain.*

Sue: *Okay, let this life come to a close. Your soul knows exactly how to do this. You've done this in many lifetimes. Your soul knows how* *to exit the physical body. You're moving away from that body. There's no pain, no struggle. You already feel free, free of that lifetime, free of any fear. Now you're in touch with your true self, your Higher Self, as you lift out of the body and expand into your highest consciousness. Moving through time and space, you recognize that there's a spirit guide standing there to help you.*

Patricia: *The guide is saying, "You must be fearless and follow the things that you really love. No one can take your power away. But in this lifetime, in the twentieth and twenty-first centuries, you've let too many people do that." Are these guides androgynous?*

Sue: *You can note whatever gender you see.*

Patricia: *Seems male.*

Sue: *Okay.*

Patricia: *He says, "There's so much more living you have to do. You can't be afraid to let people know who you are. You haven't been ready for your soulmate yet. You still hold back."*

Sue: *Ask your guide, "What else do I need to learn to be ready?"*

Patricia: *"Just be yourself. Don't try to be someone else. Just be completely yourself. Don't be afraid to let yourself show completely."*

Sue: *Ask your guide about your arc of learning.*

Patricia: *"Don't run from who you are. It's okay to be different. Your parents tried to help you with that as best they could, as best they knew how. In the time you have left, you have to embrace it and not run away from it. He wanted to kill you because you represented someone so different from him that he couldn't comprehend it."*

Sue: *Ask the guide what else you need to know.*

Patricia: *"Feel the fear then let go of it. Step into who you are. Don't hold back on your dreams. Your parents want everything good for you. Your mother's waiting for you to finish with your lists before she joins your father. She's trying so hard to wait. She's still patient. You know each other from other lifetimes. You have synchronicity together. She wants to make sure that you're fine before she leaves. She is sick. She doesn't know what she's doing now."*

Sue: *Ask the guide if there's anything you can do to help your mother release.*

Patricia: *"Keep talking to her when she's in her deep sleep and tell her that you're going to be okay."*

Sue: *Do you want to ask your guide how you're connected to other family members? If your brother or sister were in a previous lifetime with you?*

Patricia: *He said, "Yes, your sister, but not that lifetime, it was a prior lifetime."*

Sue: *What is your arc of learning with your sister?*

Patricia: *He said it twice: "Your sister was your mother. Your sister was your mother. You have to learn how to love her. She couldn't love you then. There was a lot of pain."*

Sue: *What about your brother? Is there any clarity from your guide about that?*

Patricia: *"You saved him. He didn't know what he was doing. It was an earlier lifetime. You're trying to save him again, but he's turned away. He just keeps turning away. He's got to learn. He's got to learn, but now you're moving on. You're not here to save either one of them now. You have to move on."*

Sue: *Very good. Is there anything else that you want to ask your guide before we visit the Council of Elders?*

Patricia: *I'm not sure. I guess if there are other things that need healing.*

Sue: *We can take that question to your council. As you walk toward that sacred space where your council is waiting, notice what you see.*

Patricia: *I see gold cone-shaped columns and a marble staircase.*

Sue: *How many elders do you see?*

Patricia: *Six.*

Sue: *Do they look androgynous or male and female?*

Patricia: *They're androgynous. When I was a little kid after I received my First Communion, I saw an image of an angel in my driveway, and I never forgot it. It was androgynous. That's how they look.*

Sue: *Maybe you could ask if one of them showed up in your driveway.*

Patricia: *They're nodding and smiling.*

Sue: *You can ask any questions that are coming to you now. This council knows everything about you, your soul agreements and soul lessons. What do you want to ask?*

Patricia: *What is the purpose of this lifetime with all the pain and suffering? . . . He says, "To grow stronger. Many lifetimes ago, things were quite different for you so you wanted to work harder in this lifetime. Because you had a lifetime many, many eons ago where you were very, very blessed, but you wanted to work harder, like starting from scratch. It was a long and winding road of growth. The pain makes you stronger, otherwise you couldn't help anyone else heal. You're becoming the healer. You can't heal someone if you've never been broken."*

Sue: *Ah, he's saying that you chose a lifetime that would break you so you could reassemble yourself as the healer. Is that correct?*

Patricia: *Yes.*

Sue: *Okay. Do you want to ask the council how you're doing with that?*

Patricia: *They say, "You're doing very well. Don't get discouraged. You're right on track. You have more support than you realize. All your signs are in nature. That's where you talk to the heavens. That's where you talk to God."*

Sue: *Good.*

Patricia: *The animals too. Very connected to the animals.*

Sue: *Ask your council if it would help you to move forward if you knew who the man was who killed you in that lifetime.*

Patricia: *They said, "No, you would just seek vengeance."*

Sue: *Ah, okay, good.*

Patricia: *Wow.*

Sue: *Ask if there's anything else they want to tell you or say to you before you return to your present lifetime.*

Patricia: *"You have to lift those who are not where you are; and you know who they are. They wear armor on the outside . . ." I'm just repeating what they're saying.*

Sue: *Good.*

Patricia: *"Don't be afraid to do things that others may turn away from or that may not make sense to them. You are completely on the right track. You can lessen your need to be practical and it will help you become a healer."*

Sue: *Do you want to ask your council if they will help you lift up from you practical Taurus tendencies?*

Patricia: *Oh, I need a lot of help with that. Yes. Please help me.*

Sue: *How are they responding?*

Patricia: *"You have to take time to meditate. It doesn't matter how busy you are. You have to. You must. You must. No excuses. Sometimes you make too many excuses and you're not taking care of yourself enough. You are making some progress, but we want to see more. When your mother leaves you, she will get after you all the time."*

Sue: *Okay. Is there anything else they could tell you?*

Patricia: *I guess they knew I wanted to ask about the soulmate. They said, "You don't have to make an effort to meet him. You'll meet each other energetically and you'll know when you see each other." That's good.*

Sue: *Okay. Thank them because they have always guided and loved you. Turn around and walk out. I'm going to count from one to three, and then you'll come back into your body fully. Know that you're waking up calmly and peacefully with clarity in your mind and heart to remember everything you've learned in this experience and to feel gratitude for it. One and two and three . . .*

I then used guided meditation and deep breathing to bring Patricia fully back into her physical body, after which the following conversation ensued:

Patricia: *Wow. Well, I started to cry at the very beginning . . . even before we did the countdown, I just started to cry. And I didn't know why. Probably because I was going to come upon this painful lifetime.*

It was intense. It was incredible. I mean, I know I've always felt like a champion for the underdog since I was a young kid. I always knew there was racial discrimination. But now I understand that I was a minority in another lifetime, so that's helpful to understand why discrimination upsets me so much now . . . Someone hating me for the color of my skin. Yeah, that's powerful. Everyone should experience that.

Sue: *What do you think was the most significant thing you learned in this session?*

Patricia: *Someone wanting to kill me because of my light, to put my light out. The intensity of being yourself and . . . as the elders said, my parents in this lifetime always tried to instill in me to be myself, that I was special and different. I always felt like an outsider in grade school and high school. The kid that didn't fit in. I don't know, I have to process it more, but that's really intense. The lesson of . . . I mean, people just say it randomly, "Oh, you've got to be yourself." But to know you had a lifetime where someone was enraged enough to kill you because you were different. That explains some of my fear of being vulnerable. I don't even think that it was an attempted rape thing. He just couldn't stand this young Indian girl who was somehow so different. She was this bright light. So he called her a savage and said she was ignorant and it enraged him to the point of murder. There's a lesson there in being myself no matter what.*

Sue: *Do you think that it's also a lesson about how powerful your light is—that just by being yourself you attracted a man's rage such that he wanted to kill you? If you're not a powerful soul, you're not going to attract such an experience. That's also a lesson for you of how incredibly powerful you are—powerful enough that a man could find you alone in the woods by your energy and then notice your skin and try to kill you. That's a statement about your light and your power.*

Patricia: *Yeah, I never could really see that. The first time I had a session with you, ten years ago, I wrote down what you said: "She's a divine, powerful soul. She's a powerful light being." I still have that taped to my closet door. "Let it shine." Wow. But it's so hard in this* *modern era. And to be born female, it's hard to express your power, you know?*

Sue: *Well, I think you gained a lot of insights today, especially about your mom.*

Patricia: *Yeah. Mom's very strong and she's literally just fighting her way through this dying experience. We have a very strong bond. There's such a soul agreement there. She's trying so hard to be patient with my Taurus methodical practicality: "Okay. I know you have this little list and I want everything to go right for you." It's the love that keeps her here. Now I'm trying to look for the lesson in the pain. Instead of waking up complaining, "Oh my God, this is caregiving on steroids!" I need to ask what the lesson is. My intuitive voice says you need to learn even more compassion and more love. That's for my soul growth. Whenever I think, Oh yeah, I've done it already, I have to realize that no, I'm not finished with that lesson . . . And I'm stuck in the minutiae of her dying, you know? The minutiae of caregiving. I just wrote down that I need more compassion, more love. I know when it's done she'll join my dad.*

Sue: *When you asked, "What is the purpose of this very hard lifetime?" you got a clear answer about growing stronger—that in other lifetimes you used to be very blessed with an easy life. But you wanted to become a healer and a teacher. So you've chosen in this lifetime to be broken open and heal yourself, in order to reassemble as a powerful healer. The guides told you, "You can't heal someone if you've never been broken."*

Patricia: *Thank you. It's fascinating when you look at all these soul agreements, like with my sister. The guides are basically saying, "Alright, we're going to put you two together again." It's interesting. I was the baby who came late into the family, so automatically the jealousy was set up between us. Once again, her soul was challenged to love me or not. It's like, "Are you going to love her now or are you going to be jealous?" We had a track record. Now my challenge is to love her anyway and heal that karma . . . It's amazing the evolution,* because I remember when I thought, Oh, my sister's just jealous of me. But it's not this petty human emotion of jealousy. It's like, "Okay, you're going to have this lifetime together again to break a pattern. To learn to love and to forgive." Yeah, it's deeper.

Sue: When you asked the guides to help you lift above your Taurus practicality, to lift out of the minutiae, they said you have to take time to meditate. It doesn't matter how busy you are. Take care of yourself and meditate. And I'm curious what you mean about you've got to finish your list before your mom can let go.

Patricia: When Mom was well, she used to always send cards. She was great with that, but since she's gotten sick we're not getting to the card store. So I bought the cards. Now I need to sit down and help her write them. She still has lovely handwriting and we need to write out those cards and send them to everyone. We have this list—relatives' birthdays, and my sister's and brother's. One card is a "welcome to your new house" card for my sister, who just moved. Even Mass cards, because we were the Catholics and if someone in the family dies, you send a Mass card. You may think it's corny, but I want her to hand-write them. Knowing how she always was, it's something I know she'd want to do.

Sue: Oh, okay. When you asked the guides to help you lift above your Taurus practicality, they were probably also thinking, Does Mom really need to write all those cards, Patricia? *[laughter]*

Patricia: Right. Maybe it's my need more than hers. And I have other things I want to do with Mom, like these horses that we want to go visit. They're the things to do with Mom before she leaves, you know?

Sue: Okay.

Patricia: I realize, of course, when she goes to the higher realms, it's more beautiful up there than anything down here, but being a Taurus, I still make the lists.

Sue: Right. It's so funny because you know my sister is a Taurus, too. She just got on the plane to go be with my ninety-five-year-old mom even though she was just there a few weeks ago. I asked her, "Why are *you going back? Mom's condition hasn't changed."* She said, *"Because we have this list of things we want to do before she dies. She wants to go to the shopping mall one more time, in the wheelchair, and I promised I would take her. I'm going home to do all those things on the list to help her let go so she can die."*

Patricia: *Oh, wow. I guess that's how I feel, too.*

Sue: *Just know that the guides are helping you accomplish these little things. You can ask the guides and your departed dad to help you get those cards done easily and quickly so you don't have to worry about it—and your mom can let go.*

Patricia: *Thank you. This is an amazing opportunity. I'm so grateful to you. It was amazing. I can hardly describe it. Wow!*

◉ Three Steps to Help You Shift into Your Divine Lens

1. **Focus on one thing in your life that you feel grateful for right now.** Keep focusing on it as if you're wearing binoculars and exploring it up close. See each detail of what you're grateful for. Now open your heart and send that one object or person you're grateful for a big burst of love. Wrap them in compassion. You've now shifted into your divine lens. Focus your divine lens on the challenge you're currently facing, and send compassion to the people who are troubling you.

2. **Take a deep breath with a long inhalation and long exhalation.** Say, *Divine guides, please show me the lesson of this moment and reveal the divine lens view of this story I'm telling myself today. Pull me out of the ego view and show me the wisdom of this lesson.*

3. **Then ask yourself, When I look back at this difficult moment in my life, how will I think of it?** How will I wish I had handled this challenge from my most enlightened, compassionate perspective? Write down your thoughts on this. Then, looking back at this moment in your life, describe your soul story of how you gracefully overcame this challenge by choosing love over fear. To help guide you in this, ask yourself these questions:

- What is the purpose of my life, other than financial survival? How can I change my career to fully align with this more meaningful pursuit? What baby steps can I take this month?

- Why would my soul, in choosing circumstances for my highest good and never out of punishment, have chosen to come here and experience the life I've lived?

- What gifts may have been hidden in my moments of greatest pain? These are gifts of awakening that I can only realize now as I review my past painful moments.

- What does my Higher Self know to be true about using my gifts and talents to make a difference in the world? What steps would I take to begin doing that now to make my living?

- What changes would I need to make in my life and in my relationships to move forward?

PART TWO

The Gift of Your Divine Lens

I pray to be brought into alignment with the wisdom of the Higher Self. I pray to align with the light and to separate from the ego self so that divinity inspires all my words and actions.

There's a journey you have to take, a paddle to shore, a trip through your shark-infested mind. It's your journey from dark to light, from fear to love, from nowhere to everywhere.

Reach down now and dip your hand into those dark, swirling waters. Start a ripple. Make a stir. Embrace the danger and adrenalin blending inside of you. That's the energy of your pure life force waking up. It's *you,* moving from lost at sea to found again.

Dip your hand in now, palm facing behind you. Wave away what's done and gone. You will move forward. Pain is part of this ride. You knew that going in. Let divine grace push you into the current now. Surrender. You'll find your new posse on the shore. You'll find your good work once you let go.

This ride to shore could last a lifetime. You may forget to breathe. There will be terrible storms along the way. You'll cry while you paddle.

And there will be days when the sea is calm and the sky glorious and nothing else matters. You will get lost.

But soon you'll see your loved ones standing on the shore in the glow of sunlight beckoning to you. You'll wave your arms and shout with joy. And you'll remember something long forgotten.

Once you're ashore, you won't understand what held you back—nothing. Nothing ever held you back. Maybe you forgot to breathe. Maybe you cried. But nothing ever stood in your way.

Sitting in the deep-water channel, you won't want to move. The shore will look so far away. Beyond hopeless. Your arms will ache in anticipation. You'll see the impossible journey ahead and reject it before you even begin.

"I'm not strong enough, smart enough, good enough to do this," you'll whisper to the wind. You may even turn your surfboard around to face the wide-open sea, with its unknown pleasures, invisible islands beckoning with promises of salvation. But taking that course will only lead you into a bigger storm and a longer paddle to shore through shark-infested waters.

Yes, the sharks will circle. But they're afraid of your strength. They feed on fear. When you fight back, you survive. When you quit paddling, fear will feast on your heart. Your heart is your lifejacket, your one good surfboard to freedom; your only hope. Lift your gaze from the dark shark fins. See the moon above you like a gem glistening in the night. Kiss that blessed moon. Reach up and wave your arms like the symphony conductor you came here to be. Move the stars with your grief and craft them into your healing sonata. This midnight song from the depths of your heartbreak will be the masterpiece of your life.

When the sun begins to rise, you'll find more strength. You'll push harder against the waves. You'll move forward in leaps. But nothing happens until you dip in. Dip your hand into the dark, scary water. It will save you.

Dip in. Take one stroke with your aching arms. Move forward one inch. One inch is everything. One stroke is your entire world. One more stroke is your entire future. A current will catch you. It's always something you didn't expect, didn't believe in, that suddenly moves you forward.

You'll find yourself gliding effortlessly now. You'll sit back for a moment and breathe. You'll scan the vast horizon in front of you. It looks closer than you thought. "Anything is possible," you'll whisper—even if you don't truly believe it.

Now you're beginning to feel strong. You dip into the dark water over and over again. No longer afraid, focused only on the shore. You understand now. You see the journey for what it is—a brief ride to shore that requires everything you have and makes you strong. It pulls you into light, the light you've always longed for but didn't know what you were missing. You felt homesick without knowing where your home-sickness came from. Your deep sorrow, your endless longing—it was all for this.

This *is* the journey home. It's the only journey to take. It's under-neath you and in front of you. Dip in, my friend. There's nowhere else to go. These swirling waters will soon turn into grateful tears. Those last yards to the shore are shallow and clear. You see the beauty of each life with each stroke you take.

When you come ashore, you'll fall into the arms of your beloveds. There will be bonfires and dancing barefoot in the sweet sand. Your lovers from past, present, and future will hold you. They'll whisper ten-der words. The ones who once broke your heart completely will now hold you tightly while you cry.

You'll share stories around the fire. These will be the greatest stories you've ever heard or ever told. It will all make sense—the shark-infested waters, the nights of dark despair, and the endless longing.

You will find this shore without a compass, without a lover, without a mother. You'll find your way because you once dipped your trembling hands into the dark water and shoved yourself forward into the storm.

You can lie down now, laughing, on the beach, looking up into the eyes of your beloveds. Running the soft sand through your fingers.

"Were there really sharks?" you'll ask. And you'll laugh out loud at the sound of your words.

When you find your people standing in a circle around you, the ones you thought you'd never see again and the ones you weren't sure existed, your heart will break wide open, shattering into a million tiny pieces of light, like diamonds on the open waves, guiding someone else to shore.

9
Seeing Death as Transformation

Recognizing the Eternal Soul

It's the morning of July 14, 1980. I awaken to the sounds of a mourning dove outside my window and a view of Boulder's sacred limestone slabs reaching into the clouds. These front-range Rocky Mountain slopes are where my husband and I once spent happy afternoons climbing, hiking, and feeling invincible.

Yesterday, this elegant and strong young man, my husband, Paul, died from cancer at the age of thirty-four. His death ended a year of unbearable suffering for both of us. My ego tells me this is a deplorable, soul-sucking tragedy. Paul was the most loving man I'd ever known, and he did not deserve to suffer and die before his life could unfold—before we could have our future together.

No one will ever love me like that again, my ego mind tells me. I'm alone, grief stricken, and sick with heartbreak. I'm scarred for life—just as he was at the end. But I'm still here, and he is not. This voice in my head crushes and flattens me, pushes me back into bed, feels like molten lead pouring down. It deletes my future. I feel miniscule beneath these heavy thoughts. *Why would my husband die of cancer when everyone else our age is launching careers and having babies? What kind of loser am I?* whispers the ego.

Hours later and with tremendous effort, I push out of bed and step outside on the balcony, gazing up at the jagged pink flatirons jutting into a cloudless sky. I take a deep breath and observe their beauty and remember their promise. They stir the memory of the time when I first chose Boulder, chose to come to Colorado from the flatlands, with no money or job, just courage and determination. I wanted to break away from old fear patterns, to climb these dizzying rocks, even though they terrified me. Magical things happened when I got here: an impossible mountain-climbing career, marvelous friends, soulmate love, and unprecedented happiness.

This reminiscence stirs a powerful recognition within me. I'm reminded that I have chosen the path of courage before. And it served me well.

The voice of inner wisdom that has been knocked out of me for the past year now whispers, *This is your greatest moment. Every lesson you came to learn in order to push into your soul's potential and align with your Higher Self lives in this very instant of devastating grief.* The energy of these words lights me up, gives me breath. My mind chatter quiets, and I hear my Higher Self say, *Paul was your greatest spiritual teacher. He revealed his spirit to you as he left his body. He took you on a spiritual journey disguised as a healing journey. It was your healing journey, not his. It was his gift to you.*

Over the next few months I begin to realize that all the things we experienced together in the year of his death—the meditations, the healers, the Native American ceremonies, and his fully conscious exit from his body—were all for me. He was finished with this lifetime, not meant to stay longer, just long enough to show me that I was worthy of love and could reach into my soul to find wisdom and courage. He helped me see life in a new way.

You've never been alone, whispers this inner voice of the Divine. *You've been held in love and light, even in your darkest moment.*

You must choose which path to take now. This is your choice point.

The next few years of my life play out with as many ups and downs as a roller coaster. Sometimes I'm able to embrace my divine lens view and move forward. Other times I'm lost in self-pity, self-doubt, and the blind confusion of anger and grief. Along the way, I battle fear, bankruptcy, anger, and loneliness. Yet my choice will ultimately be that of trusting my soul's wisdom and consciously taking the spiritual path that gets me here right now, writing this to you.

YOU'VE COME SO FAR

Our journeys are never one straight line of uninterrupted wisdom and enlightened action. Neither are they one continuous journey of negativity and fear. All of us vacillate between the perspective of the ego lens and that of the divine lens. We spend time viewing life through each lens so that we can make a fully realized choice. These two viewpoints battle for dominance within us until our heart finally chooses. This choice becomes the essence of who we are.

This is the point of human evolution. Before we arrive here on Earth, we're immersed in the divine realms, where the light is vivid and vibrates with love, and our heart connections are deeply satisfying. We simply wouldn't be drawn to choosing fear and darkness over love and light while existing in that sacred dimension. Yet our consciousness needed to expand—that's the nature of consciousness and energy. We created this Earth School, this dense energy realm, for the sole purpose of consciousness expansion—for all of us.

Our collective consciousness chose to push down into this Earth energy so that ultimately we'd be able to dwell simultaneously within all levels—from this luscious and sensual physical realm to the highest realms of light. There would be no death. We'd eliminate the veil between realms. Our collective souls would be pushed to new levels of awareness, love, and light. We would add a rich dimension to our existence as souls: this physical realm.

You were born here with that intention. Billions of years ago, the energy was denser on Earth, less light-filled. Our souls were still learning the basics of survival in a physical world. Our journeys to this realm were shorter, with briefer life spans.

Jesus, Buddha, and many other enlightened teachers courageously incarnated here to expand our consciousness to extraordinary new heights, merging light with dark, teaching love over fear, waking us up from the unconsciousness that had dwelled here on Earth for so long. As we collectively work on this evolution, more light is penetrating this dense realm. We've all gradually become more conscious while here on Earth. Today we stand at a pivotal moment in this awakening. It will take all of us to push the final mantle of fear and darkness away. Eventually, we'll all make a final choice for the Divine, for love over fear, and light over dark.

As impossible as it may feel sometimes, you're one of the consciousness-shifters here or you wouldn't be reading this. You wouldn't be aware enough to ask meaningful questions, to realize that you were once lost in fear and don't intend to live that way again. You wouldn't know there was a divine lens perspective unless you'd already shifted out of the ego lens.

Now you're awakening and bringing others with you. You stand on the threshold of conquering ego, fear, and darkness. You're being lifted into the light at this very moment.

Take a breath, silence your mind, and listen. Push away any thoughts that frighten you because they're not real. Breathe in the life that you came here to know—a life of love, courage, and light. This is your moment.

If grief is your greatest teacher, if right now you stand on the precipice of shattering loss, you are blessed. Your loved one, now on the other side, is trying to help you remember who you are and why you stand here on Earth. It only takes silence and listening to know that your departed lives on.

Yes, you'll still have to battle the ego mind telling you that life is meaningless and you will never love again. Listen to that song of woe that the ego mind plays. How does it feel in your body? Does it suck your life away, drain your energy, keep you in bed all day long? Does it sit on top of you like molten lead crushing your soul? That is the job of the ego self, to bury us in unconsciousness.

Yet at this very moment, your Higher Self is also speaking. It speaks with love and fearlessness. The very sound of its words stirs you, lifts the weight from your shoulders, fills you with breath and light, with inspiration: *This is the greatest moment of your lifetime! All the lessons you came to learn live in this moment of transformation. See the beauty of every misstep and every soul agreement that has brought you here. See the perfection in all of it. Choose the light. Choose the love. The rest will unfold as it should.*

Let me tell you a story . . .

In April 2015, my current husband, Gene, drove us up Four Mile Canyon, to the little Chapel of the Pines, where my first husband, Paul, and I were married in 1979. So many memories flooded back to me of that happy, sunny September day, filled with love and hope. As we drove through the canyon, we saw the little cabin beside the creek where Paul and I first lived and had our sweet wedding reception. Both places miraculously survived floods and fires and are impossibly still standing. I think Paul must have been watching over them . . .

It brought back so many powerful sensory memories to be there. I sat on the chapel steps and cried for twenty minutes. I remembered how happy my dad was that day and how much he loved Paul, our wedding, and our cabin. Dad and Paul are both watching out for me from the other side now. Sitting on those steps, I felt my dad, Paul, my best girlfriend, Crissie, and my dear friend Marv all with me. In the hard years following that amazing wedding day in 1979, I lost my dad, Paul, and Crissie to cancer, and Marv after he had a stroke at the age of forty-four. Yet I'm grateful for the heartbreak I experienced then, which sent me on my spiritual journey.

Today I have my incredible husband, Gene, our miraculous children, Sarah and Kai, and my amazing career—none of which I would have had without going through my journey.

Gene sat beside me on that visit to the chapel, listening to my memories and soaking up the experience. He understands everything about my life and where it's brought me. It was his idea to drive up there, as I hadn't been up that canyon since 1980. I was grumpy on the drive up, finding a million reasons not to go—some part of me realizing what I'd remember as soon as I saw that sacred place. Yet once I released the flood of emotion that rose up in me, I saw with great clarity the gift of my life story and the gift of loving so many amazing souls along the way.

FACING DEATH WITH GRACE

If you have been diagnosed with a terminal illness, it's an extraordinary opportunity to see each precious day through the divine lens. This is our most empowering perspective when facing death. It's where we find courage to face the unknown.

Our ego view of the world is shattered daily through illness. As the body deteriorates, we learn that the ego mind is not in charge, that it only reveals part of the picture, and that fear is our greatest challenge. Yet fear of death is natural and can be transformed into love through the process of surrendering to the moment, also known as non-resistance. Many souls choose the transformational grace of the path of terminal illness to shatter the ego, release negative patterns, and shift fully into the soul's perspective, the divine lens view. If you have chosen this path of awakening, in your final days, you'll experience visitations and dreams from departed loved ones, even if your left-brain logical mind tries to deny it. You'll slowly be pulled into expanded consciousness while you're still in the body. This can be an extraordinary awakening for anyone, especially those who've lived life unconsciously, tethered to the ego.

If you've been diagnosed with a serious illness, ask yourself, *Are you sensing things differently? Are your perceptions expanding? Do you long to talk about death but you're afraid to upset those who love you and want you to live?* This is all part of the process of returning to the higher realms.

If you're facing death, you'll find it comforting to retell the story of your life to a loved one. (If your loved one is facing death, encourage him or her to tell the story of their life.) This is a good place to start the journey of releasing the memories and attachments of earthly life. As you review your life story, consider this: What did you learn in your most painful moments? What were the gifts of your pain? What are you grateful for now? What moments of grace and divine intervention do you see today that you couldn't see then?

If you retell your story the old way, through ego lens perspective, your Higher Self will cause interference and create static to disrupt your outlook. You'll experience moments of profound and surprising wisdom as your soul reveals past hardships through a more enlightened point of view. Unresolved feelings and regrets will surface for review. Forgiveness will begin to illuminate your memories. This is your predeparture soul review. It gives you another chance to open your heart before this lifetime concludes.

Meditate for a few minutes each day, sitting quietly, eyes closed, repeating a sacred mantra or prayer, and you'll experience openings in your awareness. As you get closer to death, you may have precognitive visions of future events that will unfold for your loved ones after you're gone. These can include divorces, weddings, births, and losses. Use your precognitive awareness to initiate healing conversations. Bring wisdom and compassion to these discussions to help your loved ones face an uncertain future without you.

Past hurts will resurface into your consciousness for healing. You'll long to communicate with and forgive those you discontinued your friendships with long ago. This is your soul giving you an opportunity to see things as they are, rather than as your ego lens has distorted them.

Allow this process of surrender to unfold gracefully. Your soul wants you to finish this lifetime well, to accomplish the awakenings you came to experience. The more you quiet the mind through meditation or prayer, the better you'll use this sacred time for what it's intended to be—an opening to your Higher Self.

When you're afraid of what's coming, meditate to quiet the mind. Ask your guides or your Higher Self to reveal what happens when you die. Ask to visit the divine realms in your dreams.

Keep a journal. Writing will help you open your channel to the Divine. Write this sentence at the top of a page: "This is the graceful exit I'll experience as my soul is set free from the body and I ascend to the realm of love and light." Write that sentence several times and keep writing. Then describe the graceful exit you're about to make. Let the words flow through you. Write quickly. Let your pen move freely and don't edit or review what you've written. Writing quickly without overthinking allows you to bypass your logical left brain and download guidance directly from your Higher Self. Wisdom will channel through your words.

Try this writing exercise often until you're aware of the difference between words that come from your left-brain critic and words that flow from a source greater than your mind. When you embrace the wisdom from beyond your mind, your writing will calm your fears of death.

In your final weeks and days on Earth, allow the essence of love to fill your heart. As you surrender to the process, you'll be pulled gracefully into the bliss of transformation from this world to the Divine.

Death is an act of love. It's a surrender into greater love
than you've known on Earth. Allow this.

Your guides are here to help you. The moment you take your final breath, you are set free of your dense physical body. Your spirit returns to the happy, loving essence of the true you. This is how you began this lifetime and it's how you'll end it.

You may be greeted by departed loved ones. And you may be pulled to visit your loved ones on Earth as they learn about your death. You'll comfort them in their moments of grief. Some of them will respond to your presence and others won't seem aware of your visit. When it's time, a divine being will guide you toward the light of the highest realms.

You'll be shown the soul's perspective of your life here on Earth. You'll see objectively, in a nonjudgmental way, the soul lessons you came to learn and the great gifts you brought with you. You'll see and feel the ripple effects of your actions toward others. You'll be shown the choices you could have made but didn't. You'll feel the pain you caused others as well as the love that your positive actions and words created. This instantaneous, nonlinear viewing of your life story detaches you from your ego self and aligns you fully with your soul.

As you finish the life review, you'll be guided to another level of the higher realms, where you'll meet teachers, spirit guides, and elders who reveal more about the purpose of your journey to Earth. They'll review your soul's progress compassionately.

You'll continually be drawn back to Earth to comfort grieving loved ones. Since time is not linear, you'll feel them call you, and you'll wrap them in healing love, even as you ascend to higher levels of consciousness.

HELPING SOMEONE YOU LOVE FACE DEATH

Releasing our loved ones to the divine realms without anger or sadness or survivor's guilt is one of the hardest tasks we face on Earth. The only way to accomplish this is by viewing death through the divine lens perspective.

Your ego mind will tell you that losing your loved one is a tragedy and that you're a victim of cruel circumstances. The ego will weigh you down with sadness, depression, and grief long before your loved one actually departs. These negative feelings will hamper your ability to open your heart and love fully in their final days. You may focus on the minutiae of caregiving and miss a great opportunity for tenderness, forgiveness, and gratitude.

This simple prayer request will help you open your heart and surrender to the process of letting go: *Show me the soul's perspective on my loved one's death. Reveal to me how I can best help them.*

From this more enlightened perspective you'll understand the soul agreement you made with your loved one long before this lifetime began. You'll remember that you agreed to release them with love and courage and to remain here for your own soul's growth and evolution. Fulfilling this agreement requires all of your inner strength, but that's exactly why you agreed to it. Inner strength is exactly what you needed to develop within yourself.

You also agreed to stay here in order to fulfill your great work, which is still unborn within you. This painful lesson is a huge gift to you from your beloved; it's the gift of pain that you can transform into fuel to do your great work. Surrender to the grace of your pain, and release your loved one with wisdom and strength. Tell your dying beloved that you'll be fine without them. This helps them release the body. Say, "I love you and will love you forever. Tell me how I can help you depart with grace. Tell me how I can help you release this lifetime. Tell me how I can serve you best right now."

Whether your beloved is conscious or not, sit beside them and share memories. Discuss their childhood and reminisce over good times. If they're conscious, ask open-ended questions about their moments of greatest pain and challenge. Ask them who they'd like you to contact from their past. Ask what they learned from their hardships. Ask how they want to be remembered. These loving questions get them started on the process of surrendering.

Discuss their beliefs about where they're going. Ask how they feel as they approach death. Casually discuss differing spiritual viewpoints about the afterlife, even if these aren't the beliefs they grew up with. You might ask, "What do you think of the idea of reincarnation? Do you believe there's a hell? Do you believe you'll see departed loved ones?" Explore spirituality through books, conversations, movies, meditations, and prayer. This will help them find peace.

You'll know when it's time to directly ask, "How can I help you face death?" Listen to everything they say and follow their lead. Everyone dies in their own unique way, which is similar to how they lived. If your loved one has always been a private person, they may want to die alone. If they love being with others, they'll probably want to be surrounded by friends and family in their final hours. If they ask to die in your arms, they'll wait until you're holding them to release their body. The soul, not the conscious mind, chooses the final breath.

If you release your loved one with grace and wisdom, no matter how devastated you may feel, you'll be giving them a magnificent gift. Your loving release is an act of total surrender for another person's highest good. By doing this gracefully, you may also be accomplishing the most important task in your lifetime.

◎ Break Your Heart Wide Open

It's necessary to acknowledge you are feeling the pain of grief in order to release it and heal.

1. Start each morning with a ten- to twenty-minute meditation. During this time, quiet your mind with some deep inhalations and exhalations, followed by repeating a mantra or a prayer. I like the Sanskrit mantra *Om Namah Shivaya,* or you can repeat the Lord's Prayer or any other mantra or prayer that resonates for you.

2. Whenever your thoughts wander into your meditation, gently bring your focus back to the mantra.

3. At the end of the meditation, when your mind has settled down, ask to fully feel and release the pain in your heart.

4. Focus your attention on your heart chakra, take several deep breaths, and allow yourself to deeply experience your grief. Cry if you need to. To focus your energy, place your palm facing upward in front of your heart.

5. Whenever you feel your pain, picture it leaving your heart chakra and moving out of you and up to the Divine. Give it away to God. See divine beings taking your pain away and transforming it into love. Picture the

pain moving out of your heart as you move your palm away from your heart chakra and up to the divine realms.

6. Repeat this meditation again at the end of the day before going to sleep. By starting and ending each day with this meditation, your grief will eventually lighten, and you'll find the energy to move forward with your life.

Let me tell you a story . . .

A big part of me just wanted to run out crying into the night, to stand under the stars, to look at beauty instead of pain . . .

Last night I spent two hours having a "what happens when we die" conversation with a friend I've known since the 1980s. She's fifty years old and dying from stage-four cancer, which was diagnosed three months ago. She said her friends don't talk to her about spirituality and crossing over. She's been an atheist much of her life, although she's done amazing work for the world in her career.

She had my book *Bridges to Heaven: True Stories of Loved Ones on the Other Side* on her nightstand. She asked me to sit with her to talk about it. She said she'd spent her life not wanting to believe that kind of woo-woo stuff. But now she was having experiences that she believed were some kind of inexplicable divine order and wanted to explore ideas she'd not been comfortable with before.

She cried for most of the two hours during our talk, releasing so much of the fear and grief she's been holding on to. She's devastatingly frail and in constant pain. She lives alone. A hospice nurse visits her twice a day. It was so hard to see her suffering and so afraid of death.

I taught her to meditate (the Break Your Heart Wide Open meditation in this chapter is excellent at any time, especially for those facing death) and shared some other sacred techniques for releasing fear. I gave her a rosewood mala, which she loved. She was so grateful I'd visited and told me she will try to meditate now when she's alone and afraid. She wants me to come back. And I will. But it was so hard to be there. I'm so inadequate in these situations. The visit brought back so many memories of my husband, Paul, my best girlfriend, Crissie, and my dad, all of whom died too young, from cancer.

Afterward, Gene and I talked about my visit. It helped so much to talk to him and feel his love and support. Our views on life and death are fully aligned, and I'm so grateful for him.

But today I can't get the images and smells of the visit out of my head. All I want to do is go shopping and buy some expensive Eileen Fisher clothes that I can't afford. I know it's just a distraction to keep my grief at bay. It raises the old question as to why good people often take the path of suffering before they die. That one painful question launched my spiritual exploration journey in the 1980s, and it still fuels the work I do today.

I realize that I'm so much better at helping grieving people rather than the sick and dying. I can truly help with spiritual and emotional pain, but I can't relieve physical pain and I can't bear to see that kind of intense physical suffering, especially in young people who only months earlier were vibrant and full of life. I guess I'm still traumatized from taking care of my young husband, Paul, while still in my twenties, as he suffered through colon cancer. It's clear that I have some kind of post-traumatic stress syndrome that makes me want to run from the sight of physical suffering. And yet here I am with my dying friend, trying to help and facing my fears.

Last night I kept feeling like I might throw up when I first walked into my friend's room and saw tubes everywhere, an oxygen tank, and pain on her face as she struggled to sit up a little in her bed to greet me. I had to work so hard to focus on her spirit, her beautiful, radiant, undamaged soul, and not on her body. A big part of me just wanted to run out crying into the night, to stand under the stars, to look at beauty instead of pain. But instead I took a deep breath, opened my heart, and sat down beside her, with love as my intention. Our heart-to-heart conversation helped calm her, and I hope our future conversations will help her release fear and find an inner peace about crossing over.

I shared many stories with her of the departed coming back to show me that life continues, and that death is not the end of anything. I'm so deeply grateful to those spirits, to Paul, Crissie, my dad, and so many, many others who've made it abundantly clear that we are all souls who come here for a brief physical experience to evolve our consciousness, and that crossing over—taking the final breath—is simply an act of love, a return to the divine realms from which we came. I'm so grateful for every moment of this lifetime that has pushed me to recognize this truth and for all the sacred teachers I've had along the way.

And last night, my dying friend loved listening to those stories of departed spirits showing up, and she wanted to hear them again and again. She cried and cried as she listened, as her heart broke wide open.

To all the nurses, hospice workers, healers, and physicians who care for the dying, I honor you so much for what you do in the world. It's the hardest and best job there is. Nothing else compares.

Writing this has helped me process not just the visit to my dying friend, but my visceral reaction to seeing her in that state. Writing has always helped me heal pain and step into my wisdom in order to see things more clearly. It's why I write. And maybe now I can resist the pull of seeking superficial comfort in the face of pain, of longing for beauty instead of what is.

◉ Detoxing the Poison of Guilt

When someone dies, their loved ones usually feel guilty that they didn't do enough, that somehow they're to blame. This is also true when we lose a job or experience any kind of loss. But carrying guilt around is like drinking poison every day, and it's certainly not how your departed loved one wants to see you living, let alone how you need to live following any kind of loss. Yet we often believe we could have done something more or something different that would have prevented the loss. From a spiritual perspective, the death of anyone or anything is a soul agreement made before a lifetime begins. There is nothing you or anyone else could have done to prevent another soul from departing at their predestined time of exit, or to prevent any other uncomfortable turn of events that has impacted your life.

Begin by writing your guilt story:

- If you've lost someone you loved (or a career you cared about), what is the guilt story you carry about why this happened?
- If you're grieving a marriage or relationship that ended, what is the guilt story you carry about what you could've done differently?
- If your life hasn't turned out the way you wanted it to, what is the guilt story you tell yourself about why you went off-track?
- Do you believe our souls choose lessons for our highest good? Could these losses have been perfectly designed to push you to evolve, to live better and love better in the future? What can you do now to become your best self and use this guilt as fuel to move forward?
- From your highest spiritual perspective, what might have been your soul agreement with your departed loved one? Do you believe our souls choose their exit points? Write down your thoughts on this.

10
Using Grief to Heal Yourself and Others

The Gift of Grief

There are many souls here who are struggling with the pain of losing a loved one. The experience of heart-wrenching grief is greater now than ever before because consciousness is more evolved and human life is more valued. Love has become more altruistic and prevalent, so death is more painful to those left behind.

This is all part of the shifting of the collective consciousness. Grief is the great teacher that demands we search our souls for a wiser perspective, or else lose our way in gut-wrenching pain. Even if we turn to drugs and alcohol for comfort, it is not unlikely that we will eventually find the path of awakening. The disabling physical imbalances caused by toxic substances demand healing. Everything brings us to healing, sooner or later. You can choose your path, but the destination is the same for everyone.

Many souls agree to leave early in order to awaken their large soul posses, the loved ones they leave behind. These souls come to Earth in human form for a brief moment of recognition, a short lifetime with their loved ones. They arrive with a preplanned early exit. Once they cross over, they work hard from the other side to enlighten and heal their loved ones left behind. If you've been blessed with soul growth precipitated by the early loss of a loved one, reach out for guidance from your departed. Trust that they're around you, offering love and support when you need it. Keep moving forward on your soul journey, learning what you came here to learn so that you can join them in higher consciousness.

Consciousness is shifting. There are countless people in powerful places currently aligning with divinity and making decisions that impact everyone's growth. These evolved souls now on Earth inspire a sacred perspective; they encourage the divine view. You are part of this awakening. You're being asked to pick up your divine lens. If at first pain and grief overwhelm you and you struggle to find greater meaning, ultimately you'll learn that you can reach for the truth and activate your divine lens. Whenever you do this, your life gets better, your pain diminishes, and you begin to help everyone around you awaken.

We're reaching a tipping point of awakening right now on planet Earth. As the divine perspective spreads among us, awakening each one, it will ultimately relieve all suffering on Earth. When we shift into higher consciousness, our enlightenment will transform the darkness.

FOLLOWING THE DEATH OF A LOVED ONE

Alone with your grief, you may wonder if you'll be able to make it on your own after your beloved has died. It's completely natural to wonder this. You're in the midst of your greatest soul challenge; the lesson you planned for your Earth adventure has arrived at your doorstep. Yet within this tragic moment, within your darkest despair, lives the purpose of your journey.

Your beloved watches over you every day and walks beside you. Yet your ego lens perspective tells you the opposite. The ego tells you that you're all alone, abandoned, grief stricken, and that you'll never be truly happy again. Your Higher Self tells you a different story, but grief drowns out its inner whisperings. Going through the motions of your old life, with the same job, friends, and hobbies, now leaves you feeling empty, even though that life once filled you with contentment.

You're meant to change everything now, to shake it all up and grow. This devastating loss was designed by your Higher Self to break your old life apart, rip it down the seams, and help you start anew. This is for your highest good, even if you can't see that today.

Someday, when you've had enough despair, your brave new direction will reveal itself. Taking this path less traveled will bring you love, joy, and meaningful work. It will bring you closer to who you came here to be. You'll be guided into the dawn that you've been longing for. But it's up to you to say yes.

Deep inside, layered beneath your grief, lives your innate joy—also known as the soul. When your depression lifts, you can feel joy pulsing within. Your soul is delighted that this pivotal event has finally arrived and that you're in it now, in the thick of the lesson. Saying yes to this moment will open your heart wider than anything you've experienced before.

Your beloved's agreement was to exit before you so that you could find your power, break away from conventional thinking, and accomplish your great work. You'll find salvation through helping others. You've long known that you have healing gifts. There's miraculous love in the casual conversations you share with others who are hurting. Boldly offering your gift of wisdom to the world is your next step. Once you intend for this inner gift to become your purpose and for it to provide you with income, it will open to you. You'll offer your healing presence fearlessly and be recognized for your meaningful work. You'll quit the job that no longer serves you, and you'll find your way to the most meaningful work. This miracle will happen because it's meant to be, and your life will fill with grace as a result. Your soul desires this alignment.

On your morning walk, when you crest a hill and see the shimmer of a new sun on the lake, you can feel this joyful possibility within. You take a sip of it with your morning coffee. It waits for you to say "yes."

Just one step forward is all it takes, one prayer for guidance, one asking breath, and one moment of courage. Your departed beloved applauds you. When you step toward their soul at the end, all pain is healed. You'll feel proud of the way you walked up the final hill and stepped into the light, which changed everything. It seemed so hard at the time, you'll remember. "I know, I know," your beloved will say, holding you with love greater than you've ever known. He or she will be God, and your beloved, and your divinity, all in one moment of recognition.

On the day my father died, he appeared vividly to me while I meditated. I didn't yet know he had died, but when he appeared during my meditation, I picked up the phone and called the hospital, where my brother confirmed that he had just had a heart attack. While the doctors and nurses performed desperate CPR procedures and my family members cried and held one another, Dad was already free of his body, appearing to me as young and playful as he had been forty years earlier. He made me laugh out loud in my meditation before I realized that the apparition in front of me was his soul, and that he had just crossed over.

If you're grieving a loved one, quiet your mind and be still. It's only in the silence that your loved one can comfort you, when you're receptive and openhearted.

YOUR DEPARTED BELOVED IS NOT GONE

Why can't we see our departed loved ones all the time? Primarily because the left brain, the ego mind, distracts us with worries, doubts, and fears. We need the left-brain logical mind for this earthly lifetime. It filters out the distractions of the divine realms so we can function in the physical world and accomplish our earthly tasks. Yet our goal is to merge this dense physical realm with the highest realms of love and light. When this merger is accomplished, we can reap the sensual beauty of life on Earth while still consciously connected to our divinity.

You agreed to be part of the consciousness shift happening in the world today. The pain you feel is an opportunity to shift your perspective.

> *To connect with your dearly departed, first quiet your logical left brain. Meditation is the most effective way to consistently accomplish this.*

In my work, I see grieving clients nearly every day. When I'm aligned with my Higher Self, I feel openhearted and connected to a reality greater than our physical world. It's a dimensional shift that occurs when I listen to a grieving person tell their story of loss. As their words and tears flow, I'm pulled into another dimension, where I can sense and sometimes even see their departed loved ones. This process is like surrendering to a river of awareness that originates far beyond my mind. I hear words from their loved ones and their guides telling me what to say. It feels like a warm embrace. When I'm later asked why I said certain things, I have no idea. I can't explain the process. It's not a logical, left-brain experience. It's a dialogue with the Divine. I feel drenched in love during the experience.

You're absolutely capable of channeling this healing wisdom for yourself from your departed one and from your guides. It's a matter of simply shifting into your divine lens perspective. The ego must be surrendered to hear the truth. I often use writing as a tool for accessing this higher consciousness. Begin with a sincere request for loving guidance and clear the mind through meditation. Then pick up a pen and begin writing quickly, without editing. As your ego steps out of the way, your Higher Self takes over and writes the words that flow from beyond your conscious mind. These words of wisdom will help you heal and reopen your connection to the Divine. Trust this inner voice that comforts you when all else is stripped away, when your tears have left you quiet and empty. When you find yourself alone, broke, divorced, fired, and bereft, you may finally be willing to listen to the voice of your soul. This inner voice is your flawless navigator, your compass in the storm.

It's your ticket to happiness and your reason for being. Whenever you write from this inner voice or speak fearlessly from your heart, unconcerned about judgment, you untether your wisdom.

Your soul is a fearless, wild, beautiful bird. Your ego is a tiny cage. Open the door of your mind and set your soul free.

◎ Connecting with Your Departed One

This is a powerful meditation for connecting with a departed loved one and recovering from their loss. It has helped me when I needed relief from the pain of grief (or when I needed help in any other area of my life), and I've seen it create incredible healing for my clients and students. I recommend you practice this meditation at least once a day for seven days. If you doubt your connection and don't believe the images and whisperings you receive are real, ask your departed loved one for a sign of confirmation. You can ask for flickering lights, a phone call with no one on the other end, or that someone will say something to you that day that reflects a phrase you used with your departed one. The meditation will help you gain a new perspective on your life and see why you're still here. Remember, you have to surrender what you know and quiet the logical mind to experience this powerful connection.

1. Sit in a quiet space and close your eyes. If it's noisy, use earplugs to create quiet. Take three deep breaths.

2. Repeat a high-frequency mantra such as *Om Namah Shivaya* or the Lord's Prayer. You can do this quietly in your head. When you notice your thoughts getting in the way, gently bring your focus back to the mantra. I recommend using either this mantra or the Lord's Prayer because you're trying to raise your energy frequency and don't want to attract lost souls. Sanskrit mantras and the Lord's Prayer carry sacred energy, and they will protect you.

3. At the end of fifteen minutes, when you've noticed your mind settling down, stop repeating the mantra and keep your eyes closed. Take a deep breath and open your heart. Send loving energy to your departed loved one. Feel the love and see them feeling it and smiling back at you. Love

protects you from anything negative and strengthens your intuition. It opens your connection to the departed.

4 Speak directly to your loved one. Repeat their full name three times. Then say, "Hi, are you there?" With your eyes closed, notice the flicker of an image in front of you. Don't fixate on the image or look directly at it. Keep your eyes closed, but be aware that your loved one is taking form for you. Don't be afraid. Concentrate on feeling the love in your heart. It enhances your connection and protects you.

5. Ask your most pressing questions, such as, "Will I find love?" "Will I find work?" "Should I sell the house?" "Can you help me feel stronger?" "Why am I still here?" "Why did you have to go?" "What should I do now?" or "Can you help ease my pain?"

6. Then be quiet and listen. They will speak to you. You may doubt it because it will feel as if you're imagining the conversation. You're not. This is how they communicate. If you're feeling cynical, tell yourself that this is a fun game of imagination, but stick with it nevertheless. Take note of everything they say—the ideas that pop into your head and the images you get. This is all guidance intended for you.

7. Send them gratitude. Say, "Thank you for your help! I feel your presence and I appreciate it!"

8. Write down any ideas, phrases, images, or feelings you received or that come to you now upon reflection.

9. Get up and go about your day. Later, take time to reflect on what you experienced. Contemplate how the guidance applies to your life. Write about your experience with this reconnection meditation.

Following this meditation, ask yourself:

- If you have not felt your departed loved one's presence, could it be because your grief and pain have been so intense that they blocked the communication?
- Have you tried the "Break Your Heart Wide Open" meditation in chapter 9 to release your pain? After doing so, try once again to connect with your departed loved one.

DON'T BECOME A HUNGRY GHOST

Her face was paper-thin and stretched into deep lines of grief that widened as she spoke, telling the story of how her son, an avid hiker and a lover of mountains, came home one day with an unusual bruise and died in her arms a year later from leukemia.

She was strong—a nurse who worked all day in a hospital and cared for her son at home. *I'll find the best doctor, the best treatment,* she would say, escorting her son on rounds to places where physicians pondered the next great idea and nurses held her and cried. Now she sits before me in a room full of other grieving people. "I don't want to benefit in any way from his death," she says through choking tears. "I don't want to be happy . . ."

But beside her I see a light beam, a joyful son shaking his head at her pain, wrapping his arms around her. *No,* I hear him whisper, *that's not it . . . not the lesson . . .* He sends his thoughts through me now in a rush of words. I feel his fearless soul, unconventional, never wanting to live within the rules, not meant for a long stay, only a brief visit to tie up some loose ends and help his loved ones wake up to the deeper meaning, the big picture that they were missing in their focus on survival.

He hiked when he should have been studying. He skied when he should have worked. He knew what was essential. He broke all the rules while his parents carried on in their disappointments, working hard to pay the bills and not much more.

"Don't become a hungry ghost," he wrote to her on his last day.

"I don't know what that means," his mother cries. Her heart is fierce and her love for him is a wave of pain that crashes across the room, knocking the others over in tears.

When she's told and retold her story and is ready to sit in silent meditation, to receive, she begins writing, eventually writing furiously. And then smiling.

When the group shares their writings, they speak the profound words of their loved ones on the other side, which urge the ones left behind to live with love and embrace the divine picture of spirits on a brief visit here, some briefer than others.

"I did hear from him," she says softly. "The hungry ghost is the lost soul, forgetting that they're divine and here on purpose to grow," she says, reading from her page of notes. The others in the room nod and share the wisdom they received from their loved ones on the other side. None of the messages tell them to be sad, to give up, to be angry, even though that's how the ones left behind have felt. They pass their writings around and marvel at how the words from beyond are healing and empowering for everyone there, no matter the mess of death, no matter the suffering. The energy is playful and joyous in these writings, which are passed from griever to griever. They each tell their stories of loss again on the last day. This time their faces are plump and radiant, clear, smiling, laughing at things they've heard from their departed ones. The heavy sadness has left the room, flying out the door like a windswept fog.

"I know he's with me, and he's watching me, and I've got to get my life in gear," says the mom. "I'm going to quit my hospital job, be a nursing consultant, and work part-time at hospice," she says. "This way I can help people from what I've learned. It would make me happy to do that work."

Her face is shiny and young, like a child holding a birthday gift, excited to open it and happy to be alive. It's her beginning, her rebirth.

WHAT A LIFETIME YOU'VE HAD, BRAVE SOUL!

Many wonderful things have happened to you, but you've also experienced many painful events. You've tried to live right, learn and evolve, and bring love and gratitude to all your relationships. You've embraced yourself as a spiritual explorer and sought answers in alignment with your Higher Self.

You've also known great loss, utter heartbreak, and huge disappointment. Things beyond your control have happened that set you back, especially when you were young and struggling to find your way in the midst of fears and doubts.

When your beloved died, you fell off the edge of the world from grief and despair. But you slowly found your way back into the light. Congratulations! You're evolving exactly as you came here to do. You're experiencing the lessons you agreed to experience in order to grow and heal. You made soul agreements with your departed loved one before this lifetime began, knowing that their departure would break your heart wide open. That's exactly what you needed to experience for your highest good. Your beloved was also fulfilling their highest good through their early departure. This is the gift of your pain, though you may not see it today.

What you hold in your heart is the pearl of enlightenment that you came to awaken in this lifetime. All of us came here holding this pearl of wisdom, carrying it in our hearts, its essence vibrating within us to raise our consciousness, even while we walk here in this dense energy, beneath the heavy curtain of forgetfulness that exists in this realm. This pearl lives within each of us, waiting to be activated, awakened, so we can fulfill our mission here and evolve, helping others along the way.

You may find yourself sleepwalking through your days, filling them with routines as you follow rules handed to you by others, disempowered and feeling like a victim on your journey. At those moments you are not awake. You are asleep to who you are and why you came here—a hungry ghost going through the motions.

Love will activate your pearl. Not the act of receiving love, although that helps—the act of giving love. Open your heart in moments of great fear and offer love to those people and situations you fear the most. Now your pearl is fully activated and pulsing in divine order. You're in alignment. You're vibrating at such a high frequency that now you're an alchemist, changing the forms of people and things around you, changing your own form from dense and heavy to light-filled and translucent. You have activated your divine lens.

THIS IS THE SECRET TO ALL HEALING

You're capable of living fully through your divine lens while here on Earth, but few accomplish this. Jesus, Buddha, St. Francis of Assisi, Gandhi, and many others are examples of beings who accomplished this, and by doing so brought our collective consciousness to a higher level.

Pain—deep, heart-ripping pain—is your other option for activating your pearl, awakening fully here and shifting everything and everyone in your life. This can occur with grief—the death of a child, a sibling, or a spouse, or a career devastation, bankruptcy, and losing everything you care about. Great soul growth inevitably occurs when the person you've built your life around betrays you and leaves you lost and broken. It also occurs when you betray your Higher Self through violence, manipulation, abuse, and lies, which ultimately leave you on your knees in a terrifying moment of realization of who you've become.

When everything is stripped away, you find your soul again. You might believe that you're a victim of tragic losses. Or you might believe that life itself is tragic and random, that bad things happen to good people. You might believe that your pain has been caused by others and now you're drowning in blame and anger. Here's the truth: You brought with you a soul plan for these difficult lifetime lessons. Agreements were made before this lifetime began, for everyone's highest good. You agreed to all of this. You knew the pain would rip you apart and give you an opportunity to wake up and realign with your Higher Self. You also knew that without these painful events, you wouldn't evolve as you intended. You realized that these tragedies would break you free of old patterns that you've tried to break for lifetimes. This pain is a gift from your Higher Self.

Put on your divine lens and ask, How can I see this pain differently? What is the lesson in my pain? How can I use this pain as an opportunity to gain wisdom and connect with my soul, to love better, and to help others with what I've learned?

Once you're thinking this way, you've activated your divine lens.

Answers will flow from your Higher Self. New choices will arrive that beckon you to move in a positive direction. Fresh opportunities will allow you to live better, love better, and do work that enlightens and heals others. You'll understand how to live in alignment with your soul's wisdom. It's the only way you'll want to live.

This is, after all, what you came here to learn. Covering over your pain with drugs, alcohol, food, or sex doesn't help you become who you came here to be. These fruitless acts only muddle your journey, pull you down into the dense energy, and make it harder for you to connect to your divinity.

Ask yourself, *What if my greatest and most meaningful work is to offer to others what I wish had been offered to me in my moment of greatest pain?* Ask yourself, *What if the purpose of my grief is to confront the toughest questions: Who am I? Why am I here? Where has my departed gone?* These questions push you to align with your divinity. Asking these questions sets you on a path of growth and spiritual exploration that will change your life and carry you into the light. Asking these questions is the beginning of your true work and your soul's journey.

Ask these questions today, and don't stop asking until you find answers that resonate deep within as sacred and true. Then you'll have found a profound and powerful connection to your soul, to your divinity. Your heart will begin vibrating with fearless love for everyone, including yourself, as you recognize we are all divine beings on a sacred journey of evolution.

Now you've finally arrived at the place you've been looking for most of your life.

Let me tell you a story . . .

After traveling to San Francisco recently to teach my grief-shifting workshop Bridges to Heaven: Talking to Loved Ones on the Other Side, I discovered that when United put me on a different flight to San Francisco because of weather, they cancelled my entire ticket, and I had no flight reservation home to Colorado. My ego immediately got upset because no one at United had mentioned anything about cancelling my entire ticket when they rerouted me to a new flight.

I called United and spent forty-five minutes on the phone with an extraordinarily sweet agent, who despite my initial grumpiness, was patient and kind and fixed everything. He got me back on the same flight with no extra fees. He told me at the end of the call that he put extra energy into helping me because his departed mother whispered to him to help me out. He had no idea what I do for a living or that I'd just spent two days teaching the grief-shifting workshop. I suddenly understood the divine order that was in play to put us together on the phone. After I told him about my work, we spent another ten minutes connecting with his mom and discussing his future great work. He was crying with happiness at the end of the call.

The amazing thing is that almost everyone in the workshop I had taught earlier that day was grieving their mom. Each group I work with usually has a distinct theme that becomes apparent as we hear everyone's story of loss. We had laughingly called our group that weekend the "Dead Moms Club." I kept telling my students that the room was filled with loving mother energy. You could feel it in the air.

Through the grace of divine order, I got to end my day with this amazing conversation with another soul who was grieving his mom. I feel so blessed to do what I do in the world. And divine order blows me away, always.

ANOTHER DIVINE ORDER TRAVEL STORY

I recently taught a grief-shifting workshop at Kripalu Retreat Center in Massachusetts. When I went to board my flight home to Colorado from the Albany airport, I discovered my flight had been cancelled due to engine problems, and there were no more flights out that evening.

After waiting in line for too long to get the airline to book me into a local hotel for the night, I found my own room in a nearby hotel, where I had a lovely, relaxing evening before flying home the next morning. Back home in Colorado, I emailed the air carrier requesting financial compensation for my hotel room.

The next day, an airline agent called me and said she'd read my email to customer service requesting compensation for paying for my own hotel room when my flight was cancelled. She said she'd read the signature on my email and learned that I was the author of *Bridges to Heaven: True Stories of Loved Ones on the Other Side,* and had looked up my work on the web. She was grieving the recent loss of her dad. We had a healing conversation about her departed dad and also about her mom, who talks to Spirit. Thanks to this kind agent, the airline sent me an electronic coupon for another ticket that's double the amount I expected. As well, I got to help ease the grief of another soul.

I'm convinced that the spirits of our departed ones bring us into the presence of those who can help us, as long as we keep an open heart and take the opportunity for healing that divine order presents. I'm happy to have my travel rearranged by the spirits of these departed ones so that I can connect to those who need healing.

Soul Stories
EMMA: THE GRIEVING MOM

Here's another soul regression session, this time with a grieving mom, Emma. Her twenty-year-old son, John, departed unexpectedly while attending a local college. A couple of years had passed, and Emma was suddenly bedridden with a back injury. We'd previously done an intuitive numerology session in which she'd experienced clear communication from her son. Now she was ready for the deeper immersive experience of a soul regression.

During this session, John became an essential part of her healing. We began with the usual deep relaxation techniques and guided meditations as she moved through the tunnel of light to experience a significant past lifetime. Here's the edited transcript:

Emma: *I've been smiling ear-to-ear because I could see John's arm. In the tunnel he put his elbow out for me to hold his arm. He was standing to my right, and we walked in the tunnel together, and he had this big smile on his face and was just glowing. I just can't stop smiling. My face hurts.*

Sue: *I felt his presence, too. I saw that exact image. I was so touched.*

Emma: *Yeah, he kind of put his elbow out as if he was walking me down the aisle.*

Sue: *He looked so proud to be at your side.*

Emma: *Yes.*

Sue: *Can you look around and see where you are? Outdoors or indoors?*

Emma: *Outdoors. I'm still at the end of the tunnel. The light is so bright. I almost can't get my bearings cause it's so bright. That's why I feel like I'm outdoors. I feel I'm outside, in the sunshine.*

Sue: *Take a deep breath and see if there's anything you can smell.*

Emma: *Yeah, saltwater. It feels like the seaside.*

Sue: *Saltwater. Very good. Now look down at your feet and see what you're wearing because this helps place you in time. What are you wearing on your legs?*

Emma: *As I look down, I see my feet are women's feet because I see red toenail polish. Then I see some flowy material around my ankles; it's ragged on the bottom.*

Sue: *Can you tell if it's the bottom of a dress? Or large pants? Or a gown?*

Emma: *The bottom of a dress for sure. It's raggedy.*

Sue: *Can you tell what color that dress is?*

Emma: *It looks white, a light color, a light material. It feels like a linen, almost.*

Sue: *Imagine picking up a mirror and looking at your face. Tell me what you see.*

Emma: *In the mirror I see a woman's face, but it's more of a young woman's face, maybe in her late twenties. I have something on my head, like a kerchief of some sort.*

Sue: *Can you tell what color your skin is?*

Emma: *It's white.*

Sue: *Give me your first impression, your intuitive impression, of where you are and how you're feeling.*

Emma: *When I first looked up, I saw a bird, a seagull, fly by. I'm seeing big, white, puffy clouds and a very bright, bright blue sky. I'm not sure where I am, but if I just go with my first impression, I feel like I'm in Europe. I don't know why I'm saying that, but I just feel like I'm in Europe somewhere.*

Sue: *Very good. Can you get a sense of how you're feeling emotionally? What are the emotions that come up?*

Emma: *I feel joy. I feel like I'm looking up at this sky and I'm smiling and I feel happy. I feel happy and peaceful.*

Sue: *Are there any other people nearby?*

Emma: *No, I don't see anyone else.*

Sue: *Does this feel like a spot that you come to often or is it a spot that you've just arrived at? How does it feel?*

Emma: *It feels unfamiliar, but I keep feeling like I'm up high somewhere. I want to look down below. I feel like I'm up high looking down below, down at the ocean, like on a big cliff, like a drop-off, and then the ocean's down below and I'm up high, looking down at the ocean.*

Sue: *Beautiful. Take a moment and absorb that. Now is there anything else you think is important in this moment that we should process?*

Emma: *We can move to the next moment.*

Sue: *I'm going to count to three and when we get to three, we will be at the next significant scene in this lifetime that you're already in. One and two and three . . . When you arrive, tell me what you see.*

Emma: *The first thing that came into my head is a log cabin. Seeing the outside of a house that's made of wood, reddish brown. Literally a log cabin.*

Sue: *What else?*

Emma: *A big front porch on the house with a railing going around. It's got a wraparound porch.*

Sue: *Does it feel like your home or someone else's?*

Emma: *I feel like it's my home.*

Sue: *Who else is sharing that home with you?*

Emma: *I see John sitting on a rocking chair on the front porch.*

Sue: *Beautiful.*

Emma: *Yeah. He's sitting on a rocking chair on the front porch. If I look at the porch, he's over to the left. I can see him very clearly. He's wearing a flannel shirt. He looks to be about the same age as I feel I am, around thirty.*

Sue: *Can you tell who he is to you? What does it look like, feel like?*

Emma: *It feels like a husband, like my love. It feels like my love.*

Sue: *As you approach him, how does he respond?*

Emma: *He's not saying anything, but he has a really big smile on his face and his eyes are twinkling. He's happy I'm back from wherever I was.*

Sue: *Does it feel like it would be helpful to walk inside the cabin and see what kind of life you have there? Or do you want to just sit on the porch with him?*

Emma: *We can go in the house.*

Sue: *Okay.*

Emma: *It has a screen door. I'm opening the screen door. I'm going in the house and he's coming in behind me, and it's just a very, very modest, very simple cabin. Wood floors. I'm barefoot. I feel the wooden floors below my feet. There's no one else in the house. It's just the two of us.*

Sue: *Is there a sense of children or no?*

Emma: *No, no children.*

Sue: *Does it feel like you have everything you need or is there a sense of struggle?*

Emma: *I have a feeling of contentment. I would say it just seems very easy, simple, quiet, no needs. Everything seems good.*

Sue: *Is there anything else of significance in this moment that you need to see and understand in that moment you're in?*

Emma: *No, I don't think so.*

Sue: *I'm going to count to three and then we're going to go to the final day of that lifetime. When you get there, you'll describe what you see. One and two and three . . .*

Emma: *I see a bedroom. It's in the same house, and there's a small bed. I see myself lying on that small bed in that bedroom.*

Sue: *Can you tell how old you are?*

Emma: *I'm still feeling like I'm not much older than before. It doesn't feel like I'm much older.*

Sue: *Still in your thirties?*

Emma: *Yeah.*

Sue: *Can you get a sense of what's going on in your body?*

Emma: *I wanted to put my hand on my head right now. I think it's something with my head.*

Sue: *Perhaps fever, or does it feel like an injury? What comes to you?*

Emma: *The word* tumor *came to me. I don't know if there's something going on in my head, some kind of illness with my head, with my brain.*

Sue: *As you look at your body, do you see signs that you've been sick for a while?*

Emma: *Well, I'm in that bedroom on that small bed. I see John on the side of the bed, actually, on his knees, and he's holding my hands just as I'm ready to leave. He's crying and just brokenhearted.*

Sue: *You can lift above the body for a moment and speak to John in that scene. Wrap your arms around him. Kiss his head and say, "We are healing this moment for you because you know now that we're always connected."*

Emma: *Yes. I can imagine just kind of swirling out of that body and putting my energy over him from above. I can see him looking up and feeling my invisible presence, the way I feel him with me now in this lifetime.*

Sue: *Right. I feel the love between you two. Ask John and your soul guide what else you need to know from that moment of death.*

Emma: *That death is just a temporary separation. That's what I'm hearing. When you're out of the body, you remember that you're always connected. On Earth it feels like it's a separation, but it's not.*

Sue: *You can lift up from that body and rejoin John in the divine realms now. You two are united again. You can see him putting his arm out to escort you. Take a moment to just say whatever words you need to say to him.*

Emma: *Thank you, John. Thank you so much for being here. It's a reminder of how there's just so many more lives that we shared, so many infinite numbers of lives that we've shared, and that all those moments of love just strengthened that energetic bond, that cord that connects us.*

Sue: *Ask John if he would take you to meet your primary soul guide, the guide who has helped both of you create your life plans throughout your lifetimes.*

Emma: *I feel like he's walking me through that really bright tunnel again. It's blinding, but I know he's right next to me. He's on my right side. I can feel him. I see him. Then I get the sense of a guide or someone greeting us. It feels masculine. It feels like a man.*

Sue: *What does this guide look like?*

Emma: *This is going to sound crazy, but the first thing that came into my head is Abe Lincoln.*

Sue: *That's great! So, a beard, and tall and thin?*

Emma: *Yeah, he's got a tall hat on. He's very tall. He's wearing a black suit, and he's very thin. And he seems kind . . . Yeah, it seems like he knows me and John.*

Sue: *Okay. You can ask him what's the purpose of John dying early in your current life, and of you dying early in that past lifetime. What were you both trying to learn?*

Emma: *Well, I'm getting this sense again of that heart-to-heart energetic connection. He's reminding me that true soulmates can never be separated because of their love. This is what I'm hearing. Love is a frequency of vibration, and that energy can never be created* or destroyed. It's always there. It can never be broken. So the more love you share, the stronger that frequency of vibration connection grows and stays. It's eternal.

Sue: *Ask the guide if John is your primary soulmate.*

Emma: *I'm hearing yes, yes, yes. John's nodding his head, and the guide is nodding his head yes, too. I want to call him Abe because he looks like Abe Lincoln.*

Sue: *Good. You can ask him how you're doing with your arc of learning in your current lifetime.*

Emma: *"You have to have more confidence," he's telling me, "confidence in trusting that you are aware and awakened. Don't let yourself doubt it. Don't let fear stop you because fear is the opposite of love and it's all about love. There's no room for fear." That's what he's saying. In this lifetime, you've got to learn there's no room for fear and always trust your heart.*

Sue: *Is there a specific question you have about a life choice you have to make, whether it's career or work or family?*

Emma: *What is my purpose now that John is gone? . . . I'm getting that it is to continue helping other grieving moms feel their children beyond the veil and know that the soulmate love connection between them . . . it's really not mother-child, it's soul-to-soul. We're all souls.*

Sue: *So it's not mother-child, it's soul-to-soul?*

Emma: *Yes.*

Sue: *See what else he has to say.*

Emma: *Yeah, that we're all souls, and there's that feeling of playing a part. I feel like I was the mother to John, but in reality I'm so much more. "It's so much more," Abe's saying. "You were almost his other half. The two of you just vibrate on the same frequency. You have such a strong connection that even with him in the divine realms you won't ever lose that sense of connection with him because it's built up over thousands of lifetimes. You're so strongly connected that you can be that light now for others who are suffering in pain, feeling that they're separated when they're really not."*

Sue: *Many grieving moms struggle with guilt. Maybe you could ask the guide what is the purpose of that guilt and how can you help people heal it.*

Emma: *Well, he says guilt is a human thing. That's what I'm hearing. Guilt is a human thing. There's no room for guilt in the divine realms because it doesn't exist. Guilt is just one of those dualities that can only be experienced in a human body because it's a negative emotion that doesn't exist in divine realms. The purpose of guilt in the human body is to experience feelings, and the opposite of guilt is forgiveness. So to truly learn how to forgive, you have to learn to let go of guilt. You wouldn't be able to do that in the divine realms because guilt doesn't exist there. You have to be in a human body to be able to experience guilt and the lesson of forgiving oneself.*

Sue: *Oh, you have to be in a human body to learn this because it doesn't exist in the divine realms?*

Emma: *Yeah. I don't know where this is coming from. I'm just repeating what I hear.*

Sue: *Beautiful. Guilt doesn't exist in the divine realms. Okay, I'm vibrating from this conversation. Is there anything else you want to ask the guide before you guys go to meet the Council of Elders?*

Emma: *I'm asking him about helping the other moms with guilt. I feel like he wants to say a little more. Part of the lessons in the human body, one of the greatest lessons, is learning forgiveness—and forgiveness not of others, but of oneself.*

Sue: *Yes.*

Emma: *You can't forgive yourself if you don't realize that you are a divine being and that there is no room for any negativity . . . You have to learn to forgive yourself before you can forgive others, so the moms have to learn. Big lesson for the moms is to learn to forgive themselves.*

Sue: *To forgive oneself so you can forgive others. Yes.*

Emma: *Yes, yes, yes.*

Sue: *Do you feel complete with your guide? If you do, ask him to escort you both to the Council of Elders.*

Emma: *Yeah, let's go.*

Sue: *You, John, and this guide—Abe, we'll call him—are walking toward the Council of Elders. They meet in a special space. Look at that sacred space and see what it looks like. Describe it.*

Emma: *I see big stairs. I'm outside. I see big stairs going up to a building. They're made of gold.*

Sue: *What does the building look like?*

Emma: *It's a big, square shape. The roof is kind of arched. It's a really big, massive building. It looks like it's made of gold, too. But it's not made of gold. It looks like shiny metal.*

Sue: *As you enter, describe what you see and how many members are in your council.*

Emma: *Well, when I first walk in, I see a huge ceiling. I entered through big doors. Now I'm walking down the hallway into a room. I see people there, but I'm not seeing details. I just sense people in the room.*

Sue: *Can you tell if they're sitting in a circle or standing in a line, or is there a table?*

Emma: *A large horseshoe-shaped table with people around the table on three sides.*

Sue: *Where are they asking you to go?*

Emma: *To sit at the empty spot at the end of the table.*

Sue: *At the head of the table?*

Emma: *It's by the door when you first walk in, so yeah, it's at the head of the table by the door.*

Sue: *Very cool. Take a breath and sit down and notice where John is. Did John stand in the doorway or did he come in?*

Emma: *He stepped into the room, but he's not sitting. He's standing behind me to my right. He just put his hand on my shoulder.*

Sue: *Oh, beautiful, beautiful. The council is made up of the beings who guide all souls through every lifetime, and this is the group that has specifically guided you through every lifetime. What is the first thing you want to ask or say to them?*

Emma: *How am I doing?*

Sue: *What is their response?*

Emma: *Well, John just kind of joked and gave me a thumbs up. The council . . . I'm not getting a clear description of them. It's almost like they're ethereal. I don't sense people. It's almost like I just sense beings, if that makes sense.*

Sue: *Yes, it does. Ethereal beings.*

Emma: *Yes, they're not humans. They communicate telepathically, so you don't need to hear words. You get a sense of knowingness. I'll go by what I'm feeling. I'm feeling like they're proud of me. I'm feeling like they approve and that there are still things I could work on, but I'm doing well.*

Sue: *Do you want to ask about your current health challenge?*

Emma: *Okay. Yeah, I'm getting a sense that this is just a little blip and that it's going to heal. It's not going to affect me the rest of this lifetime. I get a feeling it almost had to happen because I needed a physical break. After John's death, I needed a break from life— almost like a time-out to kind of reset things and get back on the path. I'm going to come out of it even stronger, they're telling me. Even my intuition is going to be stronger, they say. I'm seeing my spinal column, my chakras . . . all of that needed to get strengthened. This physical break is just enough time to get things tweaked so I can continue moving forward on my path. It's going to make me stronger.*

Sue: *Is there anything else you want to ask? Is there a simple phrase they can give you to take back that helps you understand your arc of learning in this lifetime?*

Emma: *I'm hearing, "You can do it. You can do it, even when you feel like asking, 'What's the point?' and 'Why did this have to happen?'" It hurts like hell to have John in the divine realms and me here in the physical realm. I have to keep reminding myself it's just a temporary separation that I'm feeling because I'm human. But I'm really not separated from him.*

Sue: *You can ask how long you'll live in this lifetime.*

Emma: *I'm getting the sense that I still have a lot more to do, that it's going to be a while longer, unfortunately. This is hard. It's hard here in the physical world. They understand that.*

Sue: *Ask if you can establish a stronger relationship with your soul guides so they might be able to lift you up on your difficult days.*

Emma: *Right away I heard, "Reach out to the angels. The angels are always there to help you anytime. You're always surrounded by angels."*

Sue: *Beautiful. Is there any advice about lifestyle or keeping your energy in a good place to connect with the angels? Is there something you should do less of or more of in the physical world?*

Emma: *I'm sensing being down at the beach, by the ocean, being outside, walking on the sand. That's where I always feel the most grounded, the most connected to John. I can feel most connected to the Divine there, as well. I hear, "Do more of that, all year round, all the time."*

Sue: *Would it be helpful to ask about your life plan with your current husband or your daughter?*

Emma: *Well, with my daughter I'm sensing that she always seems to be more like my peer. Again, I'm feeling that it's not mother-child, it's soul-to-soul. I feel like Annie and I have that real strong soul-soul connection. Not quite the same as John's connection with me, but very strong. I'm sensing that she and I are going to do work together at some point. Now I'm actually holding my hands out in the air and there's Reiki energy coming out of my hands. I get the feeling she and I are going to be doing some significant healing work together at some point.*

Sue: *Is there any healing that you need to do in that relationship with Annie?*

Emma: *I just heard the word* trust. *I don't know what that's about.*

Sue: *Do you think it's her trusting you or you trusting her?*

Emma: *I think it's more me trusting her. I'm getting a sense of me trusting her. There's that slight fear of her leaving me because I lost John, so that's kind of the impression I'm getting.*

Sue: *Do you want to ask the council if Annie will outlive you in this lifetime?*

Emma: *Yeah. I definitely feel like she's going to outlive me. I see her living a long life.*

Sue: *What about your husband?*

Emma: *Oh, my Jim. He's my rock. He's such a strong leader.*

Sue: *Is there any healing that needs to be done in that relationship?*

Emma: *Yes. I feel like I need to work on being more gentle with him. He absorbs so much for me. I have to be more loving and giving to him. I've taken a lot of my grief out on him, and it's caused a little bit of hurt. I feel like I owe him some more love and gratitude. I need to show him more gratitude.*

Sue: *Beautiful.*

Emma: *Yeah, from me to him, because from him to me it's unconditional. It's beautiful.*

Sue: *Is there anything in particular that the guides can tell you about the core grieving mom group you meet with regularly? Is there any guidance that the council can give you?*

Emma: *Yeah. I was shown a swirling circle of energy, almost like a vortex, like a tornado. It's very symbolic. I see it started at the bottom, and then it's swirling and swirling and swirling. It's getting bigger and bigger and bigger, like a cyclone of healing, like the group of us moms came together divinely. I feel like John was at the helm of that—kind of gathering up the moms and their kids to bring everybody together for healing. I just keep getting that symbol that it started as one little point and then kept swirling, getting bigger and bigger and bigger. As our energy, as our cords of love from mom to mom grow, that frequency makes our vibrations more in line with one another. It strengthens us collectively. We're creating an energetic bond that's stronger than if one of us was working alone. We're shifting consciousness together.*

Sue: *Wow. That's beautiful. Is there anything else you're called to ask before you feel complete?*

Emma: *I am complete.*

Sue: *Okay. Thank the council and the guides. Do you want to ask John to take you to the Library of Souls?*

Emma: *Absolutely.*

Sue: *As he takes your arm and escorts you, note your surroundings.*

Emma: *Well, I'm going in the same building, but upstairs. It's like a big, open staircase, and then up to a huge, open room. There's a big square opening in the middle where you can look down below and see everything. I'm up on the second floor.*

Sue: *What do you see?*

Emma: *I'm seeing big shelves and stacks of books everywhere, racks and aisles of books.*

Sue: *Is there a certain book that you're drawn to?*

Emma: *I'm sensing the color green, so I'm going to go over to . . . Oh, okay. Yeah. It's a book about healing.*

Sue: *Wow. Is John with you?*

Emma: *He's reaching for the book because I'm too short. He's taking it down off the shelf. It's a very big book with rings on the edge, like it's bound with rings on the left side. We're walking over to a table and putting it down on the table. It doesn't look green, but I'm just feeling it's green. I can't explain it. It's just exuding a green energy from inside the book.*

Sue: *Tell me what happens.*

Emma: *I open the book and then this green mist comes out, like a green cloud. It's very mystical and magical. I get this sense of a good feeling, like a very positive feeling coming out of the book, a healing energy.*

Sue: *You can bask in that healing energy until you're ready to do something else.*

Emma: *Yeah. I'm actually inhaling it. It's crazy. It's like a green cloud. It's poofing out of the book like a green mist. I'm just breathing it in and I'm tingling. It feels so good.*

Sue: *Oh, that's so good.*

Emma: *Yeah, good for my back and for my heart. It's a book of healing. That's beautiful. I don't know where that came from. Yeah, it feels good, letting myself bask in it.*

Sue: *Yes. You can stay with that as long as you want. Just tell me when you're ready.*

Emma: *I'm good, I'm good.*

Sue: *Okay. Now is there anything else in the library that you want to do before we leave?*

Emma: *No. That was really beautiful. That's good.*

Sue: *Okay. Now we're thanking the library and closing the book. Ask John if he would escort you back through the tunnel to come back to this physical life.*

Emma: *We're walking down the stairs of the building to the first floor where we started, and we're going out through the big glass doors and down the golden steps toward that big, bright tunnel again.*

Sue: *When you're ready, you can turn and say whatever you need to say to John before you reenter this life.*

Emma: *Yeah. I'm getting teary because I don't want to say good-bye. He's holding my hands. He's assuring me I got this. "You're okay," he says. Now we're hugging. "It's okay, it's okay," he says. He's smiling.*

Sue: *Oh, good. Alright, as I count to three, we're going to come back into this physical world, knowing that you will always remember everything you've experienced here.*

I used guided meditation and deep breathing to bring Emma fully back into her body, after which we resumed our conversation:

Emma: *Thank you. Wow, I'm actually lightheaded, Sue. Wow.*

Sue: *What's your first impression of what happened?*

Emma: *It was wonderful. It was so good to see John because I've been having such a hard time feeling him around lately and feeling our connection. It felt so real. I'm just so grateful. I feel so much gratitude right now. I'm still floating. I don't feel like I'm in my body yet.*

Sue: *That's good. Take your time. Deep breaths.*

Emma: *I'm very floaty right now, yeah. I'm very lightheaded. Wow, I love it. Thank you so much.*

Sue: *Is there one sentence that you could say is the most significant thing you're taking away from it?*

Emma: *That it's really real. He really is right here. It really is real. He's not gone.*

Sue: *I can feel that. I have tears in my eyes. I saw John at every moment you described him. It was extraordinary for me, also.*

Emma: *It really was.*

Sue: *I think for me, what really stood out was the consistency of the love and dependability between the two of you, that it's eternal. In the past lifetime moment where you were dying, John was right there with you, holding you. You can trust that in this lifetime, whenever you're in pain of any kind, whether it's emotional, physical, or spiritual, you can be aware that John never leaves your side. He's right there with you, holding your hand.*

Emma: *Oh, I love that!*

Sue: *I also thought it was significant that you didn't have other children in that lifetime. It was really just the two of you. That is such a deep, profound bond you experienced in that lifetime and kind of a perfection of love. Yet at the same time, John was traumatized by your death. I think we have to keep that in our understanding because every lifetime is a give and take of lessons that need to be learned for the highest good. One of the things I think he may have learned in that lifetime in the cabin is that even after the trauma of your death, he was okay. He could go on with his life somehow. In this lifetime, perhaps you were trying to learn that even in the trauma of John's death, you can go on. You will be okay.*

Emma: *Yeah, that's true. Wow. I never thought of that, yeah.*

Sue: *I also thought it was important to note that it was a brain tumor, something in your head, because what I've always believed and what I think Louise Hay taught is that whether it's a migraine or a brain tumor, a problem with the brain means that our soul is telling us we* *spend too much time in our heads. Our soul is saying, "You've got to go to the heart." And that may have been an important part of your learning in that lifetime—to get out of your head. And that illness may have been a way of helping you do that.*

Emma: *Oh, my gosh. That's so weird because I've heard this from John in my writings. He tells me all the time you have to get out of your head and into your heart. Literally verbatim: "Get out of your head and get into your heart."*

Sue: *The other thing I found extraordinary was your guidance about guilt—that was phenomenal. The guides said guilt is a human thing. There's no room for guilt in the divine realms. It doesn't exist there. Guilt is only experienced in the physical realm, and the opposite of guilt is forgiveness. And we have to be in the human realm to learn this because guilt does not exist in the divine realms.*

Emma: *Right. Wow.*

Sue: *They said when you're having a bad day, to call in the angels, and that you and your daughter will be healers together someday. You may want to tell her about the green book that you pulled down off the library shelf.*

Emma: *Yeah. That was just so vivid. That was the last thing I ever expected to experience, and it just happened all of a sudden—it was so real.*

Sue: *I felt like I was there experiencing it with you. Thank you for the amazing journey!*

Emma: *It was really amazing. I really enjoyed every minute. I didn't know what to expect. I went into it with an open mind. Just there's no words, really. I have my good days and my bad days, but this whole back injury just has really set me back a lot because I can't get out and do my normal routine. It's hard.*

Sue: *Well, as we learned today, you're being asked to hit the reset button and just get in touch with your inner strength, to rebuild the spinal column, so to speak. Use the time to heal, to write, to embrace this gift of the pause.*

Emma: *Yeah. I have to tell you, I knew John was going to be present for this today because today was the first time in eight weeks I drove my car. I've had to wear a brace. I drove down to see where I'm going to be doing physical therapy before I signed up—to see how far it would be to drive. On the way home, the song John always played for me on the radio came on. I haven't heard it for a while. He played that song for me at the most significant times. I took a picture of it on my phone. It made my heart sing. I literally was crying in the car. I was like, "Oh, my God, I can't believe this!"*

Sue: *Oh my gosh, that's wonderful.*

Emma: *Yeah, he's so strong and present. Thank you so much.*

Chronicling Loss

Tell or write the story of your loved one's death or your career or relationship loss. In the story, answer these questions:

- What soul lesson was your departed loved one teaching you by putting you through this loss?
- What would your departed one want you to do with your life now?
- If you knew your departed one was here beside you, what would you say to them? What would they say to you?
- From your most spiritual perspective, what has been the gift of this experience?
- If you've lost a career, what gifts could be hidden in this change of direction?
- If you've lost a relationship, what positive attributes about yourself have you discovered?
- What three steps are you willing to take to bring a more powerfully spiritual perspective into your daily life and work?
- What steps are you willing to take to use your pain as fuel to accomplish your soul's greatest mission?

11
Glorious Health and Well-Being
Dis-ease Is a Nudge from the Soul

When the ego mind rules, illness occurs. This is the soul's way of getting your attention and turning your focus inward. Your body may manifest heart palpitations, high blood pressure, cancer, viruses, and chronic conditions as a nudge from your Higher Self to wake up and realign. By accessing your divine lens you can align with the wisdom of your soul and empower your immune system to flawlessly perform its job of keeping you healthy. When this alignment occurs, chronic illness heals, inflammation reverses, and viruses mend.

This connection between body, mind, and spirit is well-documented in scientific literature. You've also experienced this connection in your day-to-day life. Whenever you're behind the wheel of a car getting angry or frustrated with other drivers, your heart rate and blood pressure skyrocket. You may notice your heart pounding, your palms getting sweaty, and your breathing becoming shallow. This is proof of how your inner perspective impacts your physical body. In this moment of frustration, your immune system is diminished, and all bodily systems are thrown out of whack. You feel stressed and exhausted at the same time.

Pretend for a moment that instead of sitting in traffic, you're walking on the warm sand of your favorite beach, listening to the sound of gentle, rolling waves, feeling the soft breeze of a summer day against your skin. You have no worries. All your problems have been solved. Take a deep breath and truly feel the relief this brings. Notice your heart rate slowing, your breath regulating, and your sense of inner peace returning. You've shifted into your divine lens.

Which lens do you use most often? How is it serving you and your health? Which perspective feels better? Your divine lens elevates the immune system and reduces stress. Your ego lens sets off an inflammation response that triggers everything from heart disease to cancer. You get to choose your perspective—whether you're sitting in traffic or facing the loss of a loved one.

THE GIFT OF HEALTH CHALLENGES

Your health challenges are rich with soul lessons and perfectly designed to help you evolve in just the way you need to. Inside each unique health challenge lives the perfect solution, provided you're willing to embrace your divine lens perspective and choose that solution. When you refuse the lesson, your soul activates a more powerful wake-up call to get your attention.

Within a lifetime you're given many challenging opportunities to realign with your soul's wisdom. But if you continually fail to align with your Higher Self, your body will provide even greater nudges to get your attention until your soul has awakened. After a terrifying health diagnosis, you'll suddenly ask the good questions and look for new answers so the crisis can be used for your highest good. Your body has provided you with a major perspective shift and a moment of heart-opening possibilities.

Will you act on this opportunity? If you don't, another lesson will be graciously offered for your highest good, simply to help you awaken. You are not your body; it's only the shell holding your soul. Surrendering to the lessons of the body can bring you deeply in alignment with your soul, even in your final breath. Your last moment on Earth can be your great awakening. Nothing is over until the soul leaves the body. Each lifetime is a journey of endless reinvention and growth.

> *Your body is a vehicle for your most powerful lessons*
> *because it cannot be ignored.*

You can try to ignore your soul, but the body has a disruptive voice. You'll hear it loud and clear despite your refusal to grow. It will wake you from a deep sleep and drench you in sweat until you surrender to a new point of view. Once your body is injured or ill, you'll take action to change your life. You'd probably change your life to save the physical health of someone you love, but it's disturbing how little we risk to save our emotional and spiritual self.

The body can't be ignored, whether it's splayed across a highway, butchered in a gunfight, or ravaged with cancer. When we see a physical wound in ourself or others, we take positive action. The same should be true of our spiritual and emotional wounds.

As physical bodies in a physical world, we often ignore what we can't see. Yet when we look beyond the surface to see another person's true essence, to see beyond the physical self, we're acting in alignment with our divinity. We're connecting soul to soul. And what we find in those moments is our own divinity reflected back to us. We remember that we're all souls on a shared journey, wearing different costumes and playing different roles, all of us wounded and gifted. But our essence is the same.

The act of reaching out to save another person saves you. Our bodies are hardwired to feel good when we help others, whether we're saving them physically, spiritually, or emotionally. An act of kindness boosts the immune system. How perfectly we're designed to recognize the divine essence of others—and to align with our own sacredness.

There may be some conventional medical doctors who address the soul of healing, but many only think of the body as a machine to be fixed, a chemistry to be balanced. Spiritual, holistic, and alternative healers address both the body *and* the soul. They seek to understand the intricate interplay between our physical, spiritual, and emotional health. Any physician who looks at the body as more than just a physical system is a true healer.

Your soul is always in charge. To heal your body, you must also do the inner work of realigning with your Higher Self. Seek to understand how and why you've disconnected from the source of your wisdom. Examine your past to see choice points where you could have taken a different path. Make adjustments in your beliefs and take steps in a new direction. This is essential for healing.

Your soul is calling you to shift into your divine lens. Your previous point of view has made you sick. You're being nudged to quit the job that's toxic, start the business you've dreamed of, return to school, or walk away from a toxic relationship. Your illness won't prevent you from taking these steps. On the contrary, making these changes will save your life.

Changing your lifestyle inside and out creates a powerful paradigm shift that makes true healing possible. The energy of the food you eat affects both your physical and emotional health. Processed food, even if it carries what looks like an impressive nutritional label, has no life force. Its life-giving properties have been removed long ago. Fresh, organic foods, like vegetables from your local farmer's market, carry a high vibration, which accelerates healing. Empty, processed foods deplete the immune system because the body expends a tremendous amount of energy just trying to digest all the poisonous ingredients.

EXIT POINTS

We have several predetermined possible choice points for exiting a lifetime. At each choice point, the soul is reminded of what it came here to accomplish. We're asked if we'll be able to succeed in our mission or if we've completed the journey. We can choose to stay longer or hit the reset button, return to the higher realms for healing, and, if we desire, start another lifetime. If you have been diagnosed with a serious or terminal illness, this may be one of your predetermined exit points. Your soul may be deciding whether you accomplished what you came here to do and fulfilled your soul's mission.

The world tells us that death is random. It's not. It's the soul's choice. We exit for reasons that can't always be understood by others. If we've been living off-path, lost in fear or drowning in self-indulgence, our soul may choose to leave and regroup in the higher realms. If we've lived mostly in alignment with our Higher Self, we may have accomplished our mission and choose to exit early, knowing that our exit will launch our loved ones into the kind of tremendous soul growth that is born from pain.

This is why a child may die young. The child's soul is highly evolved, and it has accomplished what it came here to do. The early exit of the child provides their grieving loved ones an opportunity to search for sacred meaning and to experience accelerated soul growth before it's their turn to return to the Divine to reunite with the child.

When someone lives well into old age, it often means they were determined to keep learning even as their physical being disintegrated. This can either be a sign of a highly evolved soul or a stubborn ego that needed to experience physical deterioration in order to shift perspective. In the final days, this person may experience tremendous spiritual awakening, even if it doesn't appear so from the outside. The person may appear closed-off and unaware, but the soul is always processing. Things are seldom as they appear.

Your loved one may have been suffering from dementia, but their soul was hard at work, often ascending into the higher realms for guidance and returning to the body for moments of awakening. This inner growth can occur even in cases of dementia, coma, or brain damage. Consciousness does not live in the mind, only in the soul.

During coma, the soul leaves the body to regroup in the divine realms, where a decision is made as to whether the soul mission has been or will be fulfilled. The decision is made for everyone's highest good.

If a person dies from a long, lingering illness like cancer, their soul has chosen to use physical suffering to purify what needs to be brought into the light for healing. The illness allows the person to loosen their attachment to the physical and align fully with their divinity. When they cross over, the physical suffering will have served its purpose: to open the heart and cleanse any negativity.

We don't need to choose suffering. But it is a choice the soul can make for our highest good. This choice, made before the lifetime begins, is created in cooperation with the loved ones caring for the dying person. The caretakers agree to become part of this experience for their own evolution. Those who witness suffering without being able to ease it experience deep despair, which teaches divine compassion. The soul benefits whichever role we play—to suffer or to ease the suffering of others.

Soul Stories
ISABELLA: A HEALING CRISIS

Isabella is a powerful healer who runs a franchise of healing arts clinics that she launched years ago. She hires and trains staff and oversees the operation of each clinic. She has always lived a healthy lifestyle, eating well, exercising regularly, and maintaining a disciplined daily prayer and meditation practice.

Isabella was in her fifties when she was diagnosed with leukemia. During this session she was in a hospital room preparing to receive treatment. She wanted to ask her guides what the lesson was in this illness and if she could learn it any other way than through illness. During the session, she experienced a significant past life as a respected medicine woman for her tribe. Then we went to meet her Council of Elders. Here's an edited transcript of that part of her session:

Sue: *Let's ask the guide to bring us to the council of spiritual elders who have always helped you. They've prepared you for each lifetime and helped you process your lifetime when you return to the divine* *realms. And as you walk into their meeting space, describe what it looks like.*

Isabella: *There are a lot of beings, at least fifty to seventy-five. I see kind of an orange color around the walls and things. And yeah, they seem a little serious.*

Sue: *Where do they want you to sit?*

Isabella: *In front of them. A formal type of arrangement.*

Sue: *As you take your place and sit down, ask them the first question that comes to your heart.*

Isabella: *So what is the significance of what I'm going through right now? . . . I'm getting, "It's to prepare you for what's to come. To prepare you for something else. We have plans for you to do something that's not like what you've been doing. And it's very hard for you to get out of your current obligations. We can't seem to get you out of your current situation. You don't want to let anyone down or change anything because it's working for so many people, but you need to do something else. And this is going to force you."*

Sue: *Ask them if you can learn that lesson a different way.*

Isabella: *I would like to learn it without so much trauma. Can I learn it a different way?*

They're answering, "Well, you could promise to give up running your business, but you tend to cave in to people who feel sad or have expectations of you. So we feel that this illness gives you the strength to make changes."

Sue: *Are they saying that by focusing on your own body and health rather than overseeing your clinics, you can break this pattern?*

Isabella: *Yeah. Which is the way I've been teaching medicine, training my staff, and helping others for decades. I need to do it for myself.*

Sue: *Does it feel like you will be able to do it that way without the illness?*

Isabella: *They're right. I feel timid and I have a really hard time letting anyone down or not supporting them. I do, I do, but . . . I hear* them saying, "Listen to us because we're right!" I really don't want to go through all the toxic chemo and drugs.

Sue: *Can you make a promise out loud to them, right here on the spot, that with all your heart and soul you will commit to breaking the pattern of not wanting to let people down and instead you will take care of yourself, honor yourself first, and put your needs first, so that you don't have to experience this illness?*

Isabella: *Yes, because it's clear now that my life purpose is not to do what I'm doing right now. I've known that for a while, and I will do it now because I haven't been listening.*

Sue: *Do you want to ask them what your new life purpose is?*

Isabella: *Yes. It's something to do with light, using rays of light, and it's a different level of healing.*

Sue: *Are you going to pioneer this new form of healing?*

Isabella: *It will be a gift that will be given, yes.*

Sue: *And what do you have to do to receive it?*

Isabella: *I need to stop my new build-out for the expansion of the business. I need to stop my business. I need to sell the whole thing and be available for what is next.*

Sue: *Ask whatever comes to your heart.*

Isabella: *I'm worried about my stepdaughter because she's part of my business and so tied up in me doing this build-out, and I don't want to hurt her, she loves me so much. And the answer is that she will be part of this new healing someday. She may not understand it at first, but she'll be part of this new path.*

Sue: *And should we ask the guides about your departed sister and what your soul agreement with her was?*

Isabella: *It's surreal that I'm in the same hospital where my sister died of cancer. She always admired me, loved me so much. She is still looking at me, seeing how I'm going to handle this now. It's almost like she's learning something by observing my reaction to this illness, and she's very proud of me.*

Sue: *Do you have the sense that part of the reason you're going* *through this illness is because you made an agreement to go through it in a very different way than she did, and she's learning from you from the other side?*

Isabella: *That does feel true. It's part of her evolvement. She's learning and teaching me that we can do this differently. And she's seeing how I do it differently. In her lifetime here she was always trying to do everything perfectly, following the rules. I'm the complete opposite. She's saying, "You're so right to follow your heart." She suffered so much in her lifetime, and she doesn't want me to suffer.*

Sue: *Does your sister feel that you will have a miraculous healing?*

Isabella: *They say if I want it, if my soul wants it.*

Sue: *Does your soul want that?*

Isabella: *I have this little thing about changing my life—a fear. I've been afraid to disappoint the people who work for me. This illness gives me permission.*

Sue: *And if the illness were to be suddenly healed, would you still sell your business?*

Isabella: *I would, I would. I do not have to go through pain to change. I can see this pattern now, and I will change my life. I will change it in order to do what I need to do.*

Sue: *Ask your council if they had any cautions for you about this lifetime before you dove into it.*

Isabella: *"Yeah, we told you it would be hard," they say. "And you said that you would do it." And I can choose not to do it if I don't want to. I get to choose—if I want to move, which way I want to go.*

Sue: *Ask your council if your soul originated in the angelic realms. Because there are Earth-based souls who spend their incarnations on Earth, and there are souls in the angelic realm who mostly spend their incarnations as angels, working from the higher realms, and they don't spend as much time incarnating on Earth.*

Isabella: *The council says, "Angelic realm. That's why more is expected."*

Sue: *Ask the council if, as an angelic realm soul, you will be given* *the gift of channeling in a new form of healing for the world. Is there anything you need to know from them that will help you access that?*

Isabella: *I won't be given the gift until I make this first step. Then it will be revealed.*

Sue: *Ask the council to help you remember all of this knowledge when you go back to your life so that you won't forget everything you know now.*

Isabella: *Asking the council about a life partner . . . Oh yeah, it's like a "we'll see."*

Sue: *Ask them how the previous partners you've chosen have served your learning.*

Isabella: *They're saying people see me as an angelic being and try to steal my light. I haven't been valued for my soul yet. I haven't been valued by a life partner.*

Sue: *Ask what you can do to find the life partner who will not steal your light.*

Isabella: *My guide says, "If you want someone. Yeah, if you want someone."*

Sue: *And what is your answer?*

Isabella: *Hmm, I don't know . . . That's kind of my answer right now.*

Sue: *Is there anything else you want to ask this council before we leave?*

Isabella: *How can I get out of everything I'm in tactfully, without letting people down? It's hard to be tactful when you're changing a lot of things in your life . . . Yeah, they're saying there are people who aren't going to be happy with me, and it may cost me some money, but that will be made up. The money is not significant . . . My guide wants to remind me of nature. He's taking me to the mountains and showing me that nature and mountains are my strength. They're my recharge, my retreat. That's what Colorado is for me—it's where I get my energy. Where I recharge, where I find my center.*

Sue: *And does he want you to go there more often?*

Isabella: *Yeah, it needs to be scheduled in. That's a retreat place. And he says I need to read more about quantum healing.*

Sue: *Ask your guide if he wants to take you to the Library of Souls and if there's anything in there that might help you.*

Isabella: *Whoa, that feels really supreme! Yeah.*

Sue: *Let him escort you there.*

Isabella: *It feels like a really impressive energy place. So there's a door with golden light coming out, and he just wants me to stand in that light. To receive the light . . . There's purple and yellow. Purple outside the room and this golden light inside, beaming.*

Sue: *How does it feel?*

Isabella: *Like it's radiating into my cells. It's recharging me and feels really good.*

Sue: *Ask him if you can return there whenever you want to in your meditations for more healing.*

Isabella: *He says that I can.*

Sue: *Alright, is there anything else we need to know or do before we return to physical reality?*

Isabella: *If I stand in this light . . . I see my life needs to be in congruence with what my soul is telling me that it will be. A lot of times I've acted differently than what I knew in my soul to do.*

Sue: *In order to please others?*

Isabella: *Yes. It's always about not wanting to hurt other people's feelings. It was a noble intention I had, but it was keeping me from stepping into my higher purpose.*

Sue: *The great gift of this illness is that it has made you realize that your life and your future work depend on your acting in alignment with your soul's truth and letting other people be who they will be. Let them be disappointed if they need to feel that, but you need to simply live your highest truth because your life depends on it.*

After I brought Isabella back into her physical body, she shared this:

Sue: *What do you think was the biggest insight you got from that?*

Isabella: *I know it's the truth that I can either go through this painful experience and be forced to change, or commit to changing now. And* *that it's not my time to exit. I have work to do, but I need to change first. The council was strong about that. They said, "You will have a hard experience if you need to have that, because it's whatever serves your highest purpose." This is an old pattern I've had. And this is the biggest wake-up call in my world. So it's my choice. I have to change my pattern of pleasing others.*

Update: *Isabella completed a mild form of leukemia treatment and is doing well. She got an all-clear result from her latest tests. She has also taken steps to sell her businesses.*

Taking Wellness Action

A healthy lifestyle is always the best medicine. But sometimes we find ourselves facing an unexpected diagnosis that was designed perfectly by the soul for our highest good—even if we've lived a healthy life. We can work with this challenge by facing it physically (such as conventional medicine, acupuncture, and nutrition), emotionally (seeing a healer/therapist to release buried trauma), and spiritually (meditation, affirmative prayer, and energy work). Use the following to guide you.

Discuss or write the story of your health history. In the story, answer these questions:

- When in your life have you felt the healthiest?
- Describe how you felt in your body during those healthy times.
- What actions were you taking that contributed to your well-being?
- When in your life have you felt the worst physically?
- What actions were you taking that contributed to feeling unwell?
- Explain your current diagnosis from your divine lens perspective. What is your soul asking you to change? This could include lifestyle, relationships, career, as well as internal negative beliefs and feelings. Write everything that comes to mind.
- Now write out your plan for addressing these changes and set a timeline for taking action.

- Meditate and visualize your body reclaiming perfect health in whatever ways that resonate with you.
- Each morning spend a few minutes visualizing sacred white light pouring in through your crown chakra and purifying every cell, muscle, bone, tissue, and organ—filling you with health and vitality.

12

Success and Meaningful Work

Aligning Career with Your Soul's Purpose

You still have something important to do, even if you can't see it right now. Even when you feel lost and pointless, without direction, floating in grief, that great thing still lives inside of you, deep down.

When the time is right and the world is ready and you've learned what you needed to learn, your great gift will come pouring out of you like an Arkansas spring flood, like a hurricane downpour, unstoppable and urgent. It will save every heart, crack the world wide open, pour light into darkness, open minds, heal souls, and change lives—especially yours. It's the gift you agreed to bring into this lifetime. Nobody else brought it, only you. You signed up for this one. You orchestrated the precise childhood that would allow you to birth this gift. You designed the perfect pain to wake you up and break your heart wide open and turn everything you've learned into soaring wisdom that sings in just this key, this chord that nobody else can strike, that nobody else can possibly deliver, that nobody else is capable of sharing in your exact way.

This gift has your number on it and no one else's. It fits perfectly into the puzzle slot that's waiting, empty now. Not until every empty slot of this puzzle is filled can we change this world, light it up with consciousness, and shift it over into bliss. When everyone brings their unique piece to the table, we all win. And right now, everyone is wondering exactly where your piece is and when you'll bring it to the puzzle, because your gift is the tipping point, the one we've all been waiting for, and it will change everything.

SO YOU'VE BEEN LAID OFF

Maybe you've been laid off or fired, or you didn't get that new job. You feel like the wind's been knocked out of you—it's a punch to the gut. The job and career you've steadily built for years has now been taken away.

When you first hear the news, you'll notice a brief moment of calm because your ego mind is momentarily stunned into silence. This gap allows you to hear your Higher Self whispering, *Everything is okay. Something better is waiting. This is all in divine order for your highest good.* Your soul's wisdom speaks up the moment your ego mind receives a swift blow and is temporarily stunned into silence. We sometimes think of this as being in a state of shock. We feel numb and the mind goes quiet. But very soon, within minutes, the ego mind fires up and responds, *I don't deserve this! I'll never find another good job. How dare they! I'll lose my home!*

Your ego mind thus launches its battle of survival exactly as it was designed to. This is the mind you agreed to have when you took a physical body for this incarnation. Yet it's only half of your mind. The other half of your mind holds the doorway to your Higher Self, the seat of your divine intuition and your true essence. In brief gaps when the ego is silenced, you can hear your Higher Self speaking the truth. Grab hold of that deep inner voice. It's the wisdom of your soul. Listen to it before the ego mind overpowers it with fear. Shortly after you get bad news of any kind, the ego mind shifts into full-blown desperation. That brief, silent gap before ego steps in is your golden opportunity for salvation.

Unrestrained, the ego mind can push you to the edge of sanity. During crisis, your sanity will depend on how well you've learned to quiet the mind through meditation or other forms of spiritual practice. When you indulge fear, you allow it to grow stronger until it becomes your boss. If you haven't developed the mental discipline of quieting fear thoughts, ego will reign supreme over your Higher Self. It will provoke you to defend yourself at all costs and trust no one. This ego-based attitude will destroy your happiness, future success, and relationships—until you recognize that fear does not serve your highest good.

Everything changes the moment you listen to your soul's wisdom. It's a simple request: "Please show me my soul's lesson in this crisis and help me move through it with love and courage." That simple request calls wisdom to your side, fills you with light, opens your heart, quiets your mind, and will lead to an enlightening new perspective on the situation. You'll feel empowered from within. Your inner victim will settle down.

Your soul created this moment to allow you to step up to your wisdom, awaken into love, and embrace spirituality. You're not being punished. You're not a victim. You've done nothing wrong. It's simply a reinvention point designed for your highest good. By embracing the lesson of the job loss, you'll discover a new career that brings you to a greater level of meaningful work and abundance.

You're not a victim of the economy, your manager, or corrupt politicians. You're a divine being who created this moment to shake up old patterns and free yourself to become who you came here to be. You've been stuck for too long, and this is your wake-up call.

> *You didn't come here to live in fear, to be hidden or*
> *unimportant. You came to be grand and fearless, bold*
> *and awake, and infused with wisdom. When you*
> *activate your divine lens, this is who you are.*

Your ego, nurtured by teachers, priests, ministers, and well-meaning loved ones, is your "should" self. It says, *This is who you should be in order to please others. This is what I should do to be practical and survive.* Your Higher Self whispers, *This is what I know to be true about my gifts and who I came here to be. It will take courage to follow this path, but it feels right.*

Your ego self and your divine Higher Self are often in direct opposition, pulling you in conflicting directions. Your "should" voice is a truth-slayer; it's a defeater of wisdom and confidence. You can hush it with a prayer in the night or a heartfelt request for divine intervention. Everything shifts as soon as you say, *I will not live in fear. When fear arises, I'll reach for love instead. I'll find courage within my heart.* This aligns you with your Higher Self rather than the ego. Higher consciousness lives within you, always. It's part of your DNA. You've grown used to ignoring your higher consciousness because the ego mind deletes it immediately with its fear thoughts. You've allowed this pattern to continue for too long. It takes courage to break it.

What is courage to a person who trudges along untethered from their soul's longings? What is love to someone who finds pleasure only in the mundane? Those who fear the richness of fearless love and courageous choices are asleep. Their souls walk through this world unaware.

Courage is essential to living your best life. It serves you well to make "irrational" career choices as you pursue what you know to be true for yourself. A leap of faith is always required.

This world will scare you away from boldness. It will diminish your dreams with fear. You may try to set your course to be practical above all else, believing that this will save you. The opposite is true. Your compromised choices will lead nowhere. They may feel safe enough to grab hold of, yet this kind of fear never leads to success. Eventually you'll end up separated from your true self. By honoring the ego above all else, you'll lose your connection to the Divine. Without this inner compass, you'll find yourself adrift on ravaged seas, alone and hopeless. Your separation from divinity will damage relationships, destroy careers, make you sick, and empty your bank account. When everything is taken away, when you're disgusted with this mundane world, you might finally make a different choice.

At any moment, you can choose to live in alignment with your Higher Self rather than your ego self. This changes everything. As soon as you surrender your ego, you will find the fulfillment, happiness, and success you've always sought.

Each lifetime contains a series of awakenings. If we embrace the lessons within each challenge, we will find our way. We'll stay on the path. We're given many opportunities to change direction, reinvent, and rethink each time we hit a crisis.

The journey of awakening is harder if we resist it until we're in our fifties and sixties. Surrendering the ego becomes harder as we age because we've become addicted to our fear-based point of view. Our courage to choose the unknown determines our future. The sooner we choose the more enlightened perspective of the soul, the sooner we'll find happiness.

Encourage your children to search for answers that inspire them rather than diminish their self-esteem. Teach them to use the divine lens perspective whenever they face a choice. Model these wise choices for your children. They learn by watching you, not by listening to your words. If they see you living in fear, they'll absorb your negative pattern, no matter what you teach them. If they've been raised with authentic love, they'll find their way to courage.

Our children push us to the next level of soul growth, not the other way around. When we see fear reflected in our children's choices, we can realize our own shortcomings. We're meant to learn from this and redirect our lives. Children illuminate the flaws in our journey, the places where we haven't listened to our soul, the moments we give ourselves over to the ego. They respond to us by basically telling us, "Your refusal to grow is reflected in my own pain and failures. Heal me by healing yourself. Live in alignment with your divinity, so I can live in alignment with mine."

WHICH LENS DID YOU CHOOSE
THIS MORNING?

Pick your viewpoint carefully because the one you choose today determines everything. It will push you down a path that will become your story. What will it be at the end? Will it be a tale of meaningless work and choices made from fear? Or will it be a grand and bold tale of courage, wisdom, and laughter on the path less traveled? You get to choose.

Remember, it takes baby steps to climb any mountain. You may see what you came here to do and the greatness of it may overwhelm you. Instead, focus on what's right in front of you today and ask yourself, *What is one small step I can take today that will begin to turn my life in this new direction?* If you ask that question every day and keep moving forward with little steps, you will always arrive at where you're meant to be, doing great work.

If today you feel joyful about your career and you're creating abundance, you're on the path. However, in a few years changes may be required. We all have many reinvention points in our lives that are designed to nudge us forward and help us kick it up to the next level. Growth and change are required here in Earth School. They're part of our shared human experience. If you embrace these changes, trust your intuition rather than your monkey mind, and gracefully step up to the next level, your life will get better and better.

Our broken hearts and disappointments are meant to wake us up to our great potential and help us reinvent ourselves and go in a new direction—the right direction. The more off-path we are, the stronger the nudges will be.

If you're an old soul who came in to do great work and help raise consciousness (and you *are*), you'll likely get some big wake-up calls (job loss, divorce, bankruptcy, illness) until you stop hiding and start living true to your Higher Self. When you're ready to listen, your intuition will guide you flawlessly in the right direction.

We should all be thanking the bosses who fire us and the lovers who break our hearts. These are our greatest teachers. They agreed to this before this lifetime began to help us remember who we are. The pain they cause forces us to ask some good questions: Who am I? Why am I here? Where do I go when I die? Did I come here to do great work? How can I navigate differently now to find my true purpose? Until we ask these questions, we won't be able to find our way. Sometimes it takes great pain to wake us up to our purpose here, though it doesn't have to. But pain seems to be what really gets our attention,

SOUL STORIES

ROSE: THE IMPORTANCE OF SELF-LOVE

This client struggled with body weight and obesity issues for decades. She also experienced deep grief: When she was a teenager, her mom died from cancer. Then twenty years ago, she had a stillborn at thirty-eight weeks. Rose is a clinical social worker who was questioning her life's purpose. Here's the edited transcript of her session:

Sue: *Are you outdoors or indoors?*

Rose: *Outdoors. I'm in a city. Feel like it's the 1920s. I feel like everybody has their wool clothes on. It's not snowing or anything, but you can tell it's a little cool.*

Sue: *Do you have a sense of where this is?*

Rose: *New York City. People are poor. Struggling . . . All doing their own thing, very busy . . . I feel like I'm twenty years old or something. I'm just looking around, and I see people. They're kind of cold, emotionally. They're not aware, just trying to survive.*

Sue: *Allow that scene to unfold.*

Rose: *I'm going up the steps of an apartment. I see an older woman and older man, and they're supposed to be my parents, but I look at them as grandparents. We're sitting down at a table and food is being served. They don't talk to each other. There's no real communication.*

Sue: *What is the food?*

Rose: *Potatoes and soup.*

Sue: *Do you have a sense of where you were going in the city?*

Rose: *Yeah. I just left work and came home for dinner. I work at a store. I work as a store salesperson, selling merchandise. I'm friendly with the customers. I know them.*

Sue: *Are you a man or woman?*

Rose: *I am a man. I thought I was a woman, but now that I look at my body I see I'm a twenty-year-old man. I feel like I died early in that life. I didn't really have a long time to live. I got sick in my chest.*

Sue: *I'm going to count to three and we can move a little forward in time to see what happens that's significant. One and two and three . . .*

Rose: *I see a Christmas tree. It's a silver Christmas tree and we're sitting there.*

Sue: *Indoors or outdoors?*

Rose: *Inside the house. It's in the corner of the room.*

Sue: *How old you are now?*

Rose: *I feel like I'm twenty-five, not much older. I'm not happy, just cold and dismal.*

Sue: *Are you aware of having a relationship other than parents?*

Rose: *No. I feel like I'm alone, just me and my older parents . . . It's funny, I just rose up above the Christmas tree. I floated outside the window.*

Sue: *Tell me.*

Rose: *I'm kind of floating. I see that it's not a good time here. I don't know if it's war. It just wasn't a good time, not a happy time for people.*

Sue: *Was that your death scene?*

Rose: *Yes.*

Sue: *You had a feeling you were sick in your chest?*

Rose: *Yeah. I had to exit.*

Sue: *As you leave that lifetime, tell me what you're aware of.*

Rose: *I'm just sad from this suffering, so much suffering at this time. It was cold. My parents were so old. I had to leave them first. It wasn't a good time. I had more to do, but I felt stuck . . . I don't see anybody else. I'm just floating right now.*

Sue: *Your guide is arriving to help you process that life. Tell me what you sense.*

Rose: *He's telling me that I kept them company. They didn't think they were going to have a child. And then they did have a child, and it was me, but they didn't learn the lessons.*

Sue: *What was the lesson?*

Rose: *Joy, to be joyful. They were mundane. There was no happiness, so they have to come back to try again.*

Sue: *What did you learn there?*

Rose: *That we were going to have to do this again.*

Sue: *In your current lifetime?*

Rose: *Yeah. My mother and father had to come back. This time they're younger, having children younger. It's quite the opposite. They're happier than those two people, but my mother wanted to get sick because she didn't want to be with that man. So she had to exit this lifetime early, because it still wasn't working for her.*

Sue: *Is there more?*

Rose: *I'm getting that my mom died early to set me free so I could do what I needed to do here this time. If she didn't die early, I wouldn't have known what I needed to do. But because that twenty-five-year-old man wasn't really able to just become . . . He was stagnant, stuck. So here I am, coming back, and so I'm able to do what I need to do this time.*

Sue: *Is there anything else you want to ask?*

Rose: *I'm communicating with my guide. It's like I don't even have to say anything, it's like mind-to-mind.*

Sue: *Telepathic.*

Rose: *Yeah. And I'm telling him that's why I felt so stuck in my body, because I was so stuck in that life that I couldn't do what I really wanted to do. It was almost like I got ill and couldn't move my arms and legs. Do you know what I mean?*

Sue: *Yes.*

Rose: *Like I was stuck in bed.*

Sue: *Yes.*

Rose: *I'm talking to the guide. It's more of a man angel, and I'm telling him that's why I feel stuck in my body still. It's just a reminder that I don't need to feel stuck now. I'm able to move. But it's like I understand now why I feel that heavy feeling . . . It's like my body is so heavy in this life. But I want to go, go, go, and I can't. It's like I haven't healed that past lifetime.*

Sue: *Ask your guide what you can do to release the pain from that lifetime.*

Rose: *He's saying that I have to move every day. Moving is making things better. The more I stay sitting or stuck, the more I fall into the old pattern. He wants me to keep moving.*

Sue: *Ask if he can help you. Tell him about how you struggle. Ask for his help.*

Rose: *He's telling me I need to spend more time talking to him so that I can be reminded of what's important. He's telling me it's like the movie* Groundhog Day. *You just wake up and you forget, because you need to communicate with Spirit to remember. I always need to be reminded.*

Sue: *Do you want to ask him about your relationship with your husband and what you're trying to learn from that?*

Rose: *He's telling me that we're exactly the same. We come from trauma. We were meant to heal each other. And it was important to help him. And he helped me. I'm asking now, "Do I stay or do I go?" He says I still have more to learn. He says, "You'll know."*

Sue: *You can ask the guide if there's healing needed in that relationship.*

Rose: *He's trying to say that I can't judge whether there's growth or no growth within my husband. It's not my job. He's learning his own lessons. They may not be as deep or as wide as my lessons, but he's learning some things. He's saying, "Just let him be."*

Sue: *Do you want to ask about your arc of learning in this lifetime, especially when you lost a child, what that process was about for your soul?*

Rose: *That was to wake me up. He clearly said, "You know what it is, it woke you up, because you were sleepwalking."*

Sue: Do you want to—

Rose: *Nicholas [Rose's stillborn child] just came up to give me a hug. [long silence, crying]*

Sue: *Ah, good, good, good . . . Soak up that love.*

Rose: *And it's just like I understood. I understood that the lessons are so much more important than the physical people. So important. I say, "Thank you."*

Sue: *Do you want to see the Council of Elders?*

Rose: *We're just moving around these realms now.*

Sue: *Look around.*

Rose: *We're going through another tunnel. It's kind of dark. And I see sparkling, a little bit of sparkly lights coming closer. Oh my goodness, the light is brilliant! It's like it's gold. Everything is gold, shiny. I can't really see anybody, I just feel their presence . . . It's golden buildings, and golden light.*

Sue: *Wow.*

Rose: *Castles. Gold castle buildings . . . And I'm hiding behind my guide. Oh my God, oh my God . . . And he says, "Come stand beside. Not behind me, side-by-side."*

Sue: *Is he taking you to the place where the council meets?*

Rose: *He's telling me that it's going to be fine and safe. There's nothing to be fearful of. We're going inside. We're going closer, inside the gold building. Okay, they're all at a table.*

Sue: *How many do you see?*

Rose: *And they're all . . . I see six. Oh boy, they have a lot to say, I can feel it.*

Sue: *Do they want you to sit at the table or stand?*

Rose: *They're asking me to sit down. My guide doesn't need to sit. He's just standing there. Oh, my goodness, I feel the tension . . . Not tension, but I feel the strength. Some people are awarded one or two elders, but I have six.*

Sue: *You can ask how you're doing with your life plan.*

Rose: *They're telling me that I need to do more. They're not scolding me, but they're being stern with me. And they're telling me that you have all this behind you, this power. And all those moments that you disconnected from people because of your power, that's what you were supposed to do, because you were supposed to keep moving and moving to fulfill your mission.*

Sue: *Ask them what is yours to do to fulfill that mission.*

Rose: *My guide is trying to explain to me because I don't understand. He's trying to explain. It's like my guide is taking me away. He says, "I'm going to explain it to you."*

Sue: *Is he taking you outside of the council meeting room?*

Rose: *Yes, yes . . . He's telling me I have to heal others. You have to awaken them, he says. And the most important thing is teaching them how to trust their intuition so they can hear their guides and understand their purpose. I'm sitting here in disbelief because I'm saying I like that. That's what I want.*

Sue: *That's so good.*

Rose: *My purpose is to awaken people, because there has to be so much more healing on this planet. And because of the past-life experience that I had of it being so cold and so dead, so not alive, I needed to understand that. I had to leave early because I didn't feel that I could do much to heal others then. I had to come back under different circumstances and go through my experiences, to be reminded of what it feels like to be stuck—and then have an opportunity to be released from that so that I can go forth and help others. That's all. All that other stuff doesn't matter, as long as they're listening to their soul and to what they need to do here on Earth . . . And that's what the disconnect is. People are not listening. I'm thanking the guide for interpreting and explaining.*

Sue: *Wonderful.*

Rose: *He's saying, "I'm always with you, all those times when you got out of those situations, I helped you. My name is Gabriel."*

Sue: *That's beautiful.*

Rose: *He says, "When you go back, you have to remember the six people of golden light, the elders, who are with you. They gave you this power. And now that I'm explaining your purpose, you have nothing else to fear. All you need do is awaken and know that you have the power to awaken others." He's telling me that I have to go back to the physical world, but I don't want to go.*

Sue: *Is he walking you out to the tunnel? Do you feel that you're complete?*

Rose: *There's more . . .*

Sue: *Do you want to visit the pavilion where we choose our bodies?*

Rose: *Yes, I do.*

Sue: *As you move into that place of physical body selection, tell me what you see.*

Rose: *I see bodies with big hips. I don't go to any other room with different bodies. This is the room with the big hips. He's giving me information that big hips are for being grounded. That's why I chose these hips—to be more grounded. It helps me gain the knowledge that I need. They're sturdy and strong. I need this body because I'm different from others. So I chose this to have a better foundation. I can't be knocked off my feet as quickly as the skinny, slender, no-hips body. That's why I have shorter legs, because it helps me stay grounded. It was meant for me to pick this because of my journey this time. It's a very rocky world and destination . . . and the people who I'm involved with here, they're tough. I'm always rocking their boats, so the hips are sturdy so I don't fall over. So I don't wobble. I'm grounded. Because people don't really want to know why they're here. They don't want to know the message, and so I have to enlighten them. It's funny, I have tears right now because I see that it's doing me good, the body. But I fought it for so long because I didn't see its purpose. There has to be some healing around that.*

Sue: *Ask your guide for help with the healing.*

Rose: *Just knowing my body's purpose is healing in itself, because I'm* *a soul that doesn't really . . . I get people's attention, but it's not my job to just stick with them for a long period of time. I'm just supposed to meet them, shake them up, wake them up, and move on. Some people don't want that, but I don't care. It's like Jesus. Jesus just kept walking. He kept saying his message, and he didn't stick around to force people.*

Sue: *That's right.*

Rose: *He just kept moving. These people get mad at me and they try to tip me over. But because of my hips, I don't let that happen.*

Sue: *That's good. You can't be tipped over. That powerful.*

Rose: *Yeah. So I'm becoming aware that that's what I chose. I need to appreciate everything about this body—the hips, the buttocks, the thick thighs. I don't like the excess weight. I'm seeing that I put the excess weight on because I didn't understand the purpose. Now I can remove the excess weight. I will still have the hips, but I'm okay with the hips this time.*

Sue: *Beautiful.*

Rose: *I'm asking about the loose skin or the soft skin because I was never muscular. What was that about? Why do I have soft skin? Oh, because it's gentle, they say. Gentle, because the way I communicate with people is gentle. The soft skin is a reminder of gentleness in the way I communicate with others.*

Sue: *Beautiful.*

Rose: *And it's deeper than that. It's not just about bodies. This physical world is not what it's all about. It's so much more. And people have to learn to love themselves. But most importantly, to listen to their intuition. Their knowledge is already there, but they're not tuning in to the right station. I do get a sense that this is about accepting my body. But my mission is not really about helping others accept their bodies. I'm here to go deeper. The lesson is deeper. Because I always thought about that. Was I supposed to do that? Is it about their weight? Am I supposed to help them with their weight? Every signal is saying, "No, that's not it."*

Sue: *It's about their soul.*

Rose: *Yes. I'm here to understand that my body was meant for my journey this time here. And I used to beat myself up, but I don't need to do that anymore.*

Sue: *Very good.*

Rose: *My guide is saying that not that many people want to be in this room getting these types of bodies. They all want the other bodies in the other room. It's only certain people who choose this type, the brave ones.*

Sue: *Yes. Is there anything else to be learned here?*

Rose: *I just have one more thing to do.*

Sue: *Yes, what is that?*

Rose: *It's my [departed] mom, and she's standing right here. I'm telling her, "I'm sorry that I was not a good person for you when you needed me." And she says, "That's okay because that worked exactly the way it was supposed to. I was supposed to leave when you had unresolved feelings. We were supposed to bring that out in each other to help you with your mission, so you could help others."*

Sue: *Beautiful.*

Rose: *Thank you, thank you.*

I slowly guide Rose back into her physical body, then we shared our observations.

Sue: *As you come fully back into your body, what is your first insight about this that you'd like to share?*

Rose: *That whole sensation, that experience, even though I'm back in my physical body, I can still feel that tingling . . . our souls are so light. If I can remember that, my body could be light too. It doesn't have to be so heavy. Because when you're not connected, it's so dense.*

Sue: *Right.*

Rose: *So being more connected with my soul will help me feel lighter and easier in my body.*

Sue: *Does that mean daily meditation, or what does that mean to you?*

Rose: *Yes. It could be meditation, but mainly it's solitude. It's the solitude of being alone in a room, in a corner, in your car, just feeling that connection. But one thing I do notice, it was so quiet in those realms. So peaceful.*

Sue: *Yes.*

Rose: *And the lessons are so much more spectacular because we're all connected, and it's just like the ocean, right? This wave affects that wave, and that wave affects this wave. And so there's so much more love and kindness that needs to be seen or made aware of. It's just a ripple. It's just a little ripple in the huge ocean.*

Sue: *Right.*

Rose: *That was my message today. That I was fighting, trying to find purpose. But it's the thing that comes easiest to me that I'm here to do—helping people listen to their inner knowing. The guide said, "This is easy. This is who you are. This is your true nature. Don't complicate it."*

Sue: *The part about loving your body as it is may be one of the most significant things about this experience. You chose your body perfectly. It has served you for what you came here to learn and do. Now you can't be destructive in your thoughts or emotions toward your body because your soul does not see it that way.*

Rose: *Got it, very, very clearly. Thank you. Thank you so much. I'm giving you such a big air hug right now.*

◉ Your Powerful Lens-Shifting Prescription

First, to determine which lens you're wearing today, ask yourself:

- How do I feel in my body? Tense, relaxed, energized, or depleted?
- Am I feeling love for anyone? Everyone? Myself?
- Do I feel that all is well in the world, or does life feel tragic?
- Am I feeling afraid and inadequate or confident?
- Do I feel judged by others or judgmental toward others?
- Do I feel sad and heavy with grief?

- Do I feel passionate about my work?
- Do I feel exhausted and depressed?
- Do I feel joyful and grateful?

Your answers to these questions will determine which lens you're wearing today.

Feeling tense or physically depleted, afraid, insecure, sad, depressed, or angry is a sure sign of divine lens deficiency. It's time for a powerful new lens-shifting prescription:

- Imagine you've just had an interaction that has left you angry or hurt. Feel that familiar self-defense reaction.
- Now take a deep, long inhalation and exhale while focusing only on your breath. For extra credit or to help quiet the ego mind, repeat a Sanskrit mantra such as *Om Namah Shivaya* for several minutes, keeping your mental focus only on the words of the mantra rather than on your thoughts.
- When you feel your mind settling down, say to yourself, *Please show me the wisdom of this moment and reveal how my soul, not my ego, sees this challenge. Show me the soul lesson. Help me hear my soul's wisdom and quiet the chatter of my ego mind.*
- Get a notebook and pen and begin writing the following: "My soul and my spirit guides say that the lesson of this moment is . . . " and write the first thing that comes to mind.
- After you've written on that question for a while, write this: "My action step to solve this problem for everyone's highest good is . . ." Write quickly so that the words flow from your right brain, your higher consciousness, and not from your logical left-brain monkey mind, which is where the ego chatter lives.

13
Relationships Illuminated
It's All About the Soul Agreement

Have you ever recognized someone the moment you first met? If so, you're recognizing a soulmate, someone with whom you've experienced many lifetimes together and have a soul agreement. This person is part of your soul posse. The agreement, made before your lifetime began, went something like this: "I'll recognize you, embrace your true essence, and push you to evolve (through love and pain). We'll become spiritual partners exploring new ideas. We'll push each other to grow."

When your soul recognizes a soulmate, you feel the spark of the agreement you made. It awakens you. Yet the ego often misinterprets this spark as what the world considers romantic love, that "happily-ever-after" fairy-tale type of love. Both romantic love and great friendship begin with the first flush of soul recognition. You believe you've found someone who understands and supports you completely. And you have. But a soulmate embraces your soul's essence, not your ego. This relationship, whether it's a great friendship or a deeply passionate love, thrives only when the soul is honored, when the conversations are meaningful, and when you process the world together through your divine lens.

When you're with a soulmate, you experience many reinventions together in a lifetime. A soulmate will encourage you to grow and align with your highest wisdom. You will do the same for your partner. If either of you stops supporting each other's inner growth, the relationship ends. The agreement is then broken. If you prioritize money, jobs, and material possessions instead of the soul-to-soul connection, your love diminishes. You begin to feel trapped, closed-off, and afraid. When your soul's growth is no longer served, you'll both find a way to fulfill your growth elsewhere.

In any relationship, if anger, blame, fear, and criticism become the primary energies flowing between you, you'll find a way out—for your own highest good and the good of your partner. You may choose to have an affair or become depressed. Or you may treat your spouse poorly and become abusive and hypercritical. You may also manifest an illness. All of these reactions to the loss of mutual support have been spurred by your soul's longing to grow and fulfill its mission.

Choose your partner based on which lens they wear most often: ego lens or divine lens.

Ego is your greatest enemy in any relationship. Ego focuses only on the flaws of oneself and others. The ego lens prevents us from seeing the troubled soul behind any misbehavior. And it prevents you from seeing the great potential within yourself as well.

WHEN A RELATIONSHIP ENDS

Years ago, a boyfriend told me he didn't believe in anything beyond the physical, and that there is no evidence of a God. I didn't know how to respond. I live with evidence every day, in my dialogues with the Divine and through my personal intuitive experiences. This constant conversation inspires me with love and happiness.

"Who do you talk to when you're all alone?" I asked him.

"My mind. It tells me things," he said.

"What kind of things?"

"Sometimes dark and worrisome things, and I have anxiety. Other times inspiring ideas, thoughts that make me smile."

"The anxiety thoughts are from your monkey mind," I explained. "But the ones that fill you with happiness and make you smile for no reason—those are from the Divine. Try to listen to those more than to the fearful thoughts."

We broke up. He thought I needed fixing because I believed in impossible things. Today I'm happy, fulfilled, married to a man whose spiritual beliefs are in alignment with mine, and my work is meaningful. That ex-boyfriend who thought I needed fixing has fought a lifelong battle with depression and anxiety—both side effects of ego-lens living. In the end, it matters which beliefs we embrace and which ones our partners embrace.

Divorce can be an opportunity for realignment with one's soul's mission. But when negotiations get bogged down with blame and anger, it means both parties are stuck in the ego lens. No one is bringing their soul's wisdom to the conversation, and resolution can't occur until this happens. If you're going through a divorce, you can shift the energy to a higher level even if your partner is lost in blame. It's a matter of shifting your intention. During your daily meditation, silently send this intention to your partner:

I see your great potential and I'm deeply sorry I was unable to support you in fulfilling it. I will not hurt you or diminish your ability to move forward. I recognize that I have a soul connection with you and that my actions toward you come back to me a thousandfold. I won't dwell in anger, blame, fear, or depression, because that energy does not serve my highest good—or yours. I release you fully to your soul's journey, until we meet again and can make each other proud of how we've each evolved. We are now, and always will be, soulmates.

It doesn't matter if your partner reciprocates this intention or not. You're now standing in the light of your soul's integrity, which is the only place you want to be. Because of your courageous energy shift, all good things are now possible. At the end of your lifetime, you'll answer to your Higher Self for your actions and yours alone. You'll see clearly that there has never been anyone to blame. Your soul made choices every step of the way. You'll realize that within every moment of your life, including this painful divorce, there was a lesson your soul chose to experience for your highest good. The people who are hurting you the most today are acting for your highest good. They're your soul partners, taking their places exactly as you asked them to, pushing you where you need to go.

When a relationship causes you pain, use this intention:

Thank you, worthy opponent, for arriving at this moment of my greatest need, when I was finally ready for this profound lesson and ready to break old patterns that have held me back. You must love me very much to help me release these behaviors that my ego has been unable to surrender on its own. I remember now that I came here to be radiantly loving and wise. My ego was preventing me from being my best self. You've awakened me to remember my Higher Self, and I'm deeply grateful.

Now you're fully capable of healing yourself and helping others heal as you move forward. You're capable of saving a future relationship when it falls off-course, or saving a friend who has lost their way.

When people speak of forgiveness, there is sometimes a sense of one partner feeling superior to the other. But this isn't forgiveness. Forgiveness is when your soul says to the soul of the person who hurt you, *I see your soul. I realize we're both on the same journey of evolution doing the best we can. Our agreement is to help each other remember our divinity—through pain and love. I release you to your highest good, with gratitude, until we meet again.*

HERE'S WHAT YOU NEVER KNEW

The encouraging word you offered to a stranger that rainy day in a coffee shop saved him.

The heartfelt hug you gave to a friend you ran into at the party healed her.

The moment you turned your back on fear and ripped your heart wide open changed everything.

Your one simple act of courage started a ripple of consciousness that spread far beyond you.

At the end you'll see it—all the ripples spreading out, merging, and turning into waves of light. You'll see the way your words of wisdom pulled someone to shore—someone you never met, who then reached back and saved your brother, sister, child—who then saved you.

◎ Tools to Survive the Mundane World

How can you bring your soul's wisdom, your divine lens, to a day that feels scattered before it even begins? How will you listen to your inner wisdom when you're stuck in traffic, taking the cat to the vet, going to the dentist, or running to a meeting? Here's how:

- Practice daily meditation to quiet the mind, open the heart, connect to your divinity, and hear the voice of your soul.
- Bring your personal "God Guide" with you. This guide will sometimes take the form of Jesus, Buddha, Mother Mary, Lakshmi, Nityananda, some other enlightened being, or a departed loved one. When you remember to do this, you'll feel a powerfully present force of love guiding you with grace.
- Consult your personal "God Guide" for what to say whenever you're confronted with a challenging relationship. Talk out loud to the Divine; hold a daily conversation with God. Live as if you know that you are divinely guided each day.

14
Flawless Intuition
A Byproduct of the
Divine Lens Perspective

Your ego lens has been distorting reality for you and has made you doubt that anything beyond the physical world existed. But once your viewpoint is aligned with your soul rather than your ego, you suddenly have perfect vision. Nothing is distorted. You see things you've never seen before, things you didn't even know existed, including other dimensions and spirits that you've been unaware of.

You've already experienced these other dimensions, though you may not have noticed them or if you did, you dismissed them as nonsense. Whenever you opened your heart to another person, you gained access to all the inner knowledge and guidance you could ever need. This is called intuition. When you first fell in love you experienced this; when you knew when your lover would call, when you had dreams of the future that turned out to be true, you were experiencing this kind of heightened awareness.

Why didn't this heightened awareness last? Because you allowed your ego lens to take over and distort your perceptions. Your feelings were easily hurt, and you became afraid that love wouldn't be returned. You shut your heart in fear. You fell back into the habitual patterns of the ego lens, with its distorted view and fear-based limitations. Now you've grown addicted to this earthbound perspective, even though it rarely makes you happy.

> *Intuition is your gut feeling,*
> *a feeling that comes from the heart.*

Your intuition envelops you in confidence, wisdom, and empowerment, never in fear. It's the connection to your true self, your raw, unrefined truth unclouded by your monkey mind. It's the shimmer of a spirit in the corner when you turn your head. It's the dream that wakes you up and stays with you. It's the knowingness that comes when you stop talking. It's the feeling that overpowers you despite all logic. It's the voice whispering in your ear and the nudge you often ignore in deference to being "practical." It's your right-brain, expanded consciousness guiding your journey as planned.

YOU ALREADY KNOW

In the brief moments of great joy that you allow yourself to experience, you know everything you'll ever need to know. And you disappoint your Higher Self whenever you deny this. Imagine if you embraced your sixth sense of intuition as an ally and consulted it every single day for guidance:

Would I still get everything I need and want? asks the ego.

Yes, says the soul. *You would get everything you came here to experience and everything your soul needs to fulfill its great mission.*

But would I get the car, the house, the bank account, and the love that I long for? asks the ego.

Yes, if that's what your soul came to experience for your highest good and to fulfill your magnificent potential, answers the soul. *Your authentic journey is the only path to joy.*

But I long for the things that others who are more successful have, says the ego.

If those things aren't in alignment with your highest good, they'll never be yours, says the soul. *And you'll overlook the gifts of the journey you've chosen.*

Longing for a life that's not yours will push you far from who you came here to be and what you came to accomplish. You'll lose your heart and soul in someone else's life. You've already lived many lifetimes under circumstances quite different from this life. You've been rich and you've been poor. You designed each lifetime, including this one, to become the best version of you and not someone else. This is your true path. It requires feeling your feelings, opening your heart, and thinking less. You're learning to trust your Higher Self rather than follow the expectations of those around you. When you succeed, you'll realize the grace of divine order that has always flowed through your life.

You may be afraid of taking the path less traveled. Who will love you then? How will you survive? You *are* different, says your soul. You've never been like anyone else. Trying to hide your unique self and live like others will not get you anywhere good. Love does not exist in false relationships. To hide your gifts is to live the loneliest life you could choose.

Nothing is more painful than hiding your soul from the world. In the end, you'll be fully revealed as who you came here to be. You hope that this revelation won't come on your deathbed, when the illusion finally fades and it's too late to change everything. And you hope that it won't be when you're too feeble to do your soul's work. You hope it will be now. Today. Not tomorrow, although tomorrow is never too late. But today is always better. Today is always the best day to start everything, change everything, to love everyone like you've never loved before, and to drop your fear on the ground and forget to pick it up. Because today is juicy and alive, and tomorrow may never arrive.

And today is when you planned to finally listen to your soul's wisdom and use your divine lens to see what you never saw, to know everything you've needed to know. Today is the day you meant to transcend all limitations, release all fears, take the big step, throw out the old, embrace your gold, and get it done the way you came here to get it done.

Today is *that* day.

The most powerful way to quiet the monkey mind and access your intuition, which is your flawless inner guidance, is with twenty minutes of daily meditation. Everyone can find twenty minutes to sit and close their eyes and repeat either a mantra (sacred sound) or a prayer. The purpose is *not* to think, *not* to visualize, and *not* to say affirmations. Instead you're lulling the monkey mind to sleep by giving it a mantra or sacred words to focus on.

During meditation, thoughts will come bursting through the mantra. Notice them (without judgment), and then gently bring your focus back to the mantra. At the end of twenty minutes of redirecting your attention this way, you'll begin to sink into your inner knowingness, which goes beyond the mental chatter of the fear-based mind. That opens the door to your Higher Self and its inner guidance, also known as intuition.

YOU AND YOUR INTUITION

Do you recognize the importance of intuition in your life?

- Describe moments when you've felt intuitive or had intuitive experiences and dreams. Did you trust the information you received? Why or why not? What did you learn from these intuitive experiences?
- As a child, were your intuitive experiences encouraged or dismissed by your family?
- When does your intuition show up most powerfully?
- When your loved one died, did you feel them communicating with you? Have you felt their presence in your life since they died?
- Describe any dreams you've had that may have been a message from your departed loved one or from your Higher Self.
- Before heading home from work, ask yourself, *Should I take this*

route or the other route? Now close your eyes and see yourself on one of the possible routes home and note how your body feels. Do you get a good or bad feeling in response to seeing that particular drive? If it's good, take that route home. Afterward, reflect on how the commute went for you. Was it easier than usual? Was there less traffic?

• Plan an intuitively guided vacation. Visit a new city and plan your activities each morning based on your gut feelings. Keep a journal of how this works for you.

As you learn to trust your intuition for these little, everyday choices, you'll be better able to trust your intuition for the big life choices.

Four Easy Steps to Enhance Your Intuition

1. Shift your view into the divine lens perspective by taking a deep inhalation and long, slow exhalation. Pause, then connect to your Higher Self with the words: Please lift me into alignment with my soul's highest wisdom.

2 Meditate to quiet the mind. Close your eyes and repeat a sacred mantra or prayer. When thoughts arise, gently bring your mind back to the mantra.

3. Ask for divine guidance: *Please God* (or *divine guides*), *help me quiet my fear mind, open my heart, and hear my inner divine guidance.* Listen, and then write whatever comes to you.

4. Practice intuitive living. Whenever making a decision, picture yourself having already made that decision and living in that future. If it's a small decision like which restaurant to go to, picture yourself there eating a meal. See the room, smell the food. Now notice how that choice makes your body feel. Does it make you smile? Is it energizing? Or does it leave you feeling drained or anxious? Your gut is telling you what the right intuitive choice is. Practice listening to your gut for little decisions all day long. Then when you need to make a major life decision, you'll be very good at listening to and trusting your inner guidance.

15

Who Will You Become?

What I Know to Be True

A childhood full of doubts, a sweet husband's early death, countless broken hearts and flawed careers were all perfectly designed to get me where I am today, to help me evolve into my highest state of grace, to know God, and to become who I became. Sometimes I forget this.

When I'm on my path and aligned with divine order, I feel of use to the greater message, the larger truth, the highest good. It moves through me like a ray of light piercing everything, a laser beam opening my heart, filling the pages of my books, conversations with clients, and the classrooms where I teach. None of it comes from me, a flawed human, like everyone else here. I finally get out of the way.

When I forget about divine order, nothing makes sense. My sadness is legendary. My hunger is hopeless. Heartbreak brings me to my knees in despair. Everyone betrays me: my mother, brother, sister, lover, friend. I am a boat without a mooring. Fear blocks my inner voice. My mind tricks me. I let it.

When I remember the loving God-ness of our universe, my heart breaks wide open. Sacred wisdom pours through me and showers the world in diamonds, each one forged from the fire of tremendous loss. Forgiveness abounds. I feel held by the angels, kissed by the deities.

I adore my mother, brother, sister, lover, friend. I see their painful stories, their enormous grief and astounding gifts. I see how hard they've tried, how endlessly they've worked. I adore them all. The sound of their laughter is the sweetest sound I've ever known. I lift the veil and see into the other realms vividly. I speak out loud to my departed dad, to Paul, Crissie, and Marv. *It's all good,* they whisper, *very good . . .*

When I cross over, I'll apologize for all the wasted days here, the endless pain, the soaring doubts and aching exhaustion, the days when I didn't move. My divine beloveds will hold me and tell me that it was all part of the play, the dance of life, and exactly what they expected. They'll remind me that I couldn't have lived here without each moment of deeply felt pain, determined anger, and paralyzing self-doubt. These profound feelings, they'll explain, led me to moments of boundless love, soul-shaking awe, inspired wisdom, and healing grace.

What I know to be true is this: Our pain is on purpose. Our joy is the gift. Our heart is all that matters. Our mind is a great monkey loose in the forest and running amuck; he must be tamed.

Our truth is found within—always. It's the inner voice that only speaks loud enough when we turn within, tame the savage mind, and surrender assumptions; when we dip a trembling hand into the deepest water that terrifies us most and help someone who is drowning right alongside us.

> *Our truth speaks up when we see the heartbreak in everyone's journey, the struggle in everyone's life, the pain shared by each family member, the divine inner guidance within each moment. This compassion is the fabric of our universe. It guides us flawlessly through the night.*
> *This is all that matters.*

Even when we don't know it, when we feel completely alone, people who are part of our soul posse will show up in our hour of greatest need and help us in ways we may never know and never see. These soulmate agreements are always working in our favor. Even when we feel hopelessly abandoned, they're standing right where they should be standing, lending a hand in just the way that will save us.

And mostly it's only at the end of life or in brief glimpses of the Divine that we fully see this luminous connection, this brilliant pattern, and know that it's real and that we've always been held in grace. This final knowledge breaks us wide open in speechless, awestruck gratitude—even as we take our last gasping breath and our body disintegrates into a million shards of light.

LOVING THE VALLEYS

When we're at the top, at the peak of a cycle, when all is going well, it's tempting to discard our divine lens. The ego is winning. We're content to see life as a physical world because we're basking in the glow of worldly success. We're having fun! But as soon as we hit a valley—a great loss, illness, or heartbreak—we struggle to find our bearings until we reach for the divine lens. Then we remember the gift of the lesson and we reconnect with our soul's wisdom.

This is the purpose of pain—to remind us of what's important and who we really are. When we love the valleys, cherish our divine lens view, and embrace the lesson of our pain, we will soon be happy again and begin the climb toward another glorious peak. This is the sweet spot. We're still wearing our divine lens, tapping into our inner wisdom and excited to be moving forward.

If you're in a valley today as a result of job loss, heartbreak, illness, or grief, look within, meditate, ask for divine guidance, and listen to your soul's wisdom. Take a breath. You can only hear inner guidance when you're quiet, unplugged, and receptive. Become best friends with your inner wisdom and tune out the chatter all around you. Once you embrace the view from your Higher Self, you'll feel peaceful, grateful, and openhearted. This is when things will begin to shift in a better direction. You'll find yourself moving forward, with an exciting new summit just ahead. Keep wearing your divine lens and cherish the wisdom you've gained in the valley.

Yes, it takes effort to reach for your divine lens, to struggle against your cynicism, self-doubts, and fears. It's much easier to surrender to the negative forces of the world that urge you to indulge in physical experiences and ignore your soul whisperings. Everyone gives in to depression, anger, blame, or disappointment at certain points in their journey.

Why struggle to find wisdom, openhearted love, or forgiveness? Why rip your heart out and feel the pain you're terrified of feeling? Why search for the deeper meaning of a painful past when it's so much easier to become the angry victim of circumstances? Here's why: because each thought you think, each step you take, puts you on a certain path, an intended direction—until you remember who you came here to be.

The farther you move down a negative path, the harder it becomes to change directions, live fearlessly, and open your heart. The dark and cynical story you tell yourself about life's hardships gets ingrained in your essence. You become burdened with cynicism. You carry the frequency of fear in your voice. Love becomes impossible. Cynicism is then expected of you. It chooses your friends. Changing everything and living courageously becomes a choice you can't imagine making.

Once, when you were young, you could imagine taking the path of courage and hope. You could see it as a possibility. You made brief attempts to take risks, follow your heart, and change your life for the better. When you didn't immediately reap success, you decided it wasn't worth the struggle. You allowed others to influence your choices. It was easier to give up, complain, and be afraid. Cynicism is always the easier path.

Like the traveler who sets a safe course, you stayed on the path you'd become most familiar with. For a while, the other path, the one you hadn't chosen, ran parallel to yours. It wouldn't have required a major lifestyle shift to head in that direction. You told yourself that if you changed your mind later, you could still choose that riskier path. But you were having fun where you were. Life was comfortable.

As time went by, you traveled farther down the trail you'd chosen until you found yourself lost in the trees, unable to see the sky. When you looked for the upper trail that once ran parallel, you saw that it had taken a different course, winding steeply up and around the mountain, toward a peak that rose sharply into the light. This stirred a memory in you, a memory of once wanting to make that summit, of studying it on a map and dreaming of standing there in that exquisite light, feeling awesome about what you'd accomplished.

But now your trail has taken you deep into the shadows, beneath a forested sky, and somehow you're more alone than you realized. Joining the other path at this point requires a terrifying change of course. You doubt that you're still strong enough to make such a demanding hike. You've spent so many years drifting that you can barely feel your muscles. Your inner discipline has greatly diminished.

What happened to all the fun you were having? Where did those people go who were coasting along beside you? How did you end up so alone? You begin searching the horizon for an answer. You call out, "Is anyone there who can help me?" At first you hear nothing and feel extraordinary despair. Eventually, though, you see a small ray of light illuminating a different path through the woods. You can't see where it goes and you're too afraid to take it.

After days and nights of paralyzing fear, you decide the unknown path must be better than where you're at now. You walk toward the light. This uphill trail requires physical strength that you didn't know you had. But as you take each unsteady step, you slowly realize that someone or something is guiding and comforting you.

After an intense climb that pushes you to face all you've ever feared, you find yourself standing at the summit, in the place you always wanted to find but thought was impossible. You take a deep breath and enjoy the stunning view—until you notice that thousands of struggling souls are still lost in the trees below the summit, crying for help. Without hesitation, you reach your hand down to help them. You suddenly remember what joy felt like.

When a storm moves in, you build a shelter that saves lives. When you see tragedy, you bring healing grace to it. When you find yourself in the dark, you seek the stars because you know they exist. You understand that after the darkest night, the sun does indeed rise again.

You're absolutely sure now that something or someone guides you. You think back to those days of being terrified and alone in the darkness, and you realize that a loving force was always with you, even when you ignored it. When you landed in the dirt, somehow you always stood up again. You fully allow this loving force to shine through you now, to enlighten others. When you look down at the old path far below and see lost souls wandering in the shadows, you feel only compassion. You reach out to help. And you realize that the "you," the personality, the ego you worked so hard to sustain in your early years, is slipping away. Only this inner light, this awesome love, remains.

Was it worth the effort? You realize now that was never the question. The only question was: when will you make the effort? Everyone makes it eventually. It's only a matter of how long we linger in the shadows before we reach for the light. Because the light calls everyone. And the light is stronger than the dark. Whatever words you put to it, you eventually realize that there's so much divine intervention in the climb, that the darkest moments offer the greatest awakenings, and that without the darkness, you wouldn't seek the light. So you would never trade where you are now for anything, because you never understood the beauty of the climb until you stepped into the light. And here in the light is better than anywhere. And that's all that's ever mattered.

A PRESCRIPTION FOR YOUR DIVINE LENS

Do you see the shimmer of light in every moment, the possibility inside of each spoken word, the gift in every challenge? Do you see how your pain offers the perfect opportunity to awaken to your Higher Self? Do you understand that self-doubt is a temporary blindness caused by the distorted view of your ego lens blocking out the light?

If not, it may be time to get a divine lens prescription. With your divine lens in place, your view of divine order is restored. You'll find light in the darkness and feel love where you once felt pain.

Whenever you're wearing your ego lens, you'll wonder where all the darkness came from. When did unrelenting pain arrive on your doorstep? "Why do good people suffer needlessly in our meaningless world?" you'll ask. You're not alone in this distorted view. Many others, especially those in power, are aligned with this dark view. They see tragedy everywhere and believe hatred is inevitable, because someone is always to blame.

When you wear the ego lens, you feel righteous, judgmental, and superior. But this distorted viewpoint does not empower you. It encourages you to give up. "You've failed before," says the ego, "why bother now?" And for a little while you'll try to forget you have a soul. You'll fall into the temporary spell of soulless living, and your ego will have a party. When you awaken in the morning, bruised and beaten, you'll search for a better view. You'll seek the light because you have fallen so far into the darkness that it scared you.

As you pick up your other lens, the one you left buried in the drawer of your unconscious, you may be leery of the light you unexpectedly see in everything. "How can this possibly be true?" you ask. "How can there be so much light and love where before I saw none? Am I being foolish now?" You may drop your divine lens back in the drawer, saving it for another day. But one day you will find yourself alone, heartbroken, divorced, broke, addicted, grief stricken, or depressed. You'll search for that bright lens again to ease your pain. This time you'll smile when you see the light in every dark corner. You'll feel gratitude for the ones who hurt you badly, because that pain pushed you to seek the light.

TRY, TRY AGAIN

Kindness is everything. Getting back up is all that matters. Trying again is the world. Looking back, you'll see the choices you could have made.

Make them now. The road less traveled that you could have taken—take it now.

Begin by taking a tiny step into hope. It's a small clearing, mostly a break in the storm. You're not sure. Go. Put your feet on the path. Break it all wide open.

You've already lost so much, and yet you're still standing. That's all that matters. Dust yourself off. The storm actually saved you. You thought it would destroy you, but nothing will ever destroy you. Feel that searing heartbreak. Let it rise up from your chest and skim across the water like a manta ray—horrifying and yet beautiful, happy to be set free.

Take a stand and declare your truth. Your story needs to be told. Forgive that part of you that took the wrong path. It was a misguided attempt to find heaven, the divine realms from which you came. Every lost step was you trying to reclaim the love that flows so fiercely in the next realm. All mistakes are forgiven in the end.

Nothing remains the same here in this density. Everything takes effort. Trying to recreate heaven on Earth has caused you grief. You're here to feel everything and save everyone—to share your wisdom fearlessly.

Say to yourself, *I will do what is hard, what is required of me, the thing I fear, because I know doing it will save someone, lift someone out of pain, comfort a mother, brother, sister, friend. It will save me, too.*

Courage is born in your heart and not your mind. Use it, or it dies in your heart—a rosebud that never opens, a bird without a song, a light never shared. You can't see it now, but courage is everything. And trying again is the world . . .

THE DIVINE LENS VIEW OF EVERYDAY LIFE

When we're caught up in everyday life, we tend to get bogged down in drudgery and forget to reach for the divine view in each moment.

We get lost in the details. This is the unconsciousness that's caused by routine. And life here in the physical world is still mostly based on routine.

Yet your divine lens is always ready to reveal a more enlightened perspective. If you fully believe that each instant of your day is rich with divine order, with gifts and lessons, all for your highest good, how might you react differently to daily annoyances? Seeking the divinity in everything fills you with light and inspires your routine chores, transforming them into little miracles. Some examples:

Your child is crying in a crowded public place, and you're embarrassed and angry. Your ego mind tells you to control or punish because you're embarrassed. Yet hidden beneath this annoyance is an opportunity. You can choose to see a child in distress and needing love, rather than a child misbehaving. This shift of perspective opens your heart and gives you instant access to more choices in the way you react. You can choose to feel compassion despite your embarrassment. Seeing your child's tantrum as an opportunity to find love changes the behavior. Your child feels recognized. Your Higher Self takes over and calms you down. Tension dissipates, and you've gracefully risen above your anger.

Let's say you're at work and you receive a nasty email from a coworker. Your ego tells you their facts are wrong and you need to defend yourself by illuminating the errors in their complaint. While your ego points out the many flaws of your co-worker, somewhere deep inside your Higher Self is speaking up: *Stop. Breathe. Open your heart. See the insecurity, fear, and frustration of your co-worker. Respond with something helpful from your soul's wisdom that gets at the core of what they're really asking for, which is usually respect. This will create a better solution for everyone in the long run.* Does your co-worker's attack disguise what is, in reality, a need for approval and respect? Everyone is looking for that, especially in the workplace. If this person felt respected or appreciated for the work they do, they wouldn't be on the attack. How might you help? How might you offer an empowering response that helps them feel better about who they are in the workplace? This is how your soul views the situation.

Only when everyone feels honored and empowered will a workplace thrive. Before you respond to that nasty email, think of it as a moment of choice for your soul and for the future of the company. Responding with kindness might create a ripple effect that eventually changes the energy and future success of the business. Take a breath, ask for guidance, and begin writing a response from your inner wisdom. *You* are the teacher here, the one carrying the light into this situation. As you bring others into the light, you heal yourself.

You've already tried all of the possible ego responses before, and where have they gotten you? Have they created a joyful, loving home and fulfilling relationships at work? Would you consider taking a breath now, pause the ego's reaction, seek guidance, and ask to view this situation differently, through your divine lens?

See the person before you as a struggling soul on a journey just like you are, doing the best they can within their level of awareness. Try to see the pain and hurt they carry. Can you see how they look to you for love and guidance, even though their words and actions say the opposite? Can you see this soul as a divine being starved for love and healing? Once you shift into that perspective, everything changes—your mind quiets, your heart opens, your energy shifts away from fear, and you step into your wisdom.

In one moment of awareness, you can tap into your divinity, reach out to another soul, offer them a hand, and pull them out of fear. Others have done this for you. Now it's your turn to offer this gift. Reacting from wisdom rather than ego breaks the negative pattern that you're ready to release. From this moment on, you're the teacher, the light carrier capable of shifting everyone to a new level of consciousness, capable of enlightening work and family interactions and bringing everyone into love. What will you say now? How is this different from your old reactions?

Whatever problems you're facing in the external world, the

solutions lie in your inner world. When you can't pay the bills, your ego will reveal a future of escalating financial failures that lead to losing everything. But when you grasp desperately for solutions out of fear, you become the angry victim, the one who works harder than everyone else and never thrives. Each time you've chosen work for security's sake, it has eventually led you to this financial abyss. Good solutions can't be found from this perspective.

Your Higher Self says you're capable of creating abundance and comfort by aligning your work with your true gifts, by making a passionate commitment to work that empowers you and fulfills your greatest potential. Take one step today to explore a new career that might open doors you could never have imagined. Tweaking the career you already have and bringing it to a greater level of fulfillment could also change everything. It's time to consider new possibilities that have been buried under layers of fear and self-doubt. This is the moment to pick up the phone and make that call, to research a new business, to email your friend who said you might be a good fit in their new company.

It's time to reach for your divine lens and acknowledge your soul's perspective. What is your soul asking of you in this moment? Listen to the whisperings within, the solution that dissipates fear and leaves you empowered and inspired. Trust your wisdom and take steps in a new direction.

◉ A Morning Prayer to Shift into Your Divine Lens

- What is my lesson today, divine guides? What is my task? Help me step into the wisdom of my Higher Self, no matter what comes my way.
- Show me where the lessons hide today so that I may acknowledge them, open my heart to them, and make choices born of wisdom.
- Help me understand what lies beneath my pain. Teach me to hold my truth in awe. Teach me to see the dance of my ego and separate from it.
- I'm tired of fighting through painful moments and watching my ego react first. I pray for the instant knowledge that comes from my soul's highest

truth. I want the divine voice within to be louder than the ego that drives my reactions.

- Show me how the ego seeks validation instead of acting in alignment with my soul. Show me the ways I can release this ego, this flawed personality, and stand simply as a naked soul with nothing left to say except, "Thank you. I love you."
- Give me a new vocabulary, paint new memories, release me from my moments of struggle, and bathe me in divine wisdom.

16

Pain Is Your Fuel

Your Perfectly Painful Childhood

When we use our divine lens to see what lies beneath the surface, we realize that everyone experiences pain throughout life, especially during childhood. Whether we felt unloved, inadequate, rejected, unlovable, impoverished, or were abused, we all grow up hungry in one way or another. This hunger creates our desire to evolve.

You chose to be born into a family with the perfect dysfunctional challenges to push your soul in exactly the way it needed to be pushed, to help you break negative patterns you may have carried for lifetimes. The ego says this isn't true, that many people have it better than you and many have it worse. Both statements are correct. But each person's childhood has been perfectly designed for their highest good.

Look deeply and you'll see the soul story behind everyone's beautiful and terrible life. Your friend who was raised by brilliant, successful parents struggled with crippling self-doubts because she felt unworthy compared to other family members. Confidence is the lesson this soul came to learn in this lifetime. Your co-worker, who was raised in foster homes and abused as a child, struggled to find the grace in each moment of pain, to embrace his wisdom in order to thrive. He found courage because it was his only option. It was his soul's mission to find light in the midst of darkness.

Each child is here to forge his or her own unique path. The more powerful the parents, the greater the child struggles to find their true self. If you were born into great wealth and privilege, you'll struggle to find what really matters amidst the temptations of self-indulgence and addictions. These lessons are designed perfectly for your highest good. If you were born into great poverty and hardship, your soul is here to find brilliance and new solutions, to think beyond limitations. This is the mission you chose and the gifts you carry within you.

When you view your childhood from the ego lens, you may see a tragic story of injustice in which you're a victim. The ego mind will tell you that because of your suffering you have a right to be angry, desperate, afraid, or cruel. You may spend much of your life with this paralyzing viewpoint until you hit a crisis. And when your pain is great enough, you might finally choose to shift into your divine perspective. You'll realize how perfectly you chose your childhood, so that you could find your divinity, look beyond the surface, and embrace the wisdom of your soul. This is your soul story, and it's the only perspective that matters. Your ego tells you otherwise. But your soul story is the true story, and it empowers you. It's the viewpoint you'll realize at the moment of your final breath.

From my soul to yours

We want to believe that everything lasts. We last. Our loved ones last. That what we feel today is forever. But it's more like water, like waves upon waves of change and uncertainty crashing around us, causing us to go under and drink the salty brine and come up gasping for air, unsure of who we are, where we are, or whether we're alone.

We instinctively search the horizon for a landing place, safety, anywhere, until we find something solid and we feel secure again, certain that nothing will change. But we're still standing in the ocean. The next wave is always bigger and knocks us over because we had our back to it.

We learn. We open our arms wide and embrace the waves, laughing as they lift us higher to reveal the greater view, the big picture. Hungrily we drink in that vast landscape, noting the lighthouse we never saw before, the gull resting calmly on nothing halfway out to nowhere, and the long, glistening white fish jumping high above the waves, teasing us with its mystery. We marvel at the beauty, knowing that something creates this, if not the gull itself, if not the water itself. A divine poet arranges the details. But who and how? We write books about this mystery, create careers analyzing it, build dams and concrete roads and bridges, and still the water swirls around us mysteriously because we're swimming in the living sea. We *are* the living sea. That sea courses through our veins and beats in our hearts.

And just when we think we've discovered everything, that no one has ever known as much, a wave rolls toward us from out of nowhere, and we are terrified in the rush of the changing waters. We surrender once again to the power of the grand poet. We get battered by the force of the waves, our limbs dancing madly out of control, our head brushing painfully against the sand, twisting and turning with abandon, until the wave releases us. We struggle to our feet gasping, taking in raw, sobbing breaths. Calling out to the friends we may have lost in the crushing waves. And when we *do* arrive on the beach, through no efforts of our own, we realize we had a choice in how we rode those waves. There are others who floated above them, some who fought and drowned beneath them, and some who struggled endlessly when all they needed to do was surrender to the ride, resting on the salty brine instead of fighting the force of water.

And we see that when we fought the waves of change, we became exhausted, and that it would have been wiser to relax, surrender, laugh, and reach toward someone else who was going under. We realize then that all souls make it to shore one day or another, one way or another. All that ever mattered was how we rode the lovely waves, and if we brought someone along with us to reach the vast, white shore.

FACING YOUR PAIN

Peter was a forty-year-old computer programmer who hated his job and had a passion for race-car driving. He spent so much time at the racetrack that his marriage was in trouble. His doctor prescribed anti-depressants and sent him to me for career counseling. Peter's story was unforgettable.

One night when Peter was thirteen, his sixteen-year-old sister woke him up. "Mom and Dad have gone out. Get in the backseat of the car and shut up," she whispered. "We're going for a ride."

Peter followed her into the family car and fell asleep in the backseat. He woke up hours later in the darkness, in a ditch, unable to find his sister. She was pinned under the car and had died instantly. That moment changed his life forever. His parents divorced, and his father became an alcoholic. "No one ever spoke about the accident," he told me. "In fact, no one ever spoke at all." Peter became an outcast in high school and learned to bottle up his feelings. "Have a stiff upper lip and carry on" was his father's only advice.

As my client, Peter explored this memory and realized that each time he raced a car at ninety miles an hour around a race track, he was healing a childhood wound. He was reliving and reprogramming the event that had destroyed his childhood. He was taking control of his greatest pain—the loss of his sister and family.

By facing his pain, Peter gave himself permission to leave his job as a computer programmer to pursue a career as a race-car driving instructor and a race-car service shop owner. He recognized that teaching others how to navigate a speeding car was a profoundly healing experience for him. And by honestly sharing his insights with his wife and daughter, he rallied their support for his new direction. He found renewed intimacy in his marriage and gave himself permission to pursue work that he loved.

This brings me to the most powerful truth I know about meaningful work: your pain is your greatest ally for finding the work you love.

Consider that you chose (consciously or unconsciously) every job you've ever had because it was healing you. Hundreds of my clients have proven this to be true. From observing their experiences and studying the biographies of successful people, I am 100 percent sure that our pain guides us to our true work, and that our true work heals our greatest pain.

How? Our work can heal us by letting us offer to the world exactly what we need to heal ourselves. By facing our pain, we can turn it into energy. It becomes our ally and moves us forward. Ask yourself what pain needs healing now. Let the answer guide you to the work you love. Here's the secret: The more pain you feel, the more energy you have at your disposal to launch your new career. See your pain as fuel, not as something that stops you from moving forward. We have to shift into our divine lens to realize this.

When I was in my twenties and a mountaineering instructor for Colorado Outward Bound, I loved empowering people and inspiring them to overcome their fears. Throughout my own childhood as a female growing up in the South in the 1950s, I felt afraid and disempowered. This work of empowering others therefore felt very meaningful to me; it helped heal my childhood wounds. And I was having great fun too! I was married to a fellow mountaineer whom I adored, and our happy life was filled with climbing adventures and mountaineering trips.

Then my husband developed stomach problems but was told by a couple of doctors that it was nothing more than a nervous stomach or the beginnings of an ulcer. By the time we got a proper diagnosis of colon cancer, the doctors gave Paul two weeks to live. He died one year later. From that moment on, I couldn't climb or teach mountaineering anymore. My life changed, and my work changed. I went back to school to study journalism and spent years working as a health writer for a newspaper, a magazine editor writing about natural health, and then the vice president of content for various natural health websites. I was passionate about writing stories that helped people prevent disease and live healthy lives. I was healing my own pain with each story.

As my awareness evolved through my spiritual work, I became passionate about helping everyone see their greatness, their indestructible souls, and the mission they came to accomplish. I allowed my intuition to flow untethered and used it to help others. I learned to focus on my clients' luminous spirits, the great potential they each came to fulfill in this lifetime, and the beauty of their pain stories, so perfectly designed to help them evolve. This is the work I do today.

When you're unhappy in your career, it's time to face your greatest ally—your pain. The pain you're feeling deep inside of you is a beacon calling for your attention. It's telling you what you need to know so your life can move forward. Your pain needs to be recognized, listened to, and turned into fuel to move your life forward. Shifting into your divine lens reveals the blessing in your pain story.

How do you turn your pain into fuel? First by recognizing what your greatest pain is, and then by recognizing how to heal that pain through your work. Your work will then become a powerful impetus for healing yourself and others. Remember, the more pain you have, the more fuel you have. Consider your pain to be your greatest blessing, and move forward.

THE PLAY'S THE THING

When all is said and done, there's no joy without pain and no pain without joy. We have to love the play of life for what it is—a school in which to master our spiritual evolution.

Of course, like you, I long to step away from pain and live in bliss, meditating on my porch while a summer breeze stirs my heart, crying from the beauty of a tree in the morning sun, the perfect dance of light and dark, the brilliance of a mourning dove's sweet song, the song that wakes us from the sleepy bliss of higher realms.

In a moment of sudden panic at the airport, I hold my daughter tightly, kiss her lovely forehead, and never let her go. I stop her from walking toward the gate and away from me. Then, like mothers do, I blow her a kiss good-bye as she disappears from view. She too needs to see the beauty and the horror. We all must sip from this potent brew, or there's no need to be here. It's the play, and the play's the thing.

And when you take your final bow, it matters how honestly you spoke your lines, how bravely you faced the audience, and if you played your role with every ounce of heart you could muster. It matters how true your words rang out into the night, filling the audience with hope, sorrow, and understanding, your poetry drifting into a moonlit sky.

The play's the thing, and it gets me out of bed. It's the thing that holds us together, waiting for the divine "reveal." We hope for one word of unbroken truth to fall into our hearts and touch us so deeply that for a brief instant we remember who we are and leap to our feet shouting "Bravo!" For that one moment, we see the perfection of horror and beauty. We understand the play of light and shadow, and it illuminates us.

Only at the final curtain call can we say it was terrible *and* wonderful, and that we're glad we came, that the story was worth it. And the script was brilliant.

Be the player on the stage we can't forget. Pull the naked truth from your heart and lay it on the stage for all to see. Speak your untarnished wisdom that wakes us up for a brief instant of shared illumination. Because you are divine, and nothing can stop you.

When everything is stripped away, who's left inside? Your divine self. Your soul. When you've lost everything, what have you found? Your divinity.

Take the opening. Take the chance. You've got nothing else to lose. All obstacles, belongings, and attachments have been removed for your highest good—to open your heart, break your patterns, erase fear, and quiet the ego mind that's been obsessed with winning.

*Pain quiets the personality that hides our true self
from the world. When it all slips away, take a breath.
Just one breath connects you to your divinity,
to your divine perspective.*

Say this sentence out loud: "Show me my divine perspective, the lesson of my pain, the gift in this moment, and my next step." One breath, one sentence spoken out loud, and everything is revealed. Now you're ready for your next level of evolution, the next phase of your journey. Today you're being asked to release the old, step away from drudgery, throw open the windows, and kiss the unknown dawn that awaits. You're being asked to grow, to love what you fear, to embrace pain as your greatest gift. Will you consider this? Can you pray, "Help me see this differently. Pull me out of ego. Wrap me in love and understanding."

You're not weak or overly sensitive. There's nothing wrong with you. You're a divine being who came here with a plan. You may have lost your way, but that's what happens in this dense realm. None of your past matters. What you have is today. And today is your choice point. All that matters is finding your way through the fog, reaching for divinity, seeking inspired purpose, and refusing to live by the rules that others have determined for your life.

Your soul is in charge, always. Your personality is only the costume you wear. Your soul opens every door, pours love on every wound, sees beauty in every misstep. Your soul realizes this is simply the journey you chose to take on your way to higher consciousness.

Everything you touch in this physical world is infused with love—your desk, your jeans, and your drinking glass all contain energy, a vibration of consciousness capable of assisting you in your awakening. Have respect for the unseen consciousness that exists everywhere within and all around you.

You didn't come here to waste time and indulge in your pain. You had everything you needed in the higher realms. You chose this density, this layer of darkness and fog, so you could surprise yourself, awaken, and remember everything; so you could recognize your opponent as the teacher, see your heartbreak as wisdom arriving, and realize that grief calls everyone to the Divine.

Every task you perform here, every job you undertake, is calling you to your soul's true work. Nothing is meant to be drudgery, torture, or work for work's sake, even though many choose to see it this way. Our lives are meant to elevate, inspire, heal, and awaken.

Where were you when your last lesson broke you open? Do you remember? Did you pout and blame? Did you attack those who asked you to grow? If so, this was your ego acting out, your empty personality disconnected from soul, the hungry ghost inside of you.

Or did you swing the doors of your heart wide open and call out for guidance?

It's time to make amends. You get to choose again. You can open your arms with gratitude, laugh instead of cower in fear, and move through the fog into the light—the light that was always there.

All you can hope for is to take the first step and reach for a sweeter answer. Everything changes in the instant of making a new choice because everything you feared is then revealed as nothing but illusion. All that matters is your courageous heart. That's where the light lives. That's your essence, and now you can see it.

In the end, you'll see your loved ones standing in the light beside you. "You did it!" they'll cry as they hold you. You'll realize that you never truly understood there was something important to do. You forgot there was a plan that you agreed to.

Yet when life's disappointments drained you and heartbreak sucked your breath away, you finally stood up. Not fully remembering why or how, you reached for the light in that painful moment. You loved it more than you loved the darkness. And despite everything, you found your courage.

Consider the possibility that all of your pain—every wound you've ever experienced, every loss, every illness, and every disappointment— was exactly what you needed and chose in order to arrive at this point in your life, which is exactly where you're supposed to be. Your soul chose to experience loss in order to open your heart and strengthen your connection to the Divine, to push you onto your true path and inspire you to accomplish your soul's greatest mission.

Your greatest work offers to the world what you wish had been offered to you in your moment of greatest pain. Grief brings a clarity and focus to your life's purpose, which gives you a powerful advantage in everything you do. Pain of any kind will drive you to see beyond the surface and embrace a divine lens perspective in every area of your life.

Let me tell you a story . . .

I'm constantly amazed at how everyone has a story of loss. And how for too many people grief has poisoned their lives in subtle ways.

Recently, on the way to teach a grief-shifting workshop at a spiritual retreat center, my shuttle driver (we'll call him Joe) told me he spent ten years being angry at God and angry at his family for his father's sudden, traumatic death. His pain destroyed his marriage, career, and health. One day he was considering ending his life when he felt his departed father's presence. The overwhelming love and grace he felt from his father, who, tragically, had been murdered, convinced Joe that he was living in a state of anger and blame while his departed father was living in a state of pure love. Joe knew he needed to change his life and start again. He began his journey of searching for a new spiritual perspective outside of church and religion.

Today he studies with people like psychic James Van Praagh and is becoming a healer and a medium himself. He says he realizes now that there were soul agreements in place, including an agreement to learn through the pain of loss, which he resisted for years because of anger. And he talks to his departed dad every day now for guidance and healing. This brings him great comfort.

That's virtually the same story as mine and the same path I took after my first husband's death in 1980.

Whatever your pain story is, shifting into your divine lens will reveal a new way forward, illuminate your pain as fuel, clear the confusion, and open your heart.

SOUL STORIES

ELAINE: REALIZING WE'RE NEVER TRULY ALONE

Elaine's husband had a stroke five years ago and is disabled. As his primary caretaker, she feels exhausted and is often angry. This is how her experience unfolded:

Elaine: *I see a barn close by, a farm.*

Sue: *Tell me what you're wearing on your feet.*

Elaine: *Barefooted.*

Sue: *How old you are?*

Elaine: *I'm a child in overalls with blonde hair and braids. And freckles. Feels like I'm about eight years old.*

Sue: *What is your sense of what's going on?*

Elaine: *I feel like this was the place I go to escape. Something isn't right where I live. I'm running.*

Sue: *Do you have any sense of what you're escaping from?*

Elaine: *No.*

Sue: *If you're complete here we'll move forward in time. One, two, and three. Now look down and see if your feet look the same or older.*

Elaine: *I'm definitely older. I feel like I'm a teenager, more mature.*

Sue: *And as you hold up a mirror and look at yourself, what do you see?*

Elaine: *I'm not in braids anymore. I'm crying. Feeling a loss of . . . security. Just being lost. Like I'm running away from something. I'm leaving my home. Life as I know it is over.*

Sue: *Do you have a sense of the time period?*

Elaine: *Maybe early 1900s.*

Sue: *Is there a sense of where you're headed next or where you've come from?*

Elaine: *Separated from my family for whatever reason.*

Sue: *Take a moment to observe this lifetime. When you're ready, we can move to the next scene?*

Elaine: *I'm ready to go to the next scene.*

Sue: *I'm going to count to three, and you will arrive in the final day of this significant lifetime.*

Elaine: *I'm older and I'm in bed.*

Sue: *Tell me what the bed looks like.*

Elaine: *It's white, wrought iron. There's a beautiful lamp. Maybe it's a kerosene lamp. And glasses. I'm seeing a pair of glasses on the table next to me. I don't feel trauma. I just feel like I'm sleeping or at rest. It feels peaceful.*

Sue: *Are people around somewhere?*

Elaine: *Yes, a younger person in a white apron. Maybe a nurse or a caregiver. Someone caring for me. Not family. But I feel cared for . . . and I just understood . . . that I was a nurse, too. I'm in my home dying of old age. I had been a nurse.*

Sue: *What are you feeling?*

Elaine: *That sadness of no parents, no family.*

Sue: *Look into the eyes of your caretaker and see if you recognize her from your current life.*

Elaine: *Yes. I recognize my caretaker as my friend Kristen in my current life.*

Sue: *Do you feel complete with that lifetime, or is there anything else?*

Elaine: *No, it's good.*

Sue: *Okay. Take a breath with me, and as your spirit lifts out of that bed, lifts out of that lifetime, knowing that you've learned exactly what you needed to learn, tell me if you see anything significant.*

Elaine: *The beauty. Being lifted above Earth, the blue pearl. In awe of the beauty.*

Sue: *As you move away from that lifetime, we're calling in your guide to meet you.*

Elaine: *Yes, I see Archangel Michael.*

Sue: *As Archangel Michael stands beside you, ask him about the significance of that past lifetime.*

Elaine: *That you're never alone . . . you're always guided . . . He says not to be afraid. I've been afraid of going to that next level of* *communicating with Spirit. My mind says it can't be real. Archangel Michael is telling me to be in the presence of the Divine and make it the norm, not the exception.*

Sue: *Can you ask Archangel Michael to help you with that when you're back here on Earth?*

Elaine: *Absolutely.*

Sue: *When you're ready, ask Archangel Michael to take you to your Council of Elders.*

Elaine: *We're there now. It's not really a room; I'm looking at something celestial. It's just beautiful with many colors. But it's ethereal, not solid.*

Sue: *As Archangel Michael walks you into this gathering of ethereal beings, tell me how many elders you see in your council.*

Elaine: *It's a circle of seven beings. Archangel Michael brought me to the middle of the circle.*

Sue: *Take a moment to absorb it. When you feel moved to ask a question, please do.*

Elaine: *Why do I have so much anger in this lifetime? When something doesn't go right, why do I get so upset?*

Sue: *Listen and absorb . . .*

Elaine: *The anger is because I don't remember why I'm here. I've not been wrong in my assumption that I'm angry that I'm here, but . . . with the understanding and the ability to communicate with Spirit and trust that having a guide is real, if I really have that connection and communication with Spirit, I want to be lifted above to see this life at the soul level. I've been afraid to do that.*

Sue: *Ask them why you've been afraid.*

Elaine: *Why am I afraid? Power, abuse of power. I have done that. That's where my fear comes from. Teach me, guide me, show me, please . . . They won't show me how I abused power.*

Sue: *You can ask where your soul originated.*

Elaine: *Angelic keeps coming up. Angelic realms.*

Sue: *Okay. That means that you haven't spent a lot of time in physical* incarnations. Ask them why you were called from the angelic realms to incarnate into your present lifetime.

Elaine: *To aid and rescue the family I incarnated into. But I've always had this sense that I didn't belong. I wasn't wanted. But apparently at a soul level I was needed.*

Sue: *Good.*

Elaine: *Light was needed. Light and love was needed.*

Sue: *And so you agreed to come here.*

Elaine: *Apparently so. And therein lies the source of my anger, that tug of war.*

Sue: *Do you want to ask them specifically about your soul agreement with your husband, Tom?*

Elaine: *They're confirming for me what I've always known—it is not a physical relationship. It is a soul-level relationship. What attracted us and has kept us together is a soul commitment.*

Sue: *A soul commitment for what purpose?*

Elaine: *We weren't here in a physical relationship to get love. We were here to recognize and remember that we* are *love. And to share that message. Maybe that's where this anger comes from as I care for him during his illness.*

Sue: *Ask them what is the purpose of Tom's physical illness.*

Elaine: *They say it's a test of that commitment. It's a test to stand in love . . . Hmm, I'm getting a visual image of this circle of seven . . . radiant colors. And they're circling me. This immense light surrounds me. I'm in the middle, with Archangel Michael, and I am literally becoming light.*

Sue: *Very good. You can ask them to describe your arc of learning in this lifetime.*

Elaine: *Learning that love is the light, and recognizing love in the day-to-day existence gets you closer to the light. I have an image of a particle of light. I'm being shown once you were a particle of light. Now you're a being of light radiating love.*

Sue: *Good.*

Elaine: *That intense light . . . I just keep hearing,* Remember, remember, remember. Remember this moment of standing here. *Being in this space and being able to connect to it.*

Sue: *Do you want to ask them if they can make that easier for you in this lifetime with your day-to-day struggles caring for your husband?*

Elaine: *I'm asking them to take away this constant battle of wanting to end my life, to help me let go of that feeling of not wanting to be here. If I chose to be here, that's what I don't understand. If I chose to be here, why do I feel this way?*

Sue: *Acknowledging that it's been a hard, challenging lifetime. And that you came in on the sacred master soul path of the number 11 with intense sensitivity. Ask them, "If I crossed over now, if I left this life now, would I feel that I accomplished what I came to do?"*

Elaine: *No, at a soul level I would not feel like I've accomplished what I came here for.*

Sue: *Maybe what you're really asking them for is the courage to be all in this lifetime and complete what you came here to do without resisting the lesson.*

Elaine: *Yes. Help me in my day-to-day struggles with Tom. Because I know I'm here to be love. And I just feel like I'm at the end of my rope, that there's just, physically, mentally, emotionally nothing left in me. I'm on my knees every morning asking for guidance and help, anything to help ease that conflict.*

Sue: *In this moment, as you stand in front of the council and Archangel Michael, ask for the courage and grace to be in this human lifetime fully, to commit to the lesson, to embrace each moment with courage and faith. Know that they are pouring all of their strength into you.*

Elaine: *Why am I so different from everyone?*

Sue: *I sense that there's an anger at being here on Earth. As an angelic soul who came into the physical realm for a purpose and with deep sensitivity. You've been wounded, especially early in this lifetime, and it's made you angry about being here. You can ask the* guides to give you the ability to accept what this physical life is like.

Elaine: *That resonates. That is it. It has the A word,* accept. *Accept and acclimate to this. The circle, the flow. It's going with that flow. That's the image I get.*

Sue: *They're helping you release your resistance to the physical world. They're lifting that from your shoulders.*

Elaine: *Yes. That is it. 100 percent. It's that constant sense I've had that there was something wrong with me. They're taking that away.*

Sue: *Maybe you've had a constant sense that there's something wrong with this world.*

Elaine: *Yes!*

Sue: *Dropping into the physical world is very hard for you. It made you angry and resistant to the way things are done here, because it's a lower vibration. And yet, that anger and resistance about being here prevents you from accomplishing your mission.*

Elaine: *Yes! I get it!*

Sue: *If you're complete, you can ask Archangel Michael to take you to the Library of Souls.*

Elaine: *I definitely like these celestial realms!*

Sue: *Tell me what you see. What does the library look like?*

Elaine: *Archangel Michael, please help me pick out something. Okay, it's a blue book. It's about communicating in other than earthly ways—that there are other ways of communicating with Spirit. To be open and unafraid and know that I can trust Archangel Michael's presence to guide me, and that it's not my imagination.*

Sue: *Yes. Just sit with that. You can put your hand on that book and absorb it for a moment.*

Elaine: *In the last two or three weeks, I've felt energy flowing out of my fingertips. It's vibrating and I haven't known why. I know something's going on, but I don't know what it is. Opening this book and putting my hand on it is reassuring me to just trust . . . That's my way of knowing when I'm communicating with Spirit. This book, a deep, indigo blue. I don't want to close this book. I want to be able to* *access this book anytime. Is it possible to come back to this spot, open this book, and absorb this anytime?*

Sue: *Ask Archangel Michael if you can take the book with you back into the physical realm. See what he says.*

Elaine: *He says, "How can you take something that's nonphysical back into the physical? You don't need the physical reminder. You just need to go to this inner space and remember. This is not going to disappear. This is eternal, like you are. It'll always be here."*

Sue: *That's beautiful. Yes. As you look around that library, is there anything else that you need to feel or absorb or learn?*

Elaine: *The whole library! Love is real. And it truly is in this room.*

Sue: *Now we acknowledge that you have absorbed what you needed to absorb from this beautiful space. Do you feel complete?*

Elaine: *Thank you, thank you, thank you!*

Sue: *Is there a question you have for Archangel Michael, perhaps pertaining to Tom's condition?*

Elaine: *At first when he had his stroke, I wanted to be present, I wanted to be loving, because who knows how much time was left. Then as day-to-day care became harder and harder, I began wishing for his death, and that created guilt. Now I'm being told that the lesson is about accepting, and that it's not my will or my decision, it's his will and his decision.*

Sue: *Right, beautiful.*

Elaine: *So the answer is trying to see beyond the physical and come from this higher knowing . . . quietly, on my own, soul to soul. To spend time looking into Tom's eyes and sending love. Just seeing the love, regardless of how he's appearing or what he's saying or doing. Because believe me, there are days when I walk out of his room and I just want to scream at the top of my lungs. But instead, to see the true reality—that I chose this, and being grateful instead of resentful.*

When she was complete with her experience, I guided her back into her body, and the following exchange took place:

Sue: *What do you feel was the significance of that experience for you?*

Elaine: *Knowing I really do have a guide, a loving presence. Because that's always been foreign to me, not real. I've never felt like anybody truly walked beside me. So just having that image, that holy presence. Knowing I can connect in the silence. I am totally committed to reconnecting to that space daily and getting guidance. So that was huge for me.*

Sue: *What new possibility or alternatives do you see now in your day-to-day life that you gained from this experience?*

Elaine: *It's about acceptance of the moment-to-moment. No matter what physical challenges are happening, accept it. You chose this. You're learning from it. You chose this.*

Sue: *Yes. I want to share some insights I got from escorting you on this journey. The main awareness is that you are from the angelic realms, and when you arrived in this physical world, your first response, especially when you got wounded in childhood, was to shut down the heart and get angry at the world. To say, "What's wrong with me that I can't fit in here and be happy like everybody else?" Today you were being shown by the council to quit resisting the low level of consciousness here on Earth. You chose to come here. Embrace the lesson, and do what you came to do.*

Elaine: *Yes, that really resonates.*

Sue: *I feel that part of the reason for your struggle is that you're so strong and resistant, and yet you had to build that strength up just to survive here. But now, that strength, resistance, and cynicism is only hurting you. So there's a softening required, a surrender.*

Elaine: *Oh my gosh, that makes sense. Oh my God, I surrender to this life because I want to soften it. I really, really, really want to soften.*

Sue: *Yes, yes. You are doing it. You are breaking down the walls around your heart that have built up the resistance, the cynicism, and all the things that keep you from totally surrendering to what is, knowing you came to accept it all with grace and courage. Knowing you've done nothing wrong and have always done your best.*

Elaine: Grace *is a word I totally resonate with.*

Sue: *You don't have to fight so hard, my beloved.*

Elaine: *Oh my gosh, yes. Surrender—*

Sue: *—to the lesson at hand.*

Elaine: *Wow.*

Sue: *I also think that your past lifetime is important, if we can spend a minute processing it. You were a child, barefoot with braids and freckles, and not really sure if you had a family. There was a sense in that lifetime of having to learn how to survive in the physical world, to be strong. And somehow you found a way to become a nurse and live a meaningful life. Perhaps part of the lesson of that lifetime was learning how to be in this physical world and survive on your own.*

Perhaps it was your acclimating lifetime, to learn what it's like to be in the physical world and still try to remember your essence as a divine being. You did succeed, because you became a healer. And here you are in this life, being a healer again for your husband. And we're acknowledging that when you come across as forceful, cynical, or angry, that's just your defense against being here and not being comfortable here.

Elaine: *That's the key—remembering my essence, my soul.*

Sue: *You said this really important thing: "I've been afraid of going beyond the ordinary in my communication with Spirit. To believe it's real." You recognized that it's essential to experience life here in this realm and not intellectualize it; to trust your intuition. And when you're bombarded with information, to trust the Divine to guide you.*

Elaine: *Yes! That's awesome! I have to remember this.*

Sue: *You said at one point, "I have not believed that I have a guide, I've felt all alone, and that has made me angry. I want to be in this life and see it from the soul level, so I can remember that I'm not alone, and let go of the anger." You also said, "I've been afraid to see it from the soul level, because I'm afraid to abuse my power." You said your fear of connecting to Spirit comes from the fear of abusing your power. When you asked the guides to show you how you'd abused your* *power, they didn't show you. They saw no purpose in showing you how you had abused power because it wouldn't help you to see it. Take with you the understanding that you don't need to be afraid of your spiritual power now, because you've learned the lesson.*

Elaine: *Awesome, and I feel like Archangel Michael walks besides me to help me not go down that path again.*

Sue: *Exactly. We learn the lesson and move on. We never repeat the same pattern when we learn what we need to learn. We release it, and the soul moves to the next lesson. When you carry love and light from the angelic realms to Earth, it's not your job to get disappointed in other people's growth process. That's not what a healer does. That's not what an angel does.*

Elaine: *You're right, you're absolutely right!*

Sue: *You said this very profound thing as you were observing everything in the divine realms. You said, "I've got to remember that Tom's journey is not my will or my decision." There's a great surrender in that. Your only concern here is your own soul's progress.*

Elaine: *Being true to yourself, your authentic self, your internal self. Thank you, thank you, thank you!*

Update: *Elaine says she experienced great healing during this session and was able to continue in her caregiving role with less anger and more grace and acceptance.*

◉ Rewrite the Story of Your Childhood

To gain a new perspective on your life, write two different versions of your childhood, each with the same players and circumstances. In the ego story, you're the helpless victim without a choice to make things better. In your soul story, change your inner perceptions to find love and miracles in each painful moment. Use these moments of wisdom to rewrite your history and change your choices for the better, finding courage whenever you faced fear. Now you see who you came here to be. This is your new story and your new point of view moving forward. Ask yourself which version of the story makes you feel openhearted, forgiving, and empowered? Which version leaves you feeling hopeless? You get to choose your lens—the soul's view or the ego's view. Choose wisely. Your happiness and future direction depend on which lens you choose, not on the circumstances of your life.

Questions to ponder as you revisit your childhood:

- Describe two or three deeply painful moments of your childhood.
- Now write those same moments from an angel's perspective as they stood beside you unnoticed and manifested small miracles on your behalf to help you through those experiences.
- Through your soul's perspective, can you see that perhaps you were never alone and always loved even if not by the humans in your story? Write your thoughts on this.
- Write a painful scene from your childhood when someone mistreated or abused you.
- Now write that same scene but this time from the abuser's perspective (filling in their back story of pain and abuse) so that their actions are understandable in the context of their own pain and abuse.

P.S. This is what happens when our soul leaves the body at the final breath and we're held by loving guides for a soul review.

17

Joy and Gratitude

How Gratitude Shifts Us into the Divine Lens Perspective

From one moment to the next, we can shift from despair to enlightenment, from grief to gratitude, from terror to love. This is our gift as humans—the ability to choose the way we view the world and our lives, and thus we can thrive no matter what our outer circumstances. Our perception of challenge is never constant. It's always shifting. This is how we learn. Free will is essential to our evolution.

If you had incarnated into this dense realm fully remembering that you're a soul on a mission to evolve consciousness, you wouldn't learn anything here. It would be like playing Monopoly but starting out already owning all the hotels and the other properties. You'd feel nothing. There wouldn't be joy, surprise, excitement, or disappointment. There would be no point to the game and nothing learned.

We come here for one reason: to evolve and help others evolve. We arrive ready for the adventure of learning, for the adventure of new experiences. Just as we enroll in a university in order to learn, gain new experiences, and develop friendships, we enroll in Earth School for the same reasons. You signed up for your coursework before you arrived here, carefully choosing the exact lessons and gifts that would help you evolve in the way you needed to, to push you to the next level.

At certain points, all of us become angry, disappointed, or depressed over the exact lessons we come here to master. But we can shift from anger and fear to love and gratitude, no matter what we're facing. Then we step into the grace and peace of our soul's wisdom. This choice, once made, becomes a lifetime pattern that will serve us at every challenge.

We may also choose to exit this lifetime through suicide or by sabotaging our physical health, but if we haven't accomplished our soul's mission we'll still desire to do so in another lifetime or another dimension. When we cross over through intentional death, our life review reveals the choices we made and could have made. We feel the ramifications of each choice and how it affected our loved ones. Great learning occurs in this moment of ultimate realization. We see then the choices we could have made to change our life for the better. We're shown the love that was given to us that we might have denied. All of this spurs soul growth— along with the determination to try again and accomplish more. We may then choose to start over, facing the same challenges as the last time, determined to reverse the pain we caused our loved ones. Or we might choose to remain in the divine realms to do our work there.

If you feel resistant to the idea of viewing your life in a new way, with gratitude, take a deep breath, quiet your mind, and ask for a new perspective on your pain. This request is always answered. One moment of gratitude is capable of pulling you into your soul's wisdom.

Say, "I'm grateful for the lessons because I know I chose them to help me become my best self. I trust that if I embrace this pain with love and wisdom, I'll step into my divinity and experience the grace that awaits me."

JOY OVERCOMES EVERYTHING, INCLUDING PAIN

We come to this realm to experience the tastes, smells, passions, and enormous beauty of the physical world. We use contrast to push us to evolve. Fear forces us to choose love. Despair makes us reach for hope. Winter's quiet contemplation prepares us for the new growth of spring.

Your darkest despair carries a glimmer of light that will change everything—if you reach for it. In your moment of greatest fear, there's a voice of pure love singing a new song—if you listen to it. It's your choice and yours alone to pull yourself through the storm. One moment of shared laughter or unrestrained joy shatters pain into a million shards of light. When you look into someone's eyes to realize you've always known them, you're remembering your divinity. When a butterfly emerges from out of nowhere to land on your shoulder, you realize you're not alone. This is the gift of human experience.

You're in it for the beauty and the awe of an unexpected moment. But you must choose joy. Despite everything you've been through, miracles occur every day, just for you—during your daily walk, in a random conversation with a stranger, and in the sudden brush of a fresh breeze against your skin. When your soul is ready and you've learned what you came here for, you'll be pulled into the highest realms, where the light is brighter than here and the sounds are more ecstatic than you've known before. But today you're here for the joy of taking another breath.

Joy is your natural state. Your divine lens view pulls back the veil to reveal the perpetual light, love, and beauty that's always working for your highest good.

Experiencing the more enlightened view that comes with joy will break your heart wide open. Pick up your divine lens and allow a new perspective to inspire your mundane life; you'll see that all is well and there exists a higher purpose to your journey. It's this higher purpose that keeps us going as we navigate this dense realm, accomplishing daily tasks and surviving. Yet within this daily grind we often forget our divinity and do not recognize divine order. Instead we focus on details and the meaningless activities that fill our lives with drudgery. This focus on empty details blocks our joy. We briefly remember this inner joy when we hold a newborn baby, walk in nature, or fall in love.

You've evolved to the point now that you're capable of navigating this dense energy while also experiencing your divine self, your bliss, and remembering the higher purpose of your life. When challenges occur— when you lose a loved one or a job, or when you face financial hardship— you're being pushed to see the divine order even as you mourn a loss or struggle to build a new career. One breath, one moment of silent meditation, or a request for guidance opens your channel to divine wisdom.

You've accomplished so much already and in a relatively short time. But now your evolution has reached a tipping point, and your growth curve has steepened. You're awakening into the awareness that this physical world is your creation, your university of divinity. Take note of the brief moment before you react in pain, fear, or anger. Listen for the whisperings of your soul. This subtle inner voice, like a sudden breeze against your skin or a tingling up your spine, urges you to seek guidance, to step into higher consciousness and face this moment with awareness of your divinity. When you listen to the whisperings, your soul's wisdom speaks up. It says, *I will rise above my pain with grace and love, knowing that I'm not alone, that love surrounds me, and that when I ask for guidance, I'm lifted into the light, where my next step is fully revealed.*

Doing this once changes everything. It breaks a pattern. Now you know you can shift your perspective. You've begun your awakening, and nothing can stop this process. Not even your ego. This seedling of wisdom will slowly blossom in your heart despite your pain, illuminating moments of joy when you least expect them. You'll discover that you're never a victim to anyone or anything. You'll navigate this earthly realm with both sides of your brain activated; your ego mind will organize the mundane details, while your Higher Self illuminates the greater purpose.

◉ Shifting into Joy and Gratitude

Focus on one thing or person in your life that you can feel grateful for right now. Keep focusing on that thing or person as if you were wearing magnifying glasses and exploring up close. See each detail of what you're grateful for.

Now open your heart and send that one thing or person you're grateful for a big burst of love. Wrap them in compassion. You've now shifted into your divine lens. Focus your divine lens on any challenges you're currently facing, and send compassion to the people who are troubling you or the events that are throwing you off-balance.

Now take a deep inhalation and a long exhalation, and say, *Please, divine guides, show me the lesson of this moment and reveal the divine lens view of this story I'm telling myself today. Pull me out of the ego view and show me the wisdom of this lesson so I can be grateful for it.* Then write down your thoughts as you consider these questions:

- When you look back at this difficult moment in your life, how will you think of it?
- How will you wish you had handled the challenge(s) you are currently facing from your most enlightened, compassionate perspective?
- Looking back from this moment in your life, describe your soul story of how you gracefully overcame any challenges by choosing love and gratitude over fear.

18
Return to Sacred Self
Our Shared Journey

My pain is the same as everyone else's. My fear is shared by all. There is no dark night of the soul that I've had that you haven't had. We share this journey. We joined our souls long ago. We dove in. We agreed. We swim beside one another now, forgetting, fighting against the flow, resisting wisdom. Why?

Because doubt is easy. Fear is ordinary. We give up a million times, a billion times. But here's the thing: We hit the dirt but we always rise again. We reach for light after days of pacing in the dark. We long to feel love. We long to help. We want life. We breathe. We choose.

Never doubt that you have a gift. Never doubt that you walk in grace. Never doubt that every rising up and falling down is perfect and meant to be fuel for the journey of your soul. You're right on schedule. Relax. Trust your gut. You're learning what you must.

Someday when your heart is ripped open, your head thrown back in awe, and you're gasping at the light, you'll see the purpose of your whole crazy story. You'll know it was good, all good. This exact moment is good. Trust it.

Choose love. Choose what you love.
Because doubt is easy, and fear is ordinary.

Whether it appears so or not, all souls on Earth are cooperating in divine agreement for everyone's highest evolutionary good. You agreed to come here to evolve your soul and to help others in your soul family. You may have suffered greatly in your lifetime journey, but this was all agreed to ahead of time for your highest good.

It may appear that some people have everything they desire or seem untouched by hardship. Rest assured, they're experiencing exactly what you're experiencing, just wrapped in a different package. The lessons are the same for all of us no matter how things may appear on the surface.

Your divine lens provides a way to see beneath the surface. It illuminates the deeper story of the soul journey of both those you love and those you condemn. Wearing your powerful divine lens, you see divinity in everything, in each spoken word and painful moment. It reveals the hidden agreements of soul upon soul.

You may be highly intelligent, but true intelligence is the wisdom to see beyond the surface, to know the essence of things. You may consider yourself inferior or superior. But these are meaningless terms that only weigh you down with confusion. They make you doubt who you are and why you came here.

Through your divine lens, you can see the perfection in every heartbreak and the wisdom within every life story, especially your own. Your ego-lens distortion convinces you that some people are good and others are bad. Viewing the world this way is the perspective of ego, which is incapable of seeing beneath the surface. The ego is bereft of wisdom, compassion, and insight.

Shift into your divine lens view right now. Close your eyes, take a deep breath, quiet the mind, open the heart. Ask for guidance. Surrender what you think you know.

Every moment of your day is a new beginning. One fear-based judgmental action is erased in a moment of wisdom. When we trust our divine guides, they help us quiet the ego mind; this allows the heart to become the force of light that it was designed to be. Love is the radiant light that slices through ignorance to reveal the divine order in each moment.

WE COME HERE TO LEARN

We don't come here to be perfect. We come for the experience of soul expansion, growth, and consciousness evolution. If those terms seem foreign to you, if they don't speak to your pain, ask yourself, *Can I remember one moment when I felt awe at something beyond logic, beyond description, something that took my breath away and for a brief instant held me in deepest contentment, knowing all is well?* If you remember one moment like this, one brief second, then you know how you'll feel at the end when you cross the veil and view your life to see the soul lessons. You can choose to view your life this way today, even as you doubt yourself, you can look within to know your soul's story.

So many untapped gifts abound within you that when you arrive at the end of your journey and the ego lens is finally ripped away, you'll stand in awe at the brilliance and perfection of each moment of your life. The astounding gifts you brought to your lifetime will leave you stunned, and you'll realize you could have changed the world.

THE POWER OF ASKING

Great love lives within you, and your soul has taken gracious care to design this moment of heartbreak perfectly for your evolution. The joy of your unbirthed wisdom is waiting to be set free.

All of this light and possibility shimmers within, even when you fall to your knees in despair or pound your fists in anger. Sacred light shines within your heart, bright as gold, sharp as a sword, and true as the sun. Nothing ever diminishes it, not even when you deny your soul's wisdom and fail to see beyond one moment of suffering.

Hidden in the heart of your cynicism is the truth you're not speaking, the pain you're not embracing: you long for love, absolute love. Your homesickness for the Divine has caused you to feel deep misery. You feel stranded, ripped from the vast ocean of unconditional love that you once knew in the higher dimensions. How did you arrive on this earthly shore gasping for air? You swam here, poured your enormous spirit into a brief and imperfect body and a flawed personality. Your soul did this to create the exact circumstances you now find yourself in.

When you first arrived, you remembered that nothing could ever damage your essence, the diamond that is your indestructible soul. You longed to expand your consciousness, spread your wings, pour light into darkness, and transform everyone with love. You carried that love with you when you jumped into this dense realm, where you now lay abandoned on the beach of your despair.

Remember this: the sand will slap you awake and scrape skin from your bones until you clear your mind and open your heart again. It doesn't matter what you've been through or how damaged you feel. When your head clears, you'll see the beauty of your devastating loss and the gift it offers as a reminder of your divine essence, your indestructible heart, and the enormous love you came here to share. All losses disappear in the end. Some day you'll remember this.

But today, perhaps, you only feel the rough sand against your face and grieve the memory of something divine that you once knew. Perhaps your thoughts are dark at this moment. Your guides understand this and await your awakening. Your voyage must not be interfered with. But the waves of wisdom stirring within you will never stop eroding your ego and opening your eyes.

When a new tide comes, you won't be able to remember your grief and disappointment. The moment you lift your head and cry for help from something you don't even believe in, you'll find yourself cloaked in light and wisdom. The moment you seek a new answer, love arrives and changes everything.

My ego's story is terribly sad: I was abused, abandoned, and grief-stricken. I failed at many things. I was too sensitive, never perfect, and hardly lovable. Yet my soul story is filled with light. There were angels in my darkest moments. Spirits warned me of danger and pushed me into the light when I was young. Those whom I grieved showed up in my dreams to heal me, again and again. Whenever I lifted my eyes from the pain, they were standing there in the light. I felt them reaching through my grief.

Whenever I asked for divine inspiration, it always arrived, looking different from what I had expected, but I was delivered into the light nonetheless. When I didn't demand that life turn out my way, but instead surrendered to the lesson, asking only for grace and wisdom, events conspired in my favor and for my highest good. I have no regrets. I've been pushed to learn exactly what I came here to learn and rewarded abundantly for every effort I made to reach for the grace hidden inside each painful moment.

I now understand the love that surrounded me, especially when I was abandoned and brokenhearted. I acknowledge the unstoppable truth that poured through my heart once I learned to quiet my mind. I realize now that the passion and intensity I've always held within me was my gift and never my flaw, though I often believed it was a terrible weakness. And the moments I thought were easy and hoped would last forever did not serve my highest good. They were brief because I didn't come here to sleep or waste time. I planned well for the trip, choosing the perfect body type and personality for the job, even though these things were often a source of shame.

I designed the excruciating self-doubt and intellectual awkwardness I suffered from, which eventually forced me to share my wisdom fearlessly because I had learned too well the price of remaining silent, the price of people-pleasing, and the bankruptcy of living for the approval of anyone other than my Higher Self.

I recognize now that my overactive right brain and underdeveloped left brain forced me to find alternative ways to navigate my life. This worked in my favor, as an intuitive compass that delivered me into a world of endless possibilities and boundless optimism. Because I couldn't see the logic of not jumping off the cliff and instead felt, with all my heart, that the jump must be made, I took the leap. It was a leap that changed everything and brought me into the glory of a luminous world that lives within everyone and everything. And once I'd made that leap, it became so easy to do it again and again, whenever I found myself in a corner and I couldn't see the light. I discovered that the light lives in the leap, and love awaits the courageous act. And now nothing could ever keep me from the leap or dampen my courage. What a gift this has been, and I am still grateful. It's the best truth I ever learned and worth every bruise I ever suffered.

Without leaping into the abyss, we don't understand a thing. We think the glory is in the withholding of our love, the caution, politeness, acceptance, and boundaries. But none of those places hold the truth. And none of those places teach us to fly. Caution is a weighted thing and it puts us on the bench to watch the game or keeps us seated nervously on the cliff's edge, viewing everything we fear below, counting all the reasons why a leap would ruin us, explaining all the ways it could go badly, telling stories of how to conduct our lives with planning and steadfastness, without ever being foolish. At the end of the game, we see that it was us being foolish whenever we held back.

Because everything that ever mattered lived in the leap, that one moment of taking a deep breath and trusting the wind to carry us, seeing that letting go is everything—it was always the point of our existence and the reason for our story.

You always have access to your soul's wisdom, and that's the great secret here, the jewel hidden in the vault, the thing you came to find but forgot along the way. You landed here eager to find the gem of your soul's truth and view your travels through the divine lens. But then you forgot everything you knew. When others insisted that you were no more than a physical body, a personality locked in a material world, you forgot your soul. You were taught the wrong rules of behavior and given the wrong advice. You pursued things that took you further from your wisdom and made you conform to society's rules.

You were told to compete in a world where money is always the point of the story. You made choices in alignment with that, even though it bothered you. But it was all you knew. You had forgotten the point of your adventure. When your lover broke your heart or you didn't pass that exam or get the job, you tried hard to remember something essential. Sometimes you found it in music or in romantic love, when a powerful feeling stirred within your heart and couldn't be denied. But as soon as the world rewarded your ego yet again, your ego lens was restored. Off you went to relearn the rules, win the game, and become the smartest in the room, no matter the cost to your soul.

When that perfect job left you feeling empty and questioning everything, or your new lover proved unworthy, you fell back into seeking the gem you first came to find. You discovered the hidden prize wasn't money or sex or pleasure. It wasn't any of the things you were holding. You almost remembered then.

What was that thing you were looking for?

One day your inner longing became too great and you broke open. You awakened and remembered the purpose of your existence, the reason for your life. You felt schizophrenic. One day you'd know that everything was meant to happen and you felt fearless. The next day you'd wake up in fear with a sweat-drenched pillow and unpaid bills littering the floor. Then you were certain that you were headed for a tragic ending. Which viewpoint do you favor? The sweat-drenched nightmares, or the moments of clarity and purpose?

WHY CLARITY AND HAPPINESS VACILLATE FROM DAY TO DAY

We all experience lost days, when we simply can't seem to connect with anything beyond the mundane world and our pain and doubts. Yet other days are filled with light and magic, and our hearts are wide-open to feeling the Divine Presence in each moment.

Many factors contribute to the density of energy here on Earth. One is the state of the collective consciousness, which is the consciousness of all souls together at each moment of every day. At times there's tremendous collective pain among us due to international events. At those times, we feel the veil separating us from the higher realms as being thick, heavy, and impenetrable. This is caused by our collective fear, anger, and blame. During these times, focus on prayer, love, forgiveness, and reaching for the light. In this way you help shift Earth's consciousness back into a higher frequency. This shift into the light greatly benefits everyone, especially those directly suffering as a result of painful events.

At other times, the heaviness we feel is more unique to each of us, caused by our chi, or life force energy, becoming sluggish due to toxic foods and lack of movement. Sluggish body energy keeps us weighted down in the mundane and burdened with fear.

TAKE A BREATH, YOU'RE STILL IN THE GAME

As long as you're alive, you're still in the game. You may be resting on the sidelines briefly, but you're an important player, and you're needed for the next inning. Even if you're temporarily benched as you deal with fears and self-doubts, prepare to jump back in. Get up and move your body. Say a prayer for inspiration. Visualize how you'll make your next move. Show your enthusiasm to the world, and everything will begin to feel better.

There's nothing worse than realizing after the game ends that you've spent your lifetime sitting on the sidelines watching others give it their all, knowing you had it inside of you to hit that homerun, and yet you didn't jump back in. You sat watching and judging the efforts of others. You doubted your gifts. You exhausted yourself with worry and fear. But this is not who you came here to be. You didn't arrive on Earth to sit on the bench. You came to be a star, someone who passionately tries and tries again, a most valuable player, someone who makes others believe that they too can do something great to serve the world.

The players sitting on the bench don't inspire us. They never get to prove to themselves that they're gifted, that they're worthy, and that they carry a perpetual light inside that's needed in this world. How many lifetimes have you spent on the bench, doubting yourself or doubting the importance of the game, the worthiness of other players, the value of succeeding, or the ecstasy of giving your all for the greater good?

The moment you jump in and give life everything—your heart, soul, and gifts—you step into your bliss, your divine connection, which is the thrill of this realm. You remember why you came here and why all the hard work was worth it. That one moment of giving everything carries the juice, the love, and it opens your heart and pushes you into the light.

Just stand up. Move that heavy energy. Get it flowing. Call out for wisdom and love. Asking is everything, and movement allows grace to flow through you. One day you'll see it all with wisdom. You'll understand the value of a courageous heart. You'll see how courage creates miracles and accomplishes the impossible. Everything worthwhile is born of courage, the courage to move forward despite all losses and doubts. It's the one thing you truly need on Earth. This realization is a game-changer.

HOW DO I CONNECT TO MY SACRED SELF?

Your sacred self is always available. This inner frequency is active 24/7, and there's no static to block the reception unless your mind creates it. Divine guidance is always available whenever you quiet your mind.

A simple letting go of fear allows you to hear your inner wisdom. There's nothing more important than allowing your Higher Self to speak. You're one of many light beings here or you wouldn't be reading this. You've been nurtured along for this very moment, educated in the higher realms, trained in love and courage. Divinity is on your side if you embrace the lesson in front of you.

Nothing can hurt you. No one can take away your home, your love, your life, as long as you open your heart and reach for the light. Speak the words you hear in your heart and share the knowledge given to you by your Higher Self.

There are no beings who are any more or less magnificent than you, now that you've opened your channel to the highest realms and can access your soul's wisdom. It's not your imagination. This inner voice is your divine companion, the one who has always been standing beside you. You have always had a spirit posse on the other side rooting for you. They know when to push and when to comfort. You still need a little pushing, but you'll get this done just as you planned.

You wouldn't have chosen to incarnate at this pivotal time if you weren't up for the job of evolution. You don't have to remember making that choice. You don't have to struggle. Just ease forward as each step is revealed. Just do the work that's right in front of you. Truth unfolds simply and elegantly, one day at a time. When you listen to your Higher Self, everything gets easier.

What's coming in the future? Only sweet surrender will reveal that. You're not allowed to know, or growth would not occur, and it's the growth you've needed for the fulfillment of your soul's mission.

HERE'S ALL YOU NEED TO KNOW

Light is greater than dark. Always. Love is greater than fear. Always. This simple equation foretells the future of your life and the future of humanity.

Choose your side, your words, and your actions to align with the light. Move forward into grace. You are divinely blessed and deeply loved. When you choose fear and darkness, you're not in alignment with the grace that abounds within and all around you. You're lost in the static and unable to hear the ever-present loving guidance available to you at all times.

Sit in silence at least once a day or so much is missed, so many mistakes are made. Doing this is easier than not doing it, because everything shifts when you're silent and have quieted the mind. You'll barely realize the grace that surrounds you when you get up from your sacred stillness and go about your day. But at the end of the day, when you review events, you'll recognize the light that illuminated your choices.

All religions have tried to teach this in different ways, yet the ego-based ideas of humans have corrupted so much truth that was originally channeled from the Divine. Religion was meant to be a ritual of silent connection, but so much has been lost in human translations.

Your body is simply a vehicle that was perfectly designed for your particular journey. Each body and personality is thus unique in its personal vibration. All of this was orchestrated before your present life-time. You can trust that your body and your personality are carrying you exactly where you need to go.

The same is true of your brain. Your brain was perfectly designed for the gifts you carried into this lifetime. There are no flaws in the design of any brain or body. Each piece of you is in perfect alignment with your soul's mission and what you've come here to accomplish for humanity.

The older your soul, the greater your intent to accomplish something grand, to participate in the global shift to higher consciousness. You would not be reading these words if you weren't one of these old souls who came here at this time with a great purpose. Yet once you arrived, you struggled like everyone else to adapt to the dense energy here, often feeling like a fish out of water. Your body is the "Earth suit" you designed for the task of fulfilling your mission.

So stand up, brush yourself off, take a deep breath, and begin walking your path. Even if you don't know where it will take you, take a step forward. You'll be guided every inch of the way. You already have been. So take a step and trust.

NOTHING IS UNFORGIVABLE, NOTHING IS IMPOSSIBLE, NOTHING IS MEANINGLESS

You're in this now. Your soul brought you here. It takes great effort to arrive in human form and begin a new lifetime. No one sent you. No one pushed you. You asked to be put in the game. You've healed from past injuries, and you have a new and better plan: you want to help everyone.

Your guides approved your plan before you arrived here. You agreed to reduce your enormous soul into the tiniest of forms—an Earth suit called the human body. Once your feet were on the ground, though, you complained, screamed, and railed against the pain of being back in this thick density, in this diminished light, in the fog of forgetfulness. Certain people sparked you to open your eyes, to remember just a little. And you did. You reached out to anyone who shimmered. They reminded you of the beings from whence you came.

You always had a choice to reach out or not. A choice to ask for help or not. By making choices for the light, you emerged, and in your emerging, you remembered. You found your name, your song. You heard your soul's voice.

When you align with your Higher Self and take the stage to share your gifts with the world, all things are revealed. Each day, even your final one, is a moment of choice and a moment to offer healing. Your soul bears the pain and the gifts of your unique journey.

TOOLS FOR ACCESSING THE DIVINE REALMS

Throughout human history we've been given many tools for accessing our divinity. These sacred tools pull us out of the ego's grip and reveal our soul's purpose. Religious rituals such as prayer, Communion, and chanting were designed to connect us to the highest realms. Yet religion went astray when church leaders focused on sin and judgment rather than on love. God is love. When fear overshadows the sacred, we lose our connection to the Divine.

We were given many other esoteric techniques to access the Divine and help us find our way—astrology, numerology, tarot, and channeling, to name a few. When used with love and correct intention, all of these tools can reveal our divine purpose.

I've used numerology to guide clients since 1980. When my young husband died that year, I was gifted with a session from an intuitive numerologist. Her insights changed my life and impacted the future trajectory of my work. This sacred numerology technique was first shared by the Greek philosopher and mystic Pythagoras in 580 BCE, when he created the number system we still use today. He revealed that each number carries a unique energy or sacred meaning that goes beyond numerical quantity. In Pythagoras's system, we reduce the birth date down to a single number in order to reveal the soul's purpose for this lifetime. So much wisdom is revealed in these numbers that they can become a gateway to higher consciousness once they're fully understood.

To calculate your numerology to see how it points to your soul agreements as well as your work in the world, see the appendix to this book, "Calculate Your Birth Path Using Numerology."

Our elegant universe is rich with patterns and symbols that can reveal our purpose here. These patterns exist everywhere—in numbers, stars, and nature. We came into this realm knowing there would be many signposts along the way to guide us.

SOUL STORIES

VICKIE: A NEW KIND OF HEALING

This soul regression was for a mom named Vickie who had lost two children, a nineteen-year-old son named Michael and a baby girl named Eliza. Now Vickie has two grown daughters and runs an international nonprofit that provides healing services for grieving parents. At the time of this session she was in a 9 numerical year.

Vickie wanted to gain clarity about moving forward during this time of personal change. As I guided her through the usual meditation and deep relaxation techniques, she experienced the presence of her two departed children escorting her through the tunnel of light. Here's an edited transcript of her session:

Sue: *Now you've arrived in a significant past lifetime. Please take a* moment to get your bearings and see what you see. I'm going to ask you some questions. Are you outdoors or indoors?

Vickie: *Outdoors.*

Sue: *Tell me what you see.*

Vickie: *I see beautiful rocks. I stepped out into brilliant sunlight and it looks like there are rock formations all around me, but also rainbow colors. It's actually very beautiful.*

Sue: *Do you see people anywhere?*

Vickie: *No, there's no one. It's just me.*

Sue: *Can you see your feet? Are you wearing any kind of shoes?*

Vickie: *No shoes.*

Sue: *Can you tell how old you are or what color your skin is?*

Vickie: *My skin is darker. I think I'm younger than I am right now. It seems like I'm in good shape. The clothes that I'm wearing seem to be more like fabric. Not really sewn clothes. It feels like I'm in India.*

Sue: *Take a moment to allow the scene to unfold.*

Vickie: *It doesn't look like where I am is a place that I can walk down easily. It's as though I'm in a huge cave, open to the outside.*

Sue: *Is it your sense that you're a man or a woman?*

Vickie: *I think I'm a man, but my hair is long. I feel that I'm supposed to be here to meditate, and I feel very peaceful and all alone. I don't feel lonely. The place where I am is so beautiful. There are rainbow colors coming off of the rocks and the view is spectacular, but I haven't really looked to see how I got here. I'm not sure because it's fairly high up.*

Sue: *Absorb everything you can from that scene. Let me know when you're ready to move forward into a future scene in that same lifetime.*

Vickie: *I feel enormous peace here. I don't know if there's something to be learned here, but I feel very, very peaceful. I guess it would be good to move forward to see why I was here.*

Sue: *At the count of three, you will be moved forward into a future time in that same lifetime. One and two and three . . . Are you outdoors or indoors?*

Vickie: *I'm outdoors. I think I'm in a village, but on a dirt path* *between homes. I can smell food cooking outside. I think I'm in India. I can hear children. I still feel at peace. I see a sacred cow, but it's a calf. I'm reaching out to touch its nose.*

Sue: *Allow the scene to unfold.*

Vickie: *I see children coming toward me with their hands outstretched. They're forming a circle around me. They're so beautiful. I don't really know why I'm here, but I think that it might be to speak to these children and maybe to the people in the town and possibly to get supplies, I'm not sure.*

Sue: *What is your sense about this community?*

Vickie: *I feel very loved by this community. Oh, yes. I feel complete peace and happiness. I see the children with kohl under their eyes to keep the flies off. So funny, so beautiful. It's so pretty.*

Sue: *As you look into the children's eyes and faces and at the people of the village, is there anyone you recognize as someone who is currently in your life?*

Vickie: *I see my son, Michael. I think he's a child, with his beautiful eyes outlined in kohl. I believe Eliza's there as well. The girls are there as well. I think they're older.*

Sue: *They're part of this village?*

Vickie: *Yes, it feels very peaceful.*

Sue: *Do you get a sense that they're feeding you or giving you supplies?*

Vickie: *Yeah, I think they are, but I also feel that all of the children are wanting to touch me, touch my hair. It's very long. And they want to touch my hands, my face. They come to me for healing . . . [long silence]*

Sue: *Would you like to stay in this scene longer?*

Vickie: *Yes. I think that the baby sacred cow has significance. I think that it might be my sweet puppy. He's always at my side . . . I feel enormous peace and I feel very, very loved. I feel so much love for all of these kids and all of these villagers and this cow.*

Sue: *Do you have a sense of how old you are?*

Vickie: *Forty-five comes to me, but I'm not sure. Forty-five seems very* old. *I don't know how long ago this was, but it's the first number that came to me.*

Sue: *Take whatever time you need to finish experiencing what's important in that scene. When you're ready, we'll move forward to the final day of that lifetime.*

Vickie: *I look down at my hands, and all my fingertips are red. It's either the betel juice or some kind of henna tattoo. I have facial hair as well. I feel my feet on the earth, my bare feet, and it feels so good on the dusty village path. I'm putting my hand on the foreheads of the children who are coming up.*

Sue: *We're moving to the final moments of this lifetime at the count of three. And again, you can tell me what you see happening. And one and two and three . . .*

Vickie: *I'm back on that same beautiful cliff in that open cave. And I'm sitting in meditation. My legs are crossed, my hands in lotus. I must be chanting. I'm alone. I'm all by myself but not by myself. I feel very much surrounded by love and the spirits of lots of people who were family members from past lives surrounding me.*

Sue: *Do you have a sense of how old you are in this final day of your life?*

Vickie: *Fifty-one. I keep hearing the chant* "Atma namaste, Atma namaste," *but I don't know if this is from the village or from my loved ones. But I'm going to have to look up* Atma namaste. *I know what* namaste *means.*

Sue: *Do you have a sense of how your body might be ending this physical life? Is there a sense of any pain? What are you experiencing?*

Vickie: *No pain. I feel as though I'm floating, floating out and above, and just feeling so peaceful.*

Sue: *And as you lift up and above this moment, you can look down at that village, at that lifetime, at that cave, and get the bird's-eye view of it all.*

Vickie: *I don't think I climbed up. I think I came through the cave. It seems like it's possible. And it seems to me like there are villagers who are coming through, surrounding me.*

Sue: *And as you lift up above this and look at it all, is there anything else significant that you see about that place where you spent that lifetime?*

Vickie: *I see that all of the villagers are happy. They're all dressed in white. I think they all understand, like I understand.*

Sue: *As you lift out of the body, do you feel the presence of your spirit guide with you, helping you process that lifetime?*

Vickie: *Yeah, I feel very much guided.*

Sue: *Do you want to ask the guide anything about the purpose of that lifetime and what you were learning?*

Vickie: *He's telling me that it's our ultimate purpose in each lifetime to heal. That lifetime was a lifetime of healing. This lifetime is all about healing as well. And unfortunately, I think that there are things that happened during this lifetime that require healing, but we are ultimately all moving toward that divine healing.*

Sue: *Ask, "What is my purpose in this remaining part of my current lifetime?"*

Vickie: *He says it's to heal as many people as I can while I'm here and just keep moving forward, finding those who need to be healed, and helping them heal and move forward.*

Sue: *Is there a new level of healing work that you'll be doing, or will it be the same kind of grief healing that you've been doing?*

Vickie: *Oh gosh, I'm seeing a huge shift coming in the next year or so, not just for me, but for everyone.*

Sue: *What do you see?*

Vickie: *It's not all going to be easy. I think there will be a shift for everyone, not just people who have experienced the passing of a loved one, but for everyone. And I think that I will be a part of it. Not because I'm wanting to be in that, but because it feels like a tide is pulling me toward that.*

Sue: *Ask your guide about the past lifetime you just saw—why it was shown to you, and how it will help you in this current lifetime.*

Vickie: *I'm being shown that I need to shed any unnecessary things* *that are holding me back from being able to help others as much as possible.*

Sue: *Ask your guide if he'll be helping you fulfill your role in this coming shift.*

Vickie: *I keep seeing balance, that it's a question of balance—that I'm going to have to navigate balance with everyone I love in order to help as many people as I can.*

Sue: *Ask your guide if you have the same gifts in this lifetime that you had in that previous lifetime.*

Vickie: *I do, but I don't devote enough time to healing the way I used to. I've gotten away from that. I used to do a lot of Reiki healing years ago but I haven't had time for it because of my responsibilities with the nonprofit.*

Sue: *Ask how you can rekindle your healing gifts.*

Vickie: *I just need to remember I have this gift and that it's very powerful. I need to remember that all of us, not just me, but everyone who has these healing gifts needs to be using them as we move forward.*

Sue: *Ask if part of your role in the future is to help people remember how to use their own healing gifts.*

Vickie: *Yes, for any problem that is happening, not just within our bodies, but in our societies, in the world as a whole, we can help. We are guided through each lifetime. And we are all healers. I feel that we need to be doing this. Yes, it's a heavy burden. Oh my gosh, there's so much to be done! Each one of us has these gifts within us. I'm not special. None of us is special. It's just that we've had these gifts all along and we have just not allowed them to come forward the way that they need to right now. We need to be setting our doubts about these alternative healing tools aside to allow this healing to happen. Not only the healing of those around us and those who need healing because of the passing of a loved one, but also for the world as a whole—expanding beyond the world and all the way into the universe. Because right now is such a significant time, such an important time.*

Sue: *Ask your guide to take you to meet your Council of Elders.*

Vickie: *I don't feel like it's the right time right now. I feel like there are things that I need to do before I meet with them. I have a very complex road ahead of me in the next few months and much that needs to be accomplished.*

Sue: *That's significant.*

Vickie: *I feel like there are some Herculean things that are going to be coming up, which is a little awe-inspiring. Hopefully, I'll be up to the task.*

Sue: *You can ask the guide who will be helping you move through this.*

Vickie: *When you said that, I saw Michael immediately. I knew that Eliza will also be helping me, and all the departed kids. I can feel that they will be helping me figure this out. It's not going to be easy.*

Sue: *Do you want to ask your guide if you set a plan for this lifetime and if you have a certain learning arc that you agreed to?*

Vickie: *I've done what I set out to do, but I think there's still a lot more to be done. I keep seeing the number 700,000. I've been seeing that number since the beginning of this journey, and it represents a lot of grieving people I want to help. I've been told that number many times. There are only 20,000 people in my nonprofit. There's a lot more people to reach, and I'm not sure if 700,000 means parents or just people in general who need to be awakened and healed and to understand that there's more. Wow, I don't know if that means this year or if this is something that's going to be over a lifetime. I really don't know, but it's a huge task.*

Sue: *Do you want to ask your guide to take you to the Library of Souls and bring you a book that could help you understand?*

Vickie: *Okay, I think that might be a good idea. It would be nice to know why that number keeps coming up and how that goal can be accomplished.*

Sue: *You're being escorted to this beautiful library in the divine realms, where all knowledge and wisdom of human evolution has been stored. It's a sacred space. As you walk up to it, what do you see?*

Vickie: *I see a light opening. It's interesting. I felt like I was going into* *a dark library, but I'm seeing this huge light space. Different colors of purple, orange, yellow, and blue light are pouring through. I think what is being shown to me is that this light is going to be guiding and healing me and others, and that I need to be standing in the light, finding that light each day, coming from a place of light when each situation presents itself. I think that's all. Michael is taking me to a shelf and bringing out a card. It's one of those pop-up cards, and he opens it up. This beam of light comes popping out over these beautiful mountains like the ones that were in that past lifetime in India. He's closing the card. He says that's my book. It's the card with the light.*

Sue: *Is there anything else significant in the library?*

Vickie: *No, it's just that the library is filled with light. There are books in certain places. But as I say, there's this light feeding through. All different colors. I feel like this is his message to me: follow the light and be the light. I'm being told that purple can aid in my healing work. I keep getting purple, purple, purple. Violet. I feel like that's the color that's most prominent here. There's beautiful white light as well, but then there's this violet light coming through, with purple around it and some red in it as well. Oh, goodness, I think I already feel like I understand why I chose this lifetime. That it's okay because I realized that there's a lot left to do, but it was my decision with all of these other guides and soul-pod people who have been with me this whole time.*

Sue: *Ask your guide and Michael and Eliza if there's anything else you need to experience, and if not, ask them to guide you back toward the tunnel.*

Vickie: *Thank you. Thank you everyone.*

I used guided meditation and deep breathing to bring Vickie fully back into her body, then we discussed the session:

Sue: *Now that you're back in this physical lifetime, what is the most important thing you experienced today? Say the first thing that comes to mind.*

Vickie: *I learned that there's a lot to be done, and that it has to be done in the light—and that I have to develop my abilities of healing as much as possible. Not just grief healing, but healing of the body and soul, which I used to cultivate but haven't been able to do in a long time because I've been so busy with the day-to-day work of helping grieving parents. I think that it's really important that I get back to that as quickly as possible.*

Sue: *What is your overall sense about the significance of that past lifetime?*

Vickie: *I think that it makes sense because I feel that India is my spiritual home. I've always felt that way. The moment I first set foot in India, I felt I had come home. So it's understandable that I would've experienced a lifetime there. At least one, probably many lifetimes in India. It's interesting that I chose to be alone and away from society. I'm not sure why that is, but I wasn't always alone because I was also in the village.*

Sue: *I think it's really important that you developed so many sacred healing techniques in that lifetime as a sadhguru, to help others transcend the struggles of this physical world. In this lifetime, although you've had what they call in India a householder's life, it's perhaps significant that in your second Saturn return you shift back into the life of the sadhguru. Now you'll be better able to become the collective or community healer you were in that previous lifetime.*

Vickie: *Yes, that sounds right. Wow! Well, I think that's a wonderful thing to know, and again, it's a big job.*

Sue: *If you agreed to it, it means you can do it.*

Vickie: *I can. I know that I can. I think that it's interesting because I took Reiki healing and I started doing it. The things that I experienced were truly amazing. I was even able to heal my girls from across the ocean when they were in London. And then I stopped doing any of that because I have so much other stuff to do with the nonprofit. But I think that I'm going to have to start concentrating on finding ways to develop healing abilities so that I can help people that way as well.*

Sue: *Did you have a sense that when you were in the library you were learning that you can use color to heal people?*

Vickie: *Yes. I'm sure that using color and energy from the different colors is really important. It's so interesting because I was expecting to see green because green is Michael's favorite color. But there was no green whatsoever. It was all these other colors—more of an indigo color and then yellow. This white, yellow light. And then the violet light. It's interesting that those colors were so prominent. They were prominent in the first lifetime when I was sitting in the cave.*

Sue: *You spent at least one lifetime, maybe more, as a holy man in India. Perhaps you've been called into this time and place and culture to reclaim those gifts. As you probably know from your studies in India, sadhgurus in India had enormous powers. They had psychic powers and could move objects and heal anyone. That's why you were so loved in that village. Don't be afraid to reclaim all of those powers here as you move forward.*

Vickie: *Thank you. It was definitely a beautiful experience. I am truly grateful.*

◉ Shift into Your Sacred Self

- Practice daily meditation to quiet your mind, open your heart, connect to your divinity, and hear the voice of your soul.
- Remember that pain is your fuel. View your greatest pain and use it as fuel to do your great work.
- You've made soul agreements with all the important players in your life, even those who break your heart. Don't forget: all soul agreements are for your highest good.
- View your life story from your soul's perspective rather than the disempowering perspective of the ego. Apply that inner wisdom to all your worldly choices.
- Use your new perspective to create a plan for moving forward in every area of your life.

19

How Are You Doing in Earth School?

Assessing Your Progress on the Path

As this book has made clear, there are two basic ways in which we can view our lives and tell our stories. One is the ego view, which I call the ego lens. From this viewpoint, life can seem tragic and random and mostly meaningless. The other way is to see life through the divine lens. From this view we see the divine order and our soul agreements in every event that takes place in life. From this perspective, we remember that we're souls who came here to evolve and help others evolve. This perspective, although it isn't the popular or most common lens, comes from the soul and is rich with wisdom, forgiveness, and healing.

For example, when we lose a loved one, we vacillate between the ego view, which tells us a story of tragic and pointless loss and devastating pain; and the divine view, which whispers, *All is well. My loved one fulfilled his or her soul mission and made their exit exactly as their soul planned to do.* And when I quiet myself, I can feel and hear and sometimes even see these departed loved ones. When that happens, I know in my heart and soul that they're happy and filled with light and watching over me. I will join them soon enough—as soon as I fulfill my own soul mission here and live like I know they're watching, making them proud of me.

When we wear our divine lens, we are each capable of connecting to the other side of the veil for healing and guidance. When we wear our ego lens, we are stuck in the mud here, with its heavy energy and pain. Usually we're shifting between the two. When we lose a job, for example, we might vacillate between the ego lens, which views this loss as a reflection of our unworthiness and the injustice of the world, and the divine lens, which sees this as the push we've been needing in order to go in a new and more meaningful career direction.

In this moment I'm asking you to trust me and take off your ego lens. Set it down carefully because you will use it again whenever you need your left brain to work out the mundane details of life. For now I ask that you put on your divine lens to see this luminous world all around us and within us. And I will help you adjust your lens and see your soul's story of wisdom and light. If you'll join me in this perspective, you will experience healing.

Now that you've read this far, and have, I trust, integrated some of the lessons I've offered in this book, the following exercises will help you assess your progress on the path. Give them a try!

◉ Which Lens Am I Wearing Today?

How do I feel in my body today?

- Ego lens: heavy, tired, sluggish
- Divine lens: energized, alive, excited

Am I feeling love toward anyone, everyone, myself?

- Ego lens: not really, annoyed at the world and at myself
- Divine lens: feeling compassion toward everyone including myself

Do I feel that all is well with the world?

- Ego lens: No! Things are messed up and people are to blame.
- Divine lens: I see the divine order of everyone's soul journey and realize that we're all awakening to our divinity through pain and love.

◉ Seeing Life through My Divine Lens

- Which moments do I recognize as gifts of opportunity and divine guidance that I did or did not recognize at the time?
- Speaking from my soul and not my ego, what would I tell myself today to inspire me to move forward despite my fears?
- Reviewing my recent choices from the divine lens perspective, when did my choices bring me into the light of new and better possibilities and when didn't they?
- When in my life story did an opening appear and I took it, even though I was afraid, and that choice brought me into a better life?

◉ Questions to Ask Myself

- Would I feel silly consulting a source of divine guidance throughout my day, even while doing mundane things like driving in traffic, grocery shopping, doing laundry, or preparing for a meeting? Why or why not?
- Which relationship in particular will I focus on this week and bring my divine perspective to?
- Am I a fierce seeker of grace, even in the midst of chaos?
- Is it possible that within my life today there are moments of love and beauty that I might dismiss, although they could change everything?
- Do I courageously pursue the wise perspective of my divine lens even in the midst of chaos, devastating grief, or overwhelming fear?
- Do I truly understand that just one moment of fierce grace changes everything? Do I reach for that fierce grace when my heart is heavy or when I feel overwhelmed?

APPENDIX

Calculate Your Birth Path Using Numerology

Our souls choose the exact moment, place, and date of our birth because those coordinates create a unique vibration that aligns our earth journey with what our soul came to experience. These coordinates are reflected in numerology and in astrology.

To calculate the numerology of your birth date, begin by taking the numbers of your day, month, and year of birth, and then add them together to arrive at a single digit. For interpretations of each number, go to the end of this section. For example, January is a 1 month, February a 2 month, March a 3 month, and so on. Your day of birth will be factored down into a single digit, as will your year of birth.

The following are a few examples of how to calculate your numerology:

Birth date: September 15, 1951
Month is September → 9
Date is 15 → 1 + 5 = 6
Year is 1951 → 1 + 9 + 5 + 1 = 16; 1 + 6 = 7
Total of month (9) + date (6) + year (7) = 22; 2 + 2 = 4
Birth path is 4

Birth date: October 16, 1980
Month is October → 10; 1 + 0 = 1
Date is 16 → 1 + 6 = 7
Year is 1980 → 1 + 9 + 8 + 0 = 18; 1 + 8 = 9
Total of month (1) + date (7) + year (9) = 17; 1 + 7 = 8
Birth path is 8

THE MASTER SOUL NUMBERS

The master numbers 11, 22, and 33 represent sacred birth paths that we can choose at the time of birth when we're ready to take on the task of helping humanity evolve. If you get one of these numbers for your final birth path calculation (when you add the month total, the date total, and the year total, as in the examples above), you won't reduce the double digit that results to a single digit if those numbers are master numbers. (Note: double digits are reduced to single digits in the calculations that lead up to the final birth path calculation, however. For example, the month of November digits down to a 2 when you are calculating the number of your month.) The following example shows how to calculate the master soul birth path:

Birth Date: September 15, 1951
Month is September → 9
Date is 15 → 1 + 5 = 6
Year is 1951 → 1 + 9 + 5 + 1 = 16; 1 + 6 = 7
Total of month (9) + date (6) + year (7) = 22

In this example, the master soul birth path is 22. This is also referred to as a 22/4 path since the 22 is always connected to the 4 path because 2+2 = 4. Similarly, the 11 path is referred to as 11/2 path, and the 33 path is referred to as a 33/6 path.

THREE WAYS OF
ADDING BIRTHDATES

It's important to add up each birth date three different ways to check your addition and to look for hidden master path numbers. This is especially important if you've arrived at a 2, 4, or 6 birth path calculation. These birth paths often contain a hidden 11, 22, or 33 path if added two other ways. If the master soul number is "hidden" in this way, it means this person will choose when they're ready to step up to their great work—usually later in life.

For example, for the birth date of May 1, 1960, these are the three ways you would calculate the birth path number to discover that two out of three ways reveal a 22/4 path, while the other way reveals a 13/4 path.

Traditional Method #1:

Month is May → 5

Date is 1 → 1

Year is 1960 → 1 + 9 + 6 + 0 = 16; 1 + 6 = 7

Total of month (5) + date (1) + year (7) = 13; 1 + 3 = 4

Birth path is 13/4

Method #2:

$$5$$
$$1$$
$$+\underline{1960}$$

1966 → 1 + 9 + 6 + 6 = 22

Master soul birth path is 22/4

Method #3:

$$5 + 1 + 1 + 9 + 6 + 0 = 22/4$$

Master soul birth path is 22/4

Here's another example, for the birth date September 15, 1951:

Traditional Method #1

Month is September → 9

Date is 15 → 1 + 5 = 6

Year is 1951 → 1 + 9 + 5 + 1 = 16; 1 + 6 = 7

Total of month (9) + date (6) + year (7) = 22

Master soul birth path is 22/4

Method #2:

$$9$$
$$15$$
$$+\underline{1951}$$
$$1975 → 1 + 9 + 7 + 5 = 22/4$$

Master soul birth path is 22/4

Method #3:

$$9 + 1 + 5 + 1 + 9 + 5 + 1 = 31/4$$

Birth path is 31/4

Calculate your birth path from your date of birth using all three of the methods displayed above and write the results below.

First method result:

Second method result:

Third method result:

All three methods should arrive at the same final number, even if you discover you're on a master soul path of 11, 22, or 33. Those master soul path calculations result in the consistent final combinations of 11/2, 22/4, or 33/6—at least one of the ways you add the birth date. The other two ways may result in various other two-digit numbers that when added together total 2, 4, or 6. (Examples are 20/2, 13/4, or 15/6).

> Your birth month:
> Your birth date:
> Your birth year:
> Total:
> Reduced to a single digit:
> Your birth path number:

Note: Zero is more than a placeholder in numerology. It's called a *potentiator,* meaning the zero makes the number in front of it (or behind it) stronger. If your birth path calculation arrives at the number 2020, each zero strengthens the two in front of it, making this number digit down to a 22/4 master path. The same is true for 1010 or 3030, which become 11/2 and 33/6, respectively.

INTERPRETING THE NUMBERS

The following birth numbers describe the lessons and challenges you selected for this lifetime and the mission your soul intended to fulfill. After reading these descriptions, what steps would you take moving forward to align your life and career with your soul mission? How would you view the challenges you face today through the wisdom of what you came to learn on your birth path?

> **Birth path 1:** You came here to learn to believe in your uniqueness, to follow your inner voice and authentic vision no matter what anyone thinks of you or expects of you. You'll have events and relationships that cause you to doubt yourself, but your life mission is to use any self-doubt as fuel to become a great leader and visionary capable of changing the world. This will unfold once you

trust your inner wisdom, slip on your divine lens, and do work that helps others find their uniqueness and overcome their self-doubts.

Birth path 2: You have a gift for connecting with others with empathy and intuitive awareness. You're a healer as long as you don't let your sensitivity wound you. When you're focused on organizing the details of life, you're hiding from your Higher Self, running from your powerful inner wisdom, and not stepping up to your great work. If the addition of your birth date numbers ended in 11/2—even in just one of the three ways you can add it—this means you're on the 11 master soul path. Please read about this below.

Birth path 3: You have a brilliant, creative mind and are a gifted communicator through written and spoken words, movement, and other forms of creative expression. You break the rules on purpose. Meant to be an entrepreneur, you must launch that business, write that book, open your movement or healing studio, and make your living from your self-expressive path. Your challenge is to quiet the mind and open your heart, which is difficult because you've learned to trust your ideas and not your gut. To fulfill your mission, you'll need to change that pattern and learn to carry the heart of healing within you.

Birth path 4: You're strong, responsible, and determined. Your inner strength and physical strength will save your life and guide you in the right direction. Use your hard work to create new systems and foundations for the world's problems. Your passion for truth must be the guiding force for the work you do. If you think bigger than just the task in front of you, nothing will stop your success. (If the addition of your birth date numbers ended in 22/4—even in just one of the three ways you can add it—this means you're on the 22 master soul path. Please read about this further on.)

Birth path 5: You came into this lifetime to fearlessly embrace the physical world and fully experience the joys, challenges, and lessons of living in a body. Your body will be the vehicle for most of your lessons and your gifts here. You are charismatic and will attract everything you want; the lesson is to learn to pick from your Higher Self, from the divine lens instead of from the ego lens. Courage is your guide in every challenge, and it's what you came to learn. Step away from conventional careers, fear-based religions, and empty relationships to find your authentic self. Center yourself and overcome addictions with disciplined spiritual practice. Much of your lifetime does not require effort, but your spiritual work is necessary. Putting effort into meditation and spiritual studies will allow you to accomplish what you came here to do.

Birth path 6: You carry the heart of the compassionate healer and you care greatly for those around you, including family, community, and the world at large. You sense what others need and always want to help them. But losing yourself in the needs of others will poison your heart and pull you away from your own divinity. Your unique path to the Divine must come first. Channel your artistic gifts and intuitive knowingness and use your brilliance to align with your sacred self rather than your lower self. Then you can save the world as you intended. If the addition of your birth date numbers ended in 33/6—even in just one of the three ways you can add it—this means you're on the 33 master soul path. Please read about this below.

Birth path 7: You're deeply sensitive and intuitive and yet you also have an amazing analytical mind. When you use your brilliant mind to pursue spiritual knowledge (not religion), you'll find your truth. Then you can teach the world a better way to live. You can use science, nature, or the arts as your path to wisdom.

But all paths must lead to spiritual solutions, or your cynicism will destroy your life.

Birth path 8: You came to learn the lesson of power: how to own it fully in every area of your life—spiritual, physical, emotional, and financial. You intended to use that power to do good work in the world. Once you embrace this challenge and stop hiding from it, you'll find your way and become more successful and wealthy than most. But your wealth and power must eventually be used to empower others. It's what you came here to do and it's the lesson you came to learn.

Birth path 9: You're a wise old soul who chose this path to tie up the loose ends of your spiritual evolution. You agreed to face many losses and disappointments in this lifetime because your soul is ready to pass the test—to step into wisdom, compassion, and forgiveness, no matter what pain you feel. If you're avoiding your mission, you'll use your charismatic personality and many skills to manipulate and diminish others. This will leave you feeling empty, alone, and broken. When you embrace the path of wisdom, you'll become the spiritual bridge between this world and the next.

Birth path 11/2: You carry extraordinary sensitivity and beauty within, and you have a direct, wide-open channel to the Divine. You're meant to use that as your gift—to see the pain of others (not just your own pain) and to use your intuition to heal and inspire the world. If you let your sensitivity wound you, you can be paranoid and rage-filled, which is not who you came here to be. But the moment you quiet your mind, open your heart, and deepen your spiritual pursuits, your life unfolds beautifully.

Birth path 22/4: You agreed to get it done in the way it needs to get done in order to shift consciousness here on Earth. Your mission requires hard work—studying, writing, teaching, creating media, and living boldly in the world. You're perfectly designed for this task, and you brought with you all the strength and courage you need to get it done. When you step up to the challenge, your work will make a great difference in the world, helping consciousness evolve.

Birth path 33/6: You're a pure, high-vibrational channel to the Divine. You can open your heart and understand the essence of humanity and its struggles. Your intention is to use this wide-open channel to bring in your gifts of wisdom, beauty, inspiration, and spiritual awareness to help the world. You walk the path of the compassionate intuitive healer, yet if you don't embrace your inner wisdom, your sensitivities can lead to addictions and mental illness. Choosing your divine lens will save your life and allow you to then save the world.

PERSONAL YEAR CYCLES

All of your life you've experienced repeated nine-year cycles of reinvention as reflected in numerology. By understanding where you are now in your reinvention cycle, you can more gracefully heal your life, embrace your true work, and see life from your soul's perspective, which is your divine lens.

Every year of your life you've been under the influence of a particular number—1 through 9, plus 11, 22, or 33. You're working with a different type of energy each year within a repeating nine-year cycle. These nine-year cycles are designed to move you through cycles of necessary reinvention and loss, helping you to master the challenges you signed up for and accomplish the work you came here to do.

You began this lifetime under the influence of the birth-path number you chose. If that number is 3, then the first year of your life was a 3 personal year. The second year of your life was a 4 personal year, and so on.

Your current personal year is determined by the single-digit numbers of your birth month and birth date added to the current calendar year and reduced to a single digit or master number. So to calculate your personal year, you will add up the following:

Your birth month:
Your birth date:
Current year:
Total:

Reduce to a single digit to arrive at your personal year.

Here's an example:

Birthdate: September 15, 1951
Month is September → 9
Date is 15 → 1 + 5 = 6
Current year is 2023 → 2 + 0 + 2 + 3 = 7
Total of month (9) + date (6) + current year (7) = 22; 2 + 2 = 4
Personal year: 22/4

Meaning of the Personal Year

Personal year 1: This is a year to focus on *you*. It's time to launch your business, get a new job or a new title, start a graduate program, or move to a new location. Everything you do this year will influence the events of your life for the next nine years. If you don't plant seeds for a better future now, nothing will come to bloom as this cycle unfolds. Tap into all the new energy that will help you release the past and reinvent. There's never been a better time for taking steps toward your ultimate dream. Everything revolves around you and depends on you. Believe in your vision, make important decisions alone, and move forward bravely, like a pioneer.

Personal year 2: This is your year for connecting deeply with others. Your career won't be on your own shoulders anymore, as new partners will step forward to offer support for the project you started last year. It's a slower, sweeter year, one in which you nurture what you've already started rather than pushing hard to launch new things. Success hinges on opening your heart, trusting your heightened intuition, and saying yes to collaboration. It's important to be receptive. Soften the forceful energy you thrived on last year. You might feel highly sensitive now, but don't let this get in the way of love. Your solution is to become the source of love for others, even when you're feeling wounded.

Personal year 11: This is a highly charged year of personal illumination and intellectual achievement. You'll be inspired to heal the relationships in your life and accomplish your most inspired work. Your intuition, inspiration, and creativity are magnified, and so is your sensitivity. Daily meditation or prayer will enhance all of your gifts and reinforce your connection to the Divine. That spiritual connection is more powerful than ever this year. Use it as your source for actions. Spend time with evolved, conscious people who inspire you to create. Small talk and meaningless social engagements will drain you because of your heightened sensitivity. This is your best year for developing spiritual, intuitive, and artistic gifts as well as learning to love in a profoundly new way.

Personal year 3: This is the fun, sexy, playful year to create projects for your new work. Express yourself, get into the center of things, join social groups, and entertain. Forget long-term planning and just enjoy life; don't make important decisions about your future. Develop your skills with words—written and spoken. Life is your stage, so enjoy it! Whatever you started in your 1 year through hard work and diligence is now reaping enjoyment for you. It's a year to blossom.

Personal year 4: It's time to focus on your great work. Just get it done. Focus on being responsible to your career and tapping into core strengths whenever challenged. It's a serious year to fulfill obligations, get practical and organized, and build a foundation for future growth. Create your budget and do the physical work. Get your home in order, whether that means moving, remodeling, or cleaning. Get in shape physically and cultivate strength in all areas of life. Dependability, honesty, and responsibility are required in relationship and career.

Personal year 22: This is your best year for manifesting inspired work in the world. Anything is possible! Ignoring your work will leave you feeling off-balance, unfocused, and useless. Use inspiration as your fuel to get it all done. Don't waste a moment going on long vacations—you won't be able to relax anyway. Focus on your great work and trust that love and relaxation will come later. This is a year for putting personal concerns aside and doing your best for the world at large. Make big plans and introduce changes. You'll have the opportunity to ascend to your greatest career achievements and acquire abundant financial rewards. You'll also feel the sting of criticism that greatness attracts. Focus on your work and keep moving forward.

Personal year 5: This year, your charisma is amped up and your magnetism will attract everyone, from potential partners to new business opportunities. Hold steady to your true self or you'll get pulled off the path. Be open, fearless, passionate, and free. You'll have opportunities for expansion, adventure, and the unexpected in this turning-point year. Everything is vibrant and changing around you. Take trips (it's time for that long vacation), investigate career opportunities, and get rid of anything that holds you back and release anyone who restricts you with narrow, judgmental thinking. Make room for the new. Focus on freedom and adapting to change. Enjoy this sensual year with good food, relationships, and trips to exotic places. You'll be super-charged, attractive, and sexual. You can revive tedious relationships or boring work situations with your newfound energy and charisma.

Personal year 6: This year is a time of deep love and nurturing. Focus on commitment, family, and responsibility. Your heart opens wide to embrace others. Rather than focusing on yourself, adjust to the needs of others. Shift away from the passionate excesses of the 5 personal year. Relationships will blossom as you nurture them with your new openhearted energy. Reach out to understand the people in your life. Let go of superficiality and take responsibility for others. Yet don't take on more than you can carry, or you'll fall into depression or become overwhelmed. This is one year, though, when general harmony is more important than your own needs.

Personal year 33: You'll be drawn to mystical knowledge, intuition, and spiritual guidance this year. But if you're not grounded, you could become disconnected to everyday reality. Stay away from alcohol and drugs, and meditate every day. If you embrace your

Higher Self, it will be your most inspired year artistically. You'll channel genius, whether you're an actor, musician, or artist. Your pipeline to the Divine is open and flowing freely with spiritual and creative inspiration. Take a meditation retreat and create, create, create! Your finished product and enlightened ideas will change the world.

Personal year 7: This is a time for deep reflection, intuitive development, and spiritual growth. Sign up for a regular yoga class or take a meditation retreat and spend a weekend in prayer and silence. Strength will come only from your connection to the Divine. You may feel a bit lonely or isolated, whether you're in a relationship or not. Use your alone time to write a book, research higher consciousness, or take a psychology class. Focus on finding your true purpose. Withdraw from the center of things; superficial social events won't feel good. Your sensitivity and intuition is elevated, and you'll pick up on other people's feelings wherever you go. Refine what you started in the current nine-year cycle by analyzing and perfecting projects and relationships. Your intuition will be at its most powerful, so rely on it for all decisions. Pursue nothing—you'll naturally attract what is meant to be in your life.

Personal year 8: Money and career will be the topic of nearly every conversation. You'll have many opportunities to make money and advance your career, and that should be your focus. It's a year to go to the bank, not the bar. Even when you're out partying, your mind will be home crunching numbers to see how you can improve your business or pay off your debts. It's time to own your power, both financially and physically. Get back in shape, financially *and* physically. If you wrote a book last year, this is the year to promote and sell it. If you researched and developed your new business last year, now is the time to get it funded. Physical accomplishment and material success are your focus as you reap the seeds of success that you planted early in this nine-year cycle. During this powerful year, take command to get results. Think big, manage and direct others, and move forward. Beware of abusing your power in relationships, however. Be patient and generous to others, even if it feels tedious to do so.

Personal year 9: It's time to clean house, to surrender what you no longer need and what holds you back. Friends and lovers from the past will resurface to be examined, then kept or discarded for the next cycle. Your career will conclude the focus that it has had for the past nine years, even though you won't see the new cycle just yet. Open your hands and let go, with faith that something new and better will arrive in your 1 year. You may even be fired or laid off. Relationships will fall away or be transformed, and you'll grieve for your losses over the past nine years. Peace comes from higher wisdom and a greater connection to spirituality. Your insights and wisdom will be heightened. Use this awareness to benefit the people around you. Focus on artistic and spiritual disciplines, and wait for the new inspiration that begins soon in your approaching 1 year.

Map Your Own Reinvention Cycles

One of the most helpful ways you can understand your soul story is to look through all of your previous nine-year cycles and discuss what was going on during each cycle.

Starting with your birth year, write each year of your life to the left of the personal year number you were experiencing. Also include your age.

Make notations by the years when important events occurred—especially note when relationships and careers began or ended and when you experienced grief and loss.

Note any changes that took place when one nine-year cycle ended and a new one began.

Note what you learned about yourself during your Saturn return(s), which happen every twenty-seven to twenty-nine years, so most people have two Saturn returns (see the section below, "The Saturn Return"). By examining your past reinvention cycles, what insights do you have about your current challenges and how to move through them? What insights have you gained from reviewing your cycles? Ask yourself:

How did each nine-year cycle begin and end?

What was my intention at the beginning of each cycle?

What did I let go of at the end of each cycle?

When did I fall in or out of love? When did I start and end careers?

When did I have children or long to have children?

When did my loved one die?

What did I learn?

What did I learn about myself during my Saturn return(s)?

When I look at my Saturn return(s), what can I learn about the purpose of my pain and how it fuels my life and great work?

THE SATURN RETURN

Astrology is another potent tool for understanding your soul's journey. Somewhere around the age of twenty-seven to twenty-nine years, you go through your first Saturn return, an astrological transit in which the planet Saturn returns to the position it was at when you were born. The first Saturn return is a major transition point in a lifetime, your first true wake-up moment of recognizing your journey for this lifetime and what it's really about. You'll see that your life is going to turn out differently from how you thought it would be. And you'll understand that you're not here to meet the expectations of family and friends. This is your moment of seeing who you really are. You may lose a career or lose someone you love at this transition point, whether it's a parent, friend, or spouse. Or you may lose a career or reinvent your career at this point. All loss is meant to fuel your reinvention.

At the age of fifty-seven to fifty-nine, you go through your second Saturn return. This is the second major transition point of your lifetime, where you're stripped naked until you finally become your true self in the world. You're no longer allowed to hide behind limiting job titles or relationships. It's time to be the authentic self you came here to be, doing your great work in the world. This is also a time when you may lose someone you love or lose a career or a relationship, in which case you can use the pain of loss to fuel your reinvention.

Index

About the Author

Sue Frederick is a lifelong intuitive, an ordained Unity minister, a certified past-life and between-lives soul regression therapist, a certified creative arts therapist, a career intuitive coach, grief intuitive coach, and master numerologist. She's the author of *Bridges to Heaven: True Stories of Loved Ones on the Other Side*; *I See Your Soul Mate: An Intuitive's Guide to Finding and Keeping Love,* and *I See Your Dream Job: A Career Intuitive Shows You How to Discover What You Were Put on Earth to Do,* and the memoir *Water Oak: The Happiness of Longing.* Sue has taught workshops at Omega Institute in Rhinebeck, New York, and Kripalu Center for Yoga and Health in Stockbridge, Massachusetts, and she's been a faculty member at both the University of Colorado and at Naropa University.

An intuitive since childhood, Sue draws on decades of spiritual study and practice as well as powerful inner wisdom to help her clients and students fulfill their soul's mission, access their divine lens, and use their pain as fuel for a meaningful life. Sue has trained more than five hundred intuitive coaches around the world. Her work has been featured in the *New York Times, Real Simple, Yoga Journal, Natural*

Health, Fit Yoga, and *Complete Woman* magazines, and on CNN.com. She's been a guest on more than two hundred radio shows and many television shows, including *Bridging Heaven and Earth.*

For more information, visit www.SueFrederick.com
Email: Sue@brilliantwork.com